BAXTER'S GAME BOOK

BAXTER'S GAME BOOK

EDITED BY
JOHN MOWBRAYE

LINE ILLUSTRATIONS BY
JOHN ROBERTS

Produced by Elm Tree Books, Hamish Hamilton Limited,
for W. A. Baxter and Sons Limited

First published in Great Britain 1973
by Elm Tree Books Ltd.
90 Great Russell Street, London WC1

SBN 241 02244 4

Filmset and printed in Great Britain by BAS Printers Limited, Wallop, Hampshire

CONTENTS

LIST OF ACKNOWLEDGEMENTS

EXTRACTS from the following works appear by permission of the publishers in every case where it has been possible to trace them; the editor has made every effort to contact the holders of copyright, but if any have been inadvertently omitted, he proffers his apologies.

W. A. Baillie-Grohman: *Sport in Art* (Ballantyne, 1913)
Juliana Bernes (Berners, or Barnes): *The Boke of St Albans* (1486)
Richard Blome: *The Gentleman's Recreation* (1686)
Richard Blome: *Hawking or Falconry* (from *The Gentleman's Recreation*; reprinted, with an introduction by E. D. Cuming, by the Cresset Press, 1929)
John Buchan: *John McNab* (Tweedsmuir Estate, and Hodder & Stoughton, 1925)
Cameron of Lochiel: Deer Stalking (Fur, Feather and Fin Series, Longman, 1893/6)
Charles Coles: 'Pheasant' (*The Field*, January 1972)
Charles Palk Collyns: *The Chase of the Wild Red Deer* (Longman, 1862)
C. J. Cornish: *Partridge Rearing* (Country Life Library of Sport, 1906)
Rev. W. B. Daniel: *Rural Sports* (Bunny and Gold, 1802)
Charles Dixon: *Game Birds and Wild Fowl of the British Islands* (Pawson & Brailsford, 1900)
Viscount Ebrington: *Stag Hunting* (Fur, Feather and Fin Series, Longman, 1893/6)
Duke of Edinburgh: President's Foreword, *Game Conservancy Annual Review* (1970)
Pierce Egan: *Pierce Egan's Anecdotes* (Knight and Lacey, 1827)
James Fisher: *Thorburn's Birds* (Ebury Press, Michael Joseph, 1967)
Hugh S. Gladstone: *Record Bags and Shooting Records* (John Gladstone, H. F. and G. Witherby, 1900)
Herbert Byng Hall: *Highland Sports and Highland Quarters* (H. Hurst, 1847)
J. E. Harting: *Essays on Sport and Natural History* (Horace Cox, 1883)
J. E. Harting: introduction to *A Perfect Booke for Kepinge of Sparhawkes or Goshawkes* (written about 1575, reprinted by Bernard Quaritch, 1886)
Lt. Col. Peter Hawker: *Intructions to Young Sportsmen* (R. Hunter, J. Ridgeway and Sons, 1816)
Horace C. Hutchinson: *Pheasant Shooting* (Country Life Library of Sport, 1906)
Ben Jonson: *Every Man in His Humour* (1598)
Charles Kingsley: *The Water Babies* (1863)
A. E. Knox: *Game Birds and Wild Fowl* (John Van Voorst, 1850)
D. H. Madden: *A Chapter of Mediaeval History* (John Murray, 1924)
Gervase Markham: *Country Contentments* (1611)
Gervase Markham: *A Way to Get Wealth* (1623)
George Markland: *Pteryplegia, or The Art of Shooting Flying* (1727)
W. McCombie-Smith: *The Romance of Poaching in the Highlands of Scotland* (Eneas Mackay, 1904)

J. G. Millais: *Game Birds and Shooting Sketches* (Henry Sotheran, 1894)
Alexander Napier: *Pheasants at Holkham* (Country Life Library of Sport, 1906)
Ralph Nevill: *Old English Sporting Books* (The Studio, 1924)
'Nimrod' (Charles James Apperley): *The Chase, the Road and the Turf* (ed. Herbert Maxwell, 1898)
Eric Parker: *Shooting Days* (John Murray, 1918)
Sir Ralph Payne-Gallwey: *Diaries of Col. Peter Hawker* (Longman, 1893)
Hugh B. C. Pollard: *Game Birds and Game Bird Shooting* (Eyre and Spottiswoode, 1900)
Charles Richardson: *The Hare and the Lawyers* (Fur, Feather and Fin Series, Longman, 1893/6)
William Scrope: *The Art of Deer-Stalking* (1838)
'Snaffle' (Robert Dunkin): *The Image of War* (William Blackwood, 1914)
William Somerville: *The Chace* (1735)
Tom Speedy: *The Natural History of Sport in Scotland with Rod and Gun* (William Blackwood, 1920)
A Sportsman: *Essays on the Game Laws, now existing in Great Britain* (1770)
Sportsman's Dictionary (London, 1778)
Sir Dudley Stamp: *Nature Conservation in Britain* (Collins, 1970)
Martin Stephens: *Grouse Shooting* (Sportsman's Library, Adam and Charles Black, 1939)
Charles St John: *A Tour in Sutherlandshire* (1849)
Charles St John: *Wild Sports and Natural History of the Highlands* (John Murray, 1878)
Robert Smith Surtees: *Handley Cross* (1843)
George Turbervile: *The Noble Art of Venerie or Hunting* (1575)
John Henry Walsh ('Stonehenge'): *Manual of British Rural Sports* (Routledge, 1856)
John Watson: *Confessions of a Poacher* (Chapman and Hall, 1890)
John Watson: *Poachers and Poaching* (Chapman and Hall, 1891)

ILLUSTRATIONS

The publishers wish to express their thanks to the following for permission to reproduce illustrations:
Ardea Photographics: figs. 18, 33; colour plates I, II, III and V.
Bibliothèque Nationale, Departement des Manuscrites: figs. 4 and 5 (from the *Livre de la Chasse* by Gaston Phoebus, Comte de Foix, Ms. français 616, fols. 108 and 66).
British Museum, figs. 1 (Cotton Claudius Ms., D.II f. 116), 3 (*The Boke of St Albans*); 9, 14; 19 (Harley Ms. 4431, f. 144), 20 (Add. Ms. 24098, f. 28b); 24, 29, 30, 31, 32 (from *The National History of British Game Birds* by Jean Guille Millais, 1909); 34 (Royal Ms. 14 Eiv, f. 244b).
J. Dewar & Sons Ltd.: cover photo.
Mary Evans Picture Library: figs. 4 (*'Chasse au Cerf'*), 10, 11, 12 and 25.
Mansell Collection: figs. 8, 13, 16, 17, 21, 22 and 23.
W. Keith Neal: figs. 27 and 28.
Radio Times Hulton Picture Library: fig. 15.
Victoria and Albert Museum: fig. 7.
Colour Plates IV, VI, VII and VIII are from C. Dixon's *Game Birds and Wild Fowl* (1900).

LIST OF ILLUSTRATIONS

List of Colour Plates *facing page*

FOREWORD

The wild game of the British Isles are a precious part of our heritage with beginnings stretching back before recorded time itself.

Many species of British game have evolved, survived and flourished and are now part of a scene that enriches our lives. Who among us has not been stirred with an almost primeval awe on first seeing a herd of red deer crossing a snow-covered corrie, been moved with tenderness at the first spindly steps of a roe calf, or felt a pounding of the senses on being startled by the gok—gok—gok of a male grouse flushed from the August purple heather?

Such delights we may take for granted, but on reflection it is well to realise that it is not mere fortunate chance that has bequeathed to us this heritage. Man himself, for one reason or another—be it survival, sport or love of things wild—has, over the centuries, culled and husbanded nature's wild life in judicious manner to preserve the various species.

There have been many books published over the years expounding the methods of the day. In this book we have gone back to the oldest published works and traced something of the history of planned preservation through legislation and husbandry. In the end perhaps we have only shown that there is very little new under the sun, and that what passes as new is often only a different way of looking at the old. Nevertheless, it is a remarkable story and certainly well worth recounting.

Gordon Baxter
W. A. Baxter and Sons Limited
Fochabers
Scotland

BAXTER'S: A BRIEF HISTORY

This book is a kind of love-child, the natural issue of the marriage of the Baxters to their environment. In many ways their business itself is as much a romantic affair with their heritage as it is a commercial enterprise.

This will come as no great surprise to those who know the North of Scotland. If you are lucky enough to be born in one of the most beautiful spots on earth, where history and geography have become so inextricably intermixed that you cannot tell which colour's which; where you can taste the bitterness of remembered tragedy in the sweet mountain air and feel the tangible weight of sadness hanging over the empty glens like the poignant echo of a pipe lament; where the pure joy of life is caught in the gaiety of mountain streams which, even when they become great rivers, don't grow old and staid like their more solemn lowland kin; where bird and beast and man live together in a balance of resignation which composes its own sharply minor key harmony; if, indeed, it is your fortune to be native to this background the surprise would be to find your personality untouched by it, your aspirations uninformed by it.

Which is perhaps to say no more than that people are the products of their environment. Yet it is meant to say more. The Scots—and particularly the Highland Scots—are notoriously expatriate, no doubt as much from force of circumstances as from desire. Their renown is more usually won abroad than at home, as it is invariably won individually rather than corporately. Distillers aside, it is hard to call to mind many business names indigenous to Northern Scotland which have the same world-wide familiarity as Baxter's, and certainly none so firmly committed to its Scottishness and the natural harvest of its native soil.

The Baxter family tree is deeply rooted in this soil, though just how deeply seems never to have been traced. No doubt, there was an ancestor provenancing the victorious army at Bannockburn, but the earliest piece of family lore dates from much later. The story may not be apocryphal but it will certainly have gained something in the telling down the years. As the bakers of the Macmillan Clan, even the early Baxters were closely involved in culinary matters, both in terms of preparation and provisioning, and one Andrew Baxter appears to have been at the head of affairs during the time of the English Civil War. While his clan chief sat at Huntly trying to make up his mind whether he was for King or Covenanters the bold Andrew along with some other determined royalists among his clansmen, declared for Montrose.

During subsequent negotiations between Montrose and the Gordons, Andrew Baxter was responsible for the hospitality, the munificence of which moved the elder Gordon to compliment his host. He might, perhaps, have been less generous in his praise of the quality of the feast had he been aware that his own lands had provided most of the raw material. One doubts though, whether Andrew Baxter would have been pleased to have been labelled a poacher.

Curiously, this period coincides with their transition from vernerers to gardeners to grocers to manufacturers, curiously only because it appears easier to become a law-breaker in relation to the Game Laws than almost any other (except perhaps those governing motor cars), probably by virtue of their archaic nature. At any event, it seems fairly certain that the nearest a Baxter has come in recent years to being on the wrong side of the law may have been in connection with the buying, processing and selling of game. This was one of the reasons for their becoming licensed game dealers themselves in 1972, by the acquisition of two existing businesses, which coincidentally make them now one of the biggest game houses in the country. The wheel has come full circle from Willie to Ian and Gordon.

The two brothers themselves are well known sporting hosts to visitors from all corners of the globe, the one with the shooting on the Pitgaveny Estate and the other on that most famous of all salmon rivers, the Spey.

Ian is every way a production man. Aside from being in charge of the Baxter output, he farms much of the produce that finds its way into their cans and is personally responsible for the organization of the shooting over the 6,000 acres around Pitgaveny House, in his native Moray, which belong to the Dunbars. Pitgaveny, to quote Colin Willock of the *Sporting Times* is 'altogether a sporting paradise'. Willock was one of three sporting journalists invited in September 1972, jointly by Baxters and William Grant & Sons, to attempt a 'McNab'. Describing the variety of game to be found on the estate, Willock went on:

> 'Pheasants go without saying. So do pigeon. I have seldom seen so many outside the best Hampshire woodie country. Rabbits and hares, of course, and our hosts assured us that the woodlands were bursting with roe. The sea once lapped nearly up to the big house, though it has centuries since retreated, leaving behind a vast, gamey marsh. I do not care to think how many snipe, teal, mallard, let alone wild, fast pheasants, this might have turned up in a spaniel's walk.
>
> 'I have not even mentioned the loch, loud with the music of 400 greylags and where wigeon, teal, pochard and most other species of duck swam contentedly waiting for the urgings of twilight to set them on the wing.
>
> 'Oh, and I almost forgot the caper. Not the sort of setting in which I would have expected capercailzie, but there, among a flock of feeding pigeon, was a turkey-sized cock bird. We put the pigeon up. The caper gave them twenty yards' start, drove his great wings downwards four or five times and overtook them all in a climbing jet take-off that soared him over the tops of the nearest

fir trees, long before the woodies had even reached the edge of the stubbles.
"Yes," the hosts said, "there were a lot of caper." '

Thirteen varieties in three paragraphs (without mentioning partridge!) might well have earned a place in Gladstone's *Record Bags*—if not for the proliferation of game then perhaps for the speed of pen—and it is little wonder that Willock rates Pitgaveny so highly.

Ian Baxter is a modest man but he does number among the distinguished 'left and right' band (though only one of them was a woodcock). He also once got two partridge with the same shot, which no doubt gratified his national sense of thrift.

Do shooting and fishing (both with 'g's) have different personalities reflective of the people who enjoy them? Certainly in Baxterland this seems to be the case, for what Ian is to shooting Gordon is to fishing. Although, if shooting is an extrovert and fishing a quietly contemplative pastime then the reflections are inverted, for Gordon Baxter is the great extrovert. An entrepreneur with an immense flair for imaginative and creative salesmanship, he finds his relaxation in the waters of the Spey, matching the wiles of the angler against the elusiveness of the salmon. (Ironically enough, however, the family record was held for some years by his wife, Ena, who had a twenty-two pounder to her credit.)

On his beat of the river Spey Gordon plays host to Europeans, Americans, Australians and even Japanese, all of whom come to Speyside to combine business with pleasure. On one memorable occasion a party of oriental gentlemen spent an entire week on the water without landing a single fish, but, with the philosophical resignation for which they are renowned (fortified, no doubt, by the same water suitably processed a little up-stream) nevertheless returned home happy with their labours. This perhaps best sums up the charm of this romantic corner of Britain, the combination of the beauty of the place and the hospitality of its people.

In all these circumstances it is not surprising that the Baxters gave birth to this natural child nor yet that it should legitimately be called *Baxter's Game Book*.

INTRODUCTION

Anthologies are always open to criticism regarding balance. Either too many surfaces are exposed and none of them more than scratched, or just one or two aspects of the subject are explored in some depth. The only alternative seems to be a work of encyclopaedic scale which, by definition, is unreadable.

The first purpose of this anthology is to entertain. It may, therefore, err on the side of breadth, rather than depth, and will even then undoubtedly prove too narrow. It sets out to give pleasure to the informed by recalling familiar topics; and to the uninitiated by providing interesting sidelights as well as straightforward information on an unfamiliar scene. It has no pretensions to being either an instruction manual or a scholarly treatise. There is no more tuition in the art of the gun than there is tutorial on the evolution of the genus lagopus, though both are described.

The idea for this book was largely born out of the long association of the Baxter family with almost every aspect of game. From the ancestor who was gamekeeper to the Duke of Richmond and Gordon at the time of Waterloo, down to the brothers Gordon and Ian who, themselves, provide raw material for their internationally renowned products, the Baxters have never been far removed from the sporting scene in some of the finest game country in the world.

It was natural for them to be interested in this book and even more so that it should take their name.

CHAPTER ONE

Sportsmanship and Conservation

HOW LONG does it take to outbreed an instinct that is as old as the species? Does it, in fact, ever happen?

When the naked ape first came down from the trees to become *homo sapiens*, the sheer need to survive developed his predatory nature. Much the same thing can still be seen among the few remaining primitive peoples of the world, who kill primarily as a matter of self-preservation.

Modern man's mastery of his environment, however, leaves him no longer with any necessity to prey on other creatures. Civilization translated hunting from a biological to a cultural activity, formalising the natural instinct with sets of rules which allowed it to be defined as sport. Whether this is a means of satisfying a psychological need for justification is a purely twentieth-century debate – the earliest motivations were concerned simply with preserving the pastimes of privilege. The first conservationists owed nothing to ecology!

The historian William Harrison, writing in 1577, described an early attempt by King John at game preservation, in as much that 'going in progress about the kingdom in the tenth (year) of his reign, he found little or no game wherewith to solace himself or exercise his falcons. Wherefore he restrained all manner of hawking or taking of wild fowl throughout England for a season, whereby the land within a few years was replenished again'.

There is even a mild, if perhaps unconscious, irony about the two definitions of the word 'game'.

(1) 'Animals pursued or taken in the chase in sports of the field', and
(2) 'Wild animals protected by law from killing by anyone without a licence'.

This concern for conservation, maintaining the 'delicate' balance between the species (i.e. man v. the rest) is, then, by no means a new one. 'A Sportsman', writing in 1770, claimed that the reasons for the decrease in game which he had witnessed in his own life-time were, besides 'accidental causes' such as 'very dry, or very rainy seasons', four-fold: 'Poachers, Dog-breakers, Shepherd's dogs, and Vermin', and he complained that the contemporary Game Laws did very little to resolve the problem. He asserts that they had 'long been thought very inequitable, and oppressive: That they are not effective to ascertain the rights of gentlemen, or to prevent the destruction of the game, is evident, from the great number of law-suits and quarrels, that they have lately been productive of, in which some of the first rank and fortune have lost their lives . . . In every town in England, there is a qualified Poacher, some idle scoundrel of no property, no profession, without even the merit of a Dog-breaker, who has dissipated his small estate, and is the everlasting pest of every Gentleman for twenty miles round; if Game were made property, these gentry may find better sport, among their brother Savages in America, after the benefit of a free passage over.'

This polemic is followed by a short treatise in which he analyses the four main causes of trouble, and propounds some interesting solutions. His definitions of 'vermin' might particularly generate some warmth under the modern conservationist's collar.

'*Of Poachers.* All unqualified persons who kill Game, are poachers; but those are more commonly understood to deserve that name who are common fowlers, or fellows who kill Game privately, with an intention to sell it; and those vagabonds are rather encouraged than prevented by the present Laws: For if the Farmers who live upon the lands, and visit their fields every day, are not allowed to sport themselves, or licensed to kill Game upon them, for their own use; they will either destroy the Game out of resentment, or allow the Poacher to do it for them; neither will their servants prevent, or inform against a poacher, who can perhaps afford to make them a small present, which most of them would accept of, rather than a share of a large fine, accompanied with the detested name of an informer.

'Many Farmers have told me, that because they had been prevented from coursing and shooting by their landlords, they were determined that he should find nothing upon their farms; and that they would allow their Dogs to destroy every Hare, and every Bird in the breeding time, which is certainly in their power, whenever they chuse to do it.

'Some have told me, that since they durst not sport themselves, they would destroy all the Game to save their fences, and to prevent their sheep from being disturbed on the Moors.

'Others have acknowledged, that they often had entertained Poachers in their houses, and in return for their hospitality, have had a Hare, or a brace of Birds, to send a friend in town.

'I am therefore humbly of the opinion, that the Farmers *only*, have it in their power to prevent Poaching in any degree, and that they ought to be encouraged by this, by allowing them some privileges that may make it their interest, to use their best endeavours, to prevent this cause of the decrease of the Game; If they are even allowed to be the Gamekeepers of their own farms, supposing them to be ever so keen Sportsmen, there would remain double the quantity of Game, at breeding time, every season, for their own advantage . . .

'*Of Dog-breakers.* . . . Dog-breaking, or training young pointers, and spaniels, which is not prevented by the present laws, because they do not kill the Game. Gamekeepers in England, and common or licenced Fowlers in Scotland, go out with their young Dogs, in breeding time, when they often snap up a weak Hare, or a brooding Hen, or the young before they are able to fly; or if they go out earlier, in the pairing season, although they do not kill, which sometimes may happen, yet the old Birds, that are often disturbed, and driven from place to place, will not breed that season, and when taken in the net, and let go again, they lose their wildness and vigour, and become an easy prey to the meanest of the Vermin . . .

'*Of Shepherds Dogs*. . . . Of Shepherds Dogs; and I believe more Game are destroyed by them, than by all their other enemies; but I hope this will be prevented, by the attention of their Masters, the Farmers, who if they are concerned in the preservation of the Game, would undoubtedly encourage their servants to keep in their Dogs; whereas at present, they allow them to straggle out, and beat about for Game, and see them often, without remorse, pick up a whole Brood or covey, which they know will be agreeable to their master, who has oftener quarrelled with his landlord about the Game, than any thing else.

'As many fatal accidents have happened by Mad-Dogs, and many sportsmen have lost their Hounds and Spaniels, by the carelessness of Shepherds not keeping in their Dogs, during the Summer, but allowing them to go out alone, for whole days in hot weather, to feed on carrion, which occasions fevers and madness. It ought to be lawful for every person to shoot, or pursue those Dogs he may find rambling alone in the field, in Summer, and in the unlawful times . . . a high penalty ought to be against any man, who keeps a Dog that has refused to eat or drink for two days together, without shutting him up, or chaining him alone, it being usual for Dogs to refuse their meat and drink, three or four days, before they grow furious; and it is after they are gone from home, that all manner of miscief [sic] is done. They wander about biting cattle, and sometimes men, that are so unfortunate as to come in their way . . .

'*Of Vermin*. The last cause of the destruction of the Game is Vermin, by which sportsmen mean the Birds, and Beasts of prey.

'I shall propose a plan for their destruction which, if properly executed, I humbly think must, in a few years, extirpate them as effectually, as our Forefathers destroyed the Wolves; and also furnish some employment for those human Vermin, who infest every parish in the kingdom, and would rather be transported or hanged, than give up their gun.

'A Farmer who dares not kill Game, will not take the trouble to carry his gun every day, or even take it up at all, on purpose to shoot the Birds of prey, that may chance to fly past him; neither will he encourage his Dogs to attack Vermin, or keep those that are proper for it, when he has no immediate reward for them. . . . To destroy the Vermin entirely a premium ought to be given, for killing, and bringing in, Birds and Beasts of prey, over the whole island at one time. This premium might be raiséd by a small tax, in proportion to every estate . . .'

The 'Sportsman' then lists the various species of the birds and beasts of prey, and the damage caused by each. He includes every species of the Eagle which are 'destructive to the young Deer, Lambs and weak Sheep' as well as 'black Game, Growse and Wild Duck'; the Goshawk ('most destructive to the Hares, and all kinds of Game'); the Falcon, 'who as well as the Goshawk, kills a brace of Birds every day, besides the destruction they make, when they are rearing their young'; the Sparrow-Hawk ('the greatest enemy of the Partridge, and the Pidgeon'); the Merlin, 'who is swiftest of all Birds, and a deadly foe to the young Moor-Game, Partridges, Quails, Cocks, and Snipes'; the Ring-Tail, the Grey Buzzards, and the Moor Buzzard, and 'other tribes of the Buzzard kind, the Kite, . . . the whole genus of small Hawks . . . except the Stannyel, who lives entirely on Mice, and is therefore an useful bird, like the Owl'; Carrion Crows, and Magpies ('the Carrion Crow is very destructive to young Game on the Moors, as the Magpie is to young Partridges, Quails, and Rails'). The beasts of prey are the Fox, 'more destructive to the Farmer, and the Game in the pairing season, than any of the other vermin; I humbly think the highest premium ought to be given

1. King John hunting the stag

for him'; the Wild Cat, particularly destructive to the Moor Game, Lambs and Poultry; the Pole Cat, Fitch or Foumart, and the Martin which live on game; the Weasel ('I have seen this little animal kill an old Growse, and have been credibly informed, that they will attack a Hare; that they eat the eggs of all kinds of Game, is well known to most sportsmen, but I suppose the Farmers will chuse to save him, because he is an enemy to Rats and Mice'); the Otter, for his onslaughts on the fish of ponds and rivers; and lastly the 'Snakes, Vipers or Adders' which destroy eggs in birds'-nests and sometimes kill the hen-bird too. The writer concludes his treatise with a fervent plea for responsible action.

> 'I am an old Sportsman, and have seen the Game gradually decrease every year, not only from the causes I have mentioned, but from the increase of luxury in trading towns, the additional demand for Game, the great rewards given to Poachers for Game to send to London, and the great number of Gentlemen that can now shoot flying; which is the most certain way of taking all kinds of Game, at least the whole season round. I hope I shall not survive the Game of this island, or be obliged to banish myself from my native country to enjoy the pleasure of the chace in my old age: I will rather hope that the Lords and Gentlemen of parliament, will soon consider the necessity of preventing the farther decrease of the Game, and constitute such penalties, and premiums, as will in a few years restore them to their original plenty; when every man who has land, may have a share of the sport, at least upon his own land, and every man that can afford to pay for them, may have them on his table.'
>
> (*Essays on the Game Laws,* 1770)

Another eighteenth-century sportsman who claimed to have a proposition 'for making a Game Law both useful and effectual' suggested that, 'surely' there would be 'no hardship, in banishing such food from the tables of the meaner sort of Mechanicks, and poor Labourers'.

As far back as the Conqueror, when the Norman nobles exalted venery almost into a religion, there were laws protecting game, and an awareness that unless such legislation was observed, both numbers and quality of the game available would deteriorate rapidly. Gamekeepers, eventually, were appointed, but the very crude form of wild life control at first practised was shockingly inhumane.

> 'How crude it was may be judged by the wide differences of opinion among gamekeepers themselves. At one extreme the old type was both indiscriminate and cruel: any bird with a hooked beak was a predator with designs on game chicks, in fact almost any non-game bird and a range of animals would be found strung up on his nauseating gibbet. The sight of a decomposing corpse presumably was to deter others by reminding them of impending fate. Often animals were caught in gin traps infrequently visited, and so left to die lingering deaths. Even if the old type disappeared, many gamekeepers retained a special hatred for hawks and had most exaggerated ideas of the amount of damage a pair of peregrines might do. Another maxim was that the first essential condition, to quote from *The Keeper's*

Book, 'in order to increase a stock of game on an estate, is the destruction of vermin', and one must remember the wide range covered by 'vermin' – rats and mice yes, also rabbits, foxes, stoats, weasels, polecats, otters, as well as wood-pigeons and crows. Indeed the noblest of birds are 'vermin' to many gamekeepers – the golden eagle, the osprey, the kite, all owls. All, according to the old type of gamekeeper, to be shot in the interests of the grouse and his fellow noblemen.'

In the late nineteenth century, the situation began to change, with government legislation for game conservation and a growing awareness of the need for discrimination on the part of shooters. Eric Parker, writing in 1918, describes the changing attitude and defends the gamekeepers of his own day.

'It is the fashion to blame the gamekeeper always, and nobody else but the gamekeeper, for the destruction of the rarer forms of wild life in these islands; and I doubt if he deserves all that is said of him. It is true that if you go back fifty or a hundred years – to any time up to the 'eighties', say, of the last century, before the Wild Birds Protection Acts began to be operative, and before books on shooting like the *Badminton* were published – you will find that gamekeepers as a class were destructive and ignorant, and trapped and shot indiscriminately on the principle that what was not game was, therefore, the enemy of game. It is true, too, that the less observant and less well-educated keeper of to-day shoots if he is doubtful, just because it is less trouble to shoot than to wait and watch. But the unobservant and ignorant among keepers tends to disappear, just as he does in other callings which need skill and thought for success, and the keeper who shoots owls and who regards all hawks as vermin is a vanishing type.

'But in any case, stupid or unobservant, of the ancient school or the modern, who and what, after all, is the gamekeeper? Whom does he represent? He represents the average countryman – the sportsman, farmer, smallholder, labourer, cottager with chickens, geese, ducks. He is the countryman with a difference – just that he has a gun in his hand. He has killed hawks for generations because hawks kill young pheasants and partridges; and if he had never existed, the farmer would have killed hawks, and would be still killing them, because hawks kill chickens. It is not only the gamekeeper, who asks, 'Does this bird or beast interfere with my food?' It is the ordinary, plain, average human being, producing food from the soil, obeying the ancient and simple law that if a man will not work, neither shall he eat. He sees his food being destroyed, and he destroys the destroyer, with the better justification probably, the savager and grander the destroyer may be. Eagles, kites, and ravens have been killed down not because they devour pheasants, but because they feed on poultry and lambs; and the same process of reasoning which has all but exterminated the kite, menaces already the badger and the fox. Both may some day go down to the dodo; but when they go, it will be not because they have robbed the rearing-field but because they threaten the chicken-run.'

(*Shooting Days*)

Nowadays, the survival of many of these birds and beasts depends on positive action to protect them, not from the consequences of predatory incursions into 'chicken-runs' or rearing-fields, but from the inexorable pressures of 'growth' economy. The eagle apparently does not find the power station cooling tower a congenial nesting site. The badger sets very little store by shopping centres: the disappearance of hedgerows, chemical fertilisers, pest control, industrial waste, the simple need for more living space for people, all add to the complexity of the problem without contributing much to the solution.

This is not to deny that some control is sometimes needed. Unfortunately, until very recently 'control' seems to have been capable of being interpreted as indiscriminate persecution. In 1920 Tom Speedy observed:

> 'The peregrine, as already observed, is the most dashing of our birds of prey, and to see him making a quarry is a sight to be remembered. He is, however, a meaningless murderer, and few people have the slightest idea how destructive he is. As is well known, grouse indigenous to the British Islands realise a pound per brace [sic] on our Scottish moorlands, and shooting rents pay a large percentage of local taxes. The peregrine pays neither rates or taxes, but it would be interesting to ascertain how many grouse a pair annually destroys. This will never be ascertained, as every grouse killed between February and June means the destruction of a covey; and I have seen peregrines, when catering for their young, bring five grouse to the eyrie in six hours. Grouse, blackgame, curlews, duck, and plover constitute the staple food of peregrines on inland moors . . .
>
> 'Since game preservation has become so common in Scotland, the peregrine falcon has been justly persecuted; yet he holds his own despite every effort to destroy him. It is only in the solitude of deer-forests, where grouse are not wanted, that he is allowed to harbour. Incredible as it may appear, it is nevertheless a fact that a pair of these birds, if allowed to rear their young on an inland grouse moor, will soon immensely reduce its value. For some time before nesting they generally take up their abode on a rock selected for their eyrie, and it is not too much to say that a brace of birds daily fall victims to their destructive habits. When the young are hatched, more are necessarily required for the nestlings.'
>
> (*The Natural History of Sport in Scotland*)

And less than fifty years later, James Fisher records:

> 'Family *Falconidae*, Peregrine: Breeding population of Britain/Ireland order (less than 1,000 pairs): decrease under human persecution from the nineteenth well into the twentieth century, a stabilisation just before the Second World War, further decrease in the war years under special persecution, a rapid recovery from the late 1940s under protection, and a crash since 1955, with convincing evidence of toxic chemicals as a major factor, as summarised by the work of Ratcliffe and Parslow. By 1961 two-fifths of the *c*.1939 British population of *c*.650 pairs had gone and only 82 reared young; only 68 pairs reared young in 1962. In Ireland *c*.190 breeding pairs in 1950 may have fallen to under 70 in the mid-1960s. There

were signs of some arresting of the decline in Britain in 1964.'

(*Thorburn's Birds*)

This seems to raise questions about the definition of 'control'. Who, in fact, controls the controllers?

In the case of the red deer, a species which needs strict regulation, Sir Dudley Stamp summarised the situation in his *Nature Conservation in Britain.*

'The problem of controlling the deer population in Britain has some points of comparison with the grey seal problem, with the added complications that deer-stalking and hunting has long been a part of the social life of Britain, albeit a sport for the privileged few, and that venison is a highly appreciated and valuable food. The red deer (*Cervus elaphus L.*) standing about four feet high at the withers, and the much smaller roe deer (*Capreolus capreolus L.*) of about half that height, are the only true wild deer in Britain. The red deer, formerly occurring over the whole country, but now restricted to the Highlands and Islands of Scotland, the Lake District, Exmoor, the Quantocks and the New Forest (though there possibly re-introduced) is a gregarious animal of the moorlands; the roe deer is a nocturnal woodland animal living in small family groups and has been extending in the new forests of the Forestry Commission. The reign of Edward VII (1901–1910) saw the recognized and demarcated deer forests of Scotland increase in numbers to over two hundred and the acreage to over 3,850,000 acres. At the peak period of 1912–13, just before the outbreak of the First World War, the deer population may have reached 175,000: the annual kill reached 12,500 (all stags should be seven years or more), the 'industry' employed 12,000 persons and the rental of deer forests was over £100,000 per annum. Although probably 50–60,000 were killed for food during the war, the present situation began to emerge: too many deer, little disturbed by the extinct race of wealthy deer-stalkers, chasing too little food on too little land, and competing for that land with the growing economic needs in lamb, mutton, beef and timber. The townsman, thinking of the deer in Richmond Park, is very easily led to be sentimental about Britain's wild deer. He should see the emaciated carcases, two-thirds of them last year's calves, on the ground in the Highlands after severe frosts as in the winter of 1962–3. Again comes the obvious need for positive control and how our red deer should be managed under today's conditions.

'Even in Southern Britain the increase in numbers both of our native deer and of the several introduced feral species is creating major problems. One thing becomes clear: the worst cruelty is that inflicted by failure to take positive steps to control the deer population.'

Throughout the Middle Ages the roe deer was an important species among the 'beasts of chase'. It is mentioned by Turbervile in his *Booke of Hunting* and by Archbishop Aelfric in his famous *Colloquy*:

'I take harts, boars, and deer, and roes, and sometimes hares . . . I braid nets and set them in a convenient place, and set on my hounds that they may pursue the beasts of chase, until they come unexpectedly to the nets . . .'

(The practice of taking roe-deer with nets is even noted in the *Domesday Book*, as being in vogue in Lancashire at the date of the Norman Conquest: 'Rogerius de haci teñ Cortune. Ibi est haia capreolis capieñd.')

By the nineteenth century, however, J. E. Harting in his *Essays on Sport and Natural History* is surprised to find that the animal has become extinct:

> 'It is not a little curious that of the three species of deer which were once plentiful in England the smallest should be the first to become extinct.
>
> 'One would have supposed that its diminutive size, its timid disposition, and retiring habits, combined with fewer requirements as regards food, would have enabled it to linger on and hold its own in the remnants of our ancient forests.'

Happily Harting was mistaken and the roe deer, though its numbers were much diminished during the eighteenth and nineteenth centuries, has survived to re-establish itself throughout Britain.

Inevitably changes in agriculture have dramatic effects on wild life. While in 1973 environmentalists lament the consequences of grubbing up hedgerows, disenclosing the land as it were, A. E. Knox, in 1850, put the disappearance of the black grouse from Southern England down to enclosures.

> 'It must be admitted that the chief obstacle to the existence or increase of the black grouse in the south of England is the genius of modern agriculture. The rage for enclosing and draining waste lands and commons – where the soil, frequently sandy and poor, can never repay the first outlay of the wealthy experimentalist or the subsequent labour of the husbandman – has expelled it from many districts where it was of frequent occurrence, even within the memory of the present generation. But besides the ancient forest moors, there are still several extensive heaths – as for example, in West Sussex – which, from their peculiar situation and the present depreciated state of all farming produce, are not as likely, at least for many years, to be absorbed in the surrounding tillage. Many of these are intersected by clear streams, and broken here and there with clumps and plantations of alder, birch, hollies and fir trees, and adjoin, or are included in, the manorial rights of extensive neighbouring preserves. Pheasants, partridges, a few snipes, and even woodcocks, are found during different periods of the shooting season; but the black grouse is unknown. Doubtless he was here the representative of the *tetraonidae* in former days, but the very memory of his existence has since faded away. Now, reasoning from analogy, it has often struck me that he might without much difficulty be restored or introduced into these beautiful wastes by simply reversing the process that has already . . . proved successful in the North with the pheasant.'
>
> (*Game Birds and Wild Fowl*)

It is only now, faced with prophecies of doom and destruction, including the extinction of our *own* species, that the realisation is beginning to dawn that so long as technological improvements on natural processes are informed only by economic motives, there is a very real danger that natural resources will be either irreparably damaged or exhausted completely. The argument that nature should be allowed to take its course without the dubious advantages of man's intervention appears to be gaining strength, even leaving aside any moral considerations. It would be ironic if the Anti-Blood Sports campaign were now to succeed on technical grounds.

Meanwhile the moral battle rages as strongly as ever and apparently over much the same ground. Knox was busy with it 120 years ago.

> 'It would be useless to deny that all field sports, even when conducted on the most humane principles, are attended with a certain degree of cruelty, but it is obvious that none should venture to prefer such a charge except those who rigidly, and from conscientious motives, abstain from all kinds of animal food. All other persons afford an indirect encouragement to the deprivation of life, and are as deeply implicated in the culpability as the actual perpetrator of the deed. How unjust, then, to abuse the grouse shooter and the angler while we encourage the poulterer and the fishmonger, or to condemn the deerstalker while we patronize the butcher.
>
> 'An instinctive love of the chase seems to be innate in man. It prevails equally amongst the most barbourous savage tribes and the most enlightened cultivated nations, and exists as strongly at the present moment as in the days of Nimrod. But while, on the one hand, the maudlin complaints of modern sentimentalists may be treated with contempt or derision; on the other, it must not be forgotten that "the quality of mercy" is the noblest attribute of the "true sportsman", an appellation of which the mere bird murderer and the cold-blooded pot-hunter are utterly unworthy, while even the well-meaning but thoughtless gunner who indulges in a long range – where game is sufficiently plenty to admit of his picking out his birds within a moderate distance and "killing them clean" – must abandon the cruel though occasionally tempting custom before he can justly lay claim to the title.'

In common with most writers on the subject, particularly those of the nineteenth century, Knox is concerned with good manners and the essential sporting ethic is that of the 'fair fight'. He deplores indiscriminate shooting by inexperienced guns (as much as the targets themselves, no doubt).

> 'I am aware that it is easier to preach than to practise, and readily admit that "in my hot youth" I was no better than my neighbours; but the very recollection of these juvenile delinquencies renders me now the more anxious to make some amends by endeavouring to dissuade others from a habit so mischievous yet so easily corrected. With this view I have occasionally, during the last few years, preserved a specimen of a pheasant or partridges, which at some period prior to its death had been mutilated or disfigured by a random shot, and whenever a youthful visitor to my museum shows symptoms of sporting propensities by a marked admiration of the game birds, I generally venture to read him a lecture on the subject, and to draw his attention to my assemblage of cripples which I call

the "Chelsea Hospital" of the collection. I also tell him that it is a bad practice to fire at a pheasant the moment it rises from the ground, if it springs within a few yards of him; for the shot not being spread until it reaches a certain point, the bird in all likelihood receives the whole charge or none of it; and the consequence is that it is either woefully mangled or missed altogether. On the other hand, if a bird should rise out of distance, it is essentially wrong to let fly at it on the chance of a stray shot bringing it down; the probability is very great that, if hit at all, it will only be wounded and lost.

'Most of my specimens furnish examples of the former error. There is one miserable looking hen pheasant in particular which never fails to attract attention. Her entire beak had been shot away. Indeed, both mandibles and the tongue were gone, leaving a wide aperture, the edges of which, under the healing influence of dame Nature, had hardened into a pair of horny lips; and thus the poor bird – unable to procure its usual insect food, or to pick up any scattered grains of corn – was compelled to haunt a small barley stack, near the keeper's house; the sheaves of which being loosely placed together, she contrived to extract the ears separately, and to provide herself with sufficient food, for she was by no means in bad condition when killed by chance at the close of the season.

'But the number of birds thus maimed or disabled, are as nothing compared with those, which, appearing scarcely to wince under the effects of a long shot, are fated to perish miserably in some remote corner of a wood, unless the fox or the stoat should fortunately discover the spot, and charitably anticipate the wretched end. The amount of mischief occasionally perpetrated by the novice, who is thoughtlessly permitted to shoot at every thing, because he seldom succeeds in bagging a bird – and is therefore erroneously supposed to commit less havoc than a good shot, is really incalculable. The lord of the manor, if he is himself no sportsman, but merely preserves a head of game for the amusement of his friends, will perhaps say to his keeper, "Now, Smith, here are Captain Hawthorn and Lord Tyro going out today. You will take them to the hanger, where the tame birds were turned down this year. I don't want more than ten brace killed in that quarter, as I wish to leave a good stock for next year. The Captain is a dead shot. Put him on the hill at the top of the cover; none but old birds will fly that way, and they will run to the end, and perhaps be off before he gets there. So much the better. As to Lord Tyro, he is only a beginner. Place him in the bottom between the hanger and the gorse, where you have the barley stack. Most of the birds will go over his head. He will have two guns, and you may let him blaze away at every thing. I am told he can't touch a feather; but I wish him to have plenty of shooting." '

(*Game Birds and Wild Fowl*)

Since Knox's day, time has eroded some positions which appeared to be fixed and the definitions of both 'sportsman' and 'preservation' have undergone some modification. The once despised 'tradesman' (paying handsomely for the privilege) is now a vital figure on the sporting scene and 'preservation' has ramifications reaching far beyond the grouse moors.

The Duke of Edinburgh in his President's foreword to the Game Conservancy's Annual Review for 1970 expresses a characteristically unequivocal view.

> 'Contrary to what many uninformed people seem to think, European Conservation Year has made it more and more apparent that the man who shoots over his land is usually the most active supporter of the conservation movement. He fights to retain hedgerows and a sensible pattern of crops; he will protect ponds and marshes for duck; he is careful of the effect of chemicals. He is concerned with living things.'

CHAPTER TWO

'Dunghill' Gentlemen and the Game-Hunting Tradition

'. . . before I proceed any further, I will tell you what *Hunting* is; and from the true definition thereof, make your way more easie and plain in to the hidden Art of the same. Hunting is then a curious search or conquest of one Beast over another, pursued by a natural instinct of enmity, and accomplished by the diversities and distinction, or smells onely, wherein *Nature* equally dividing her cunning, giveth both to the offender, and offended, strange knowledge both of offence and safety . . .'

(Gervase Markham, *Country Contentments*)

THE CLASSIFICATION of animals as game depends principally on two qualities in the creatures themselves; first, that they shall provide good sport while alive; and second, that they shall provide good eating when dead. Thus the chicken, while making good table, is too domesticated and stupid a bird to offer challenge in the chase, while the fox, a wily quarry, remains as indigestible as Oscar Wilde.

Modern game, therefore, consists principally of birds* of the orders *Galliformes* (pheasant, partridge, grouse particularly but including also capercaillie and black game) and *Anseriformes* (wild fowl), with only the deer and the hare remaining to represent the quadrupeds. With the progressive urbanisation of society over the last 200 years and the parallel development of highly sophisticated agriculture, this reverses the earlier order of things.

The first book on field sports printed in England was also, curiously, the first book by a woman to be printed in England. The *Boke of St Albans* by (Lady) Juliana Bernes was published in 1486. D. H. Madden in *A Chapter of Mèdiaeval History*, sees it as a kind of gentlemen's primer, almost a *sine qua non* for aspiring gentry.

> 'The publication of the *Book of St Albans* marks an epoch in the social history of England, for in it we find the earliest recognition of a class which grew in importance throughout the succeeding centuries.
>
> 'There had come into existence a kind of "gentlemen whose ancestors are not knowen to come in with William duke of Normandie (for the Saxon races yet

*Pheasants, Partridges, Grouse, Heath or Moor Game, Black Game, Bustards, Woodcocks and Snipes are the protected species.

remaining we now make none accompt, much lesse of the British issue)''. Harrison tells how such a man takes his beginning in England, and how when he is able to ''beare the port, charge and countenance of a gentleman, he shall for monie haue a cote and armes bestowed vpon him by heralds (who in the charter of the same doo of custome pretend antiquitie and seruice, and manie gaie things)''. He is then called master, which is the title that ''men giue to Esquiers and gentle men, and reputed for a gentleman euer after''.

'But if the *novus homo* (called by plainspoken Master Stubbes ''a dunghill gentleman, or gentleman of the first head'' in the *Anatomie of Abuses*, 1583) is to pass muster as a gentleman, something more must be done than the obtaining for money of a coat-of-arms. He must learn to speak the language of the caste to which he has been admitted; and the literature of the sixteenth and seventeenth centuries teems with references to his endeavours to reach this standard with the aid of a book of sport.

'The best known one is in Ben Jonson's *Every Man in his Humour*:

STEPHEN: Uncle, afore I go in, can you tell me an we have e'er a book of the sciences of hawking and hunting, I would fain borrow it.

KNOWELL: Why, I hope you will not a hawking now, will you?

STEP.: No, wusse; but I'll practise against next year, uncle, I have bought me a hawk and a hood and bells, and all; I lack nothing but a book to keep it by.

KNOW.: O most ridiculous!

STEP.: Nay, look you, now you are angry, uncle; why you an a man have not skill in the hawking and hunting languages nowadays. I'll not give a rush for him; they are more studied than the Greek or the Latin. He is for no Gallant's company without them. (Act I, Sc. i).

'The great popularity of the *Book of St Albans* was largely due to the assistance which it gave to the growing class of those gentry who were, in Ben Jonson's words, ''in the cradle of their gentry''.

'In Ben Jonson's *Speech according to Horace*, the old nobility, the ''Beauchamps and Nevills, Clifford Audleys bold'', ask:

Why are we rich, or great, except to show
All licence in our lives? What need we know
More than to praise a dog or horse? Or speak
The hawking language?

'This, their gentle language, must needs be learned by study, as a foreign tongue, by the

Hodges, and those newer men,
As Stiles, Dike, Ditchfield, Millar, Crips and Fen.

'But it must be undertaken by the would-be gentleman of the Tudor Age, for it would have been as difficult for one living in that age to be regarded as a learned clerk without knowledge of Latin as to pass muster as a gentleman without acquaintance with a mode of speech derived from the Norman French of the Conqueror.

'I have elsewhere noted the difficulties with which the learner of this language had to contend, and his obligation to the *Book of St Albans* and its successors. "To him the Book of Sport served as grammar, dictionary, and exercise book in one. The task was no trifling one. There was a separate word for every conceivable act done by, or to, each beast of venery or of the chase, and for every incident of sport; with an endless array of appropriate verbs, nouns, and adjectives, the mis-application of any one of which stamped the offender as no gentleman . . . Many of these terms have survived to the present day, and lingering traces may yet be discerned of the old-world ideas associated with them. We still speak of a herd of

2. Lady Juliana Bernes, author of The Boke of St Albans

deer, a bevy of ladies, a congregation of people, a host of men, a flight of pigeons, a brace and leash of greyhounds, a couple of hounds, a litter of whelps, a covey of partridges, a swarm of bees, a cast of hawks, a flight of swallows, a stud of mares, a drove of cattle, and a flock of sheep. Few of us are conscious that in so speaking we are correctly using the gentle terms appropriated by the *Book of St Albans* to the various 'compaynys of beestys and fowlys'. And even now – so inveterate are ideas wrought into our blood – while the misuse of scientific terms suggests nothing more than ignorance, we can hardly avoid associating the idea of vulgarity with a man who would speak of a flight of partridges, a flock of grouse, or a pair of hounds''. (*Diary of Master William Silence*).'

If this presents Dame Juliana as a medieval Nancy Mitford, that may not be too much of an exaggeration, for she is very precise about 'dew termys', as for example, 'an Esquyer lodgeth' but 'a yoman beddeth'. Indeed, in the third part of the book 'is determined the lynage of coute armuris and how gentilmen shall be knowyn from ungentillmen'. The fourth section is a continuation of part three and was subsequently absorbed into it.

3. Frontispiece of The Boke of St Albans: *woodcut showing birds both heraldic and real*

D. H. Madden says that although our knowledge of the author is scanty, it 'is enough to secure for her immortality as the author of the earliest book on hunting written in the English language, and the Englishwoman who first gave her writing to the world in print'.

In the following extract she defines the categories of animals which could be hunted:

Foure maner bestys of venery there are:
The first of theym is the hert. The seconde is the Hare.
The Bore is oon of tho, the wolff and not oon moo.
And where that ye com in playne or in place.
I shall tell you which be bestys of enhace.
Oon of thym is the bucke, a nother is the doo.
The fox and the martion and the wilde roo,
And ye shall my dere chylde othe bestys all
Where so ye hem fynde rascall ye shall hem call.

Both the Buck and the Doe qualify as beasts of chase, but the Hind seems either to be omitted or to be included, by implication, with the Hart; while the distinction between Venery and the Chase appears fairly fine. Are the animals classified in order of nobility? The noble boar? Of ferocity then? Scarcely a fierce hare! Edibility perhaps? Even that suggests an improbable subtlety in the medieval palate, though it offers a neat and tidy line of descent from venery to game.

In fact the terms and forms of hunting belong to the age of chivalry. The earliest works on the subject are all French and one of the first *Le livre du Roy Modus*, lists the 'ten beasts of venery' under

Doulces	*Puans*
Stag	Boar
Hind	Sow
Fallow Buck	Wolf
Roe Buck	Fox
Hare	Otter

the distinction being made by Royne Racio (Queen Reason) between 'sweet' (*doulces*) and 'stinking' (*puans*) beasts, as she moralises the practical lessons given by Roy Modus (King Method). D. H. Madden argues persuasively in favour of Jean de Malon, Comte de Tancarville, as the 'maker' of the book which was written by an unknown scribe and probably first appeared about the year 1338.

Charles Collyns in *The Chase of the Wild Red Deer* quotes an even earlier reference which suggests a further refinement, between 'beasts of the forest' and other beasts of venery.

> 'The old book called *Antiquitas Britanniae* written before the Conquest, says that there were five wild beasts of venery that are called beasts of forest: the hart, the hind, the hare, the boar, and the wolf. The same statement is to be found in Hollinshed, and other old writers; and would my readers ask why the hart and the hind are both mentioned as beasts of forest, their query shall be resolved by

Manwood. "And whereas they say, the hart and the hind, being both beasts of one kind, and yet they do accompt them for two several beasts; it seemeth that it is because that although they be both of one kind, yet they are beasts of several seasons; for the hart hath his season in summer and the season of the hind doth begin when the season of the hart doth end".'

What is certain is that the conventions were strictly laid down and the hunt was required to be conducted with the same attention to manners as if it were a pavane. Viscount Ebrington (Master of the Devon and Somerset, 1881–7), writing in 1896, refers to the French origin of the earliest rules of etiquette.

4. 'Bestys of Venery': a medieval stag-hunt

'The fullest and most complete description of the arts of woodcraft and stag-hunting is found in the writings of Gaston, third Count de Foix, who died in 1394. He was a mighty hunter and his book seems for centuries to have been the standard work on sport. It was the basis of the earliest practical treatise on hunting in the English language, the "Mayster of Game", published at the end of the 14th century, and is quoted wholesale by Jacques de Fouilloux, a French author who wrote in 1561: whose book in turn became the parent of nearly every other volume written on the subject since . . .

'Stag hunting in the middle ages was a stately and solemn affair: "rude and furious cries", though permitted in boar hunting, were forbidden as derogatory to that science of venery in which men then took their degrees. Even Louis XV had to hunt first hares, then roe, then fallow deer for five years before he was allowed to hunt a stag . . .

5. 'Bestys of Venery': boar-hunting in the Middle Ages

'Du Fouilloux even gives quaint directions as to the place which is suitable for the meet.

' "A pretty, well-shaded spot should be selected, near a spring or stream: thither should the butler bring three good horses (no more and no less) laden with fluids and the cook should follow him with cold meats to grace the cloth which has been laid on the turf. So shall the king or great lord, with his companions, refresh themselves; and if there is an attractive lady within reach, she should be brought thither likewise, to help pass the time till the harbourers return and make their report. This heard, the great personage will decide which of the stags he will hunt, and will inform the favoured harbourers accordingly. . ." '

How, then, might our sporting ancestors have gone about the actual pursuit of the animal? In Elizabethan times, huntsmen were instructed to 'find out your game . . . early before Sun rise, at which time the Deer goeth to his food: from whence you shall watch unto his Leir; and have logded [sic] him, you may return home and prepare all things for the dayes hunting: for be assured, except violently compeld, he will not stir untill Evening'. So, for those without an entourage of servants, or 'an attractive lady' with whom to pass their time in sweet dalliance until the time was ripe for the chase (of the deer), a long period of waiting was likely (though few sportsmen of more recent years would agree that it is necessary to wait until evening before giving chase to a stag).

'Now for the manner of his hunting: you shall first cast off your finders, near his place of lodging, and after they have hunted him about a ring or two, you shall cast in the rest of your hounds; and being in full cry and main chase, you shall give them comfort both with Horn and sight of the Deer, and take what especiall notes or marks you can from him, so that as much as possible you may know him from any other Deer; then at every default, as soon as the hounds are in cry again, you shall make in to the hunted Deer, and view him, and if you find it to be a fresh Deer [i.e. too young to be hunted] you shall rate the Dogs, and bring them back to the default, and there make them cast about again, untill they have undertaken the first hunted Deer, and then give them comfort by hollowing and Gibelts [sic], and so continue the chase till you have either set up the Deer or slain him, ever and anon having a watchfull eye unto change: for it is the nature of a Deer, when he is once imbost, or weary, to seek where he may find another Deer, and to bear him up and lay himself down in his place.'

(Gervase Markham, *Country Contentments,* 1611)

Though seventeenth-century game included buck, roe, hare, fox, badger, otter, boar and goat, the stag was 'the most Princely and Royal Chase of all Chases'. But he was also much more than the most princely chase, he was a royal treasure chest of valuable specifics.

'He is of all Beasts the goodliest, stateliest and must [sic] manly; and for the use of Man, the fullest both of outward and inward profit, as in his flesh for the nourishment of Mans body, and in his other members for helps in Physick; As the bone in his heart, which is Soveraign for all inward faint sicknesses, for Poyson, the Plague, and hard Travail in women; his blood excellent for all kinds of Fluxes, and to make the skin white and smooth; his pizle good for the Colick and bloody-Flux; his Horn a most soveraign Cordial againgst venome, his suet for swellings, Gouts, and Humors; and his skin, which is ever a during and Gentlemanly cloathing: and of Staggs, the oldest and greatest is the best.'

(ibid.)

The hare, whose 'shifts and sleights, . . . doublings and windings' made her no easy quarry, likewise supplied sundry remedies and aids to health. Hares were, indeed, 'full of good profit for Mans Preservation'.

6. *From Gaston de Foix's* Livre de la Chasse: *questing with limer for wild boar (early 15th century)*

7. *Detail from Roe Deer Hunt, a tapestry woven at Tournai (15th century)*

'For though the beast be but little, yet are the members worth injoyment, as the flesh, which is good for all manner of Fluxes; the brains good to make children breed their teeth with ease; the wool excellent to staunch blood; the Gall sovereign for sore eyes; the blood which will kill Rheume, and Worms; the stifling bone, which being worn, taketh away the pain of the Cramp, with many other good things besides.'

(ibid.)

Food, sport and 'Physick' were, then, three properties of those species we classify as game. Another was rent! Loyal subjects of the realm were frequently obliged to contribute generous quantities of simple produce (fish, fowl and game, fruit, vegetables, honey, ale and wine) for their monarch's comfort and also, according to the season, fine linen and furs for his person, firewood and straw for his household, in return for secure tenure of property. J. E. Harting explains how the various monarchs kept their sporting instincts, as well as their appetites, well satisfied.

'Many [subjects] contributed . . . to the King's amusement by furnishing him with hounds for hunting, and with falcons for hawking, which they did annually at stated times by way of quit rent for the land they held. In the reign of Edward I, Henry de la Wade held ten pounds of land [i.e. as much as paid a yearly rent of ten pounds] at Staunton, in the country of Oxfordshire, by the serjeanty of carrying a Gerfalcon every year, before the King whenever he should please to hawk with such falcons, at the cost of the King.

'The Isle of Man was granted by Henry IV, to Sir John Stanley and his heirs for ever, to be held of the King, his heirs, and successors, by liege homage; rendering to the King two falcons, once only, viz. immediately after the homage done; and rendering to his heirs, Kings of England, two falcons on the day of the coronation of the said heirs, for all services, customs and demands; as freely, fully and entirely as William Scrope, Knight, or any other, held the same. (Patent Roll. 7th Hen. IV., par. 2, m.18.) The island was afterwards held by the Duke and Duchess of Athol (in right of the Duchess, lineally descended from Sir John Stanley) by the same honorary service of rendering two falcons on the day of the coronation of the Kings of England. (Stat. 5 Geo. III, c.26.)

'The tenants of Tey Magna, in the county of Essex, were formerly bound to maintain a number of *hawks* for the lord's use, till they were a year old. This service, however, was turned into a rent of 30s., and in 1782 this rent was paid to Thomas Astle, Esq., Chief Clerk of the Records in the Tower.

'Sir Robert Broughton, Kt., held the manor of Wellwyn in Hertfordshire of the King *in capite*, by the service of annually rendering a sparrowhawk, or two shillings, yearly, by the hands of the sheriff of Hertford for the time being. This form of tenure was not an uncommon one.

'The manor of Sutton, within the purlieus of the forest of Macclesfield, was formerly held by the service of free forestry, the owner being bound to follow the king's standard in war, with the same arms (bows and arrows) with which he guarded his balliwick of the forest, and whilst a tending in the wars he was exonerated from the custody of his balliwick.

'The foresters were entitled to timber and firewood, within their own districts, with other perquisites, and they had the liberty of fishing within the forest, and of taking Foxes, Hares, Squirrels, Bawsons (Badgers), Otters, Muskets (Sparrow-hawks), and Eagles.

'From the depositions of some old persons taken in the year 1720, it appears that the manor of Taxall, in the county of Chester, was anciently held by the service of blowing a horn on Midsummer Day at a high rock near Taxall, called Windgather; and that there was a tradition that the lord of this manor was to hold the king's stirrup and rouse the stag when he should come to hunt in Macclesfield Forest.'

(*Essays on Sport and Natural History*, 1883)

Such, then, were the customs of another age, long since fallen into disuse or replaced by a money payment to acknowledge the rights of the king. The traditions of another age, and those monarchs who perpetuated them, are also strongly associated with the subject of the next chapter, falconry.

CHAPTER THREE

The Age of Falconry

'The fawning Dog full of sagacitie;
Excelling in sense and capacitie,
The hardieMastife and nimble Greyhound,
The ornament of *Floras* blessed round,
Whose use we know, the Hart doth feare his might,
The squatting Hare doth tremble at his sight.
The noble chaunting hound with pleasing throat,
With bace and treble, meane, and tenor noat.
Warbling his voice, making the horne to sound,
Orderly tunes t'immortalize the Hound:
Quicke senting Spannels, fit for Princelie game,
To pearch the Pheasant, and rare Birds of name.
To set the Heath-cocke, Partrich and the Quaile
The Snype, the Woodcocke and the dainty Raile.
To serve the Spar-hawke, Faulcon and Laneret,
The Gosse-hawke, Ger-faulcon and young Eglet.
TheMarlyon, Hobby, Hawkes of swiftest wing,
Which many pleasures unto Ladies bring.
Deserveth praise of the best fluent Pen,
That ever wrote the benefits of men.'

(From *'Ourania'* by Nathaniel Baxter, 1606)

ALTHOUGH IT is not possible to date precisely the introduction of hawking into England, several sources provide evidence that it was practised in early Saxon times, perhaps through the influence of merchants and adventurers who became familiar with the art in the orient and brought falcons and falconers with them on their return home. (It is known that falconry was in vogue in the period of Sargon II (722–705 B.C.) in Assyria.) In a letter addressed by King Ethelbald to St Boniface, Archbishop of Mainz, who died in 754, the monarch asks that two falcons should be sent over that would serve to fly at the crane, for, he asserted, 'there are very few birds of use for this flight in this country'.

According to Asser's account of this king, 'His felicity in hunting and hawking, as well as in all the other gifts of God, was really incomparable, as I myself have seen'. The same author, writing of Ethelred (866–871), says that 'the King . . . continued to carry on the government and to exercise hunting in all its branches, to teach . . . his falconers, hawkers and dog-keepers' (under date 884 in Asser's *Life of King Alfred*).

Whether or not the Saxon falconers learned the art of taming and training hawks from eastern immigrants and imported birds cannot be proved, but the great falconry expert J. E. Harting found a remarkable similarity between the systems of treatment and the appliances used in Asiatic countries of old, and the more recent West.

Other theories suggest that Wales may have been the country of origin, from details given in the Venedotian Code of Laws applicable to North Wales and the many references in Saxon manuscripts to hawking with Welsh birds. William of Malmesbury, extolling Athelstan's gift for training hawks, claims that this royal devotee procured his hawks from Wales. And he also describes Edward the Confessor's love of hunting and hawking: 'It was his chiefest delight to follow a pack of swift hounds in pursuit of their game, and to cheer them with his voice, or to attend the flight of hawks taught to pursue and catch their kindred birds. Every day, after divine service, he took the field, and spent his time in these beloved sports.'

The practice of falconry was so prevalent and so widespread in Saxon times that the monks of Abingdon were obliged to procure a charter from King Kenulph to restrain the activity in harvest-time, in order to prevent their lands being trampled by neighbouring sportsmen. Archbishop Aelfric in his *Colloquy* (written in the tenth century) reveals that it was then a common custom in falconry to let the birds fly off to breed in the woods during the spring, in order to save trouble and expense of keeping them throughout the summer, and then to catch their young in the autumn. This practice was apparently still followed five centuries later, according to the famous fifteenth-century *Paston Letters*.

The early importance accorded to falconry cannot be over-estimated. According to E. D. Cuming, the Venedotian Code of Precedence ranked the King's Chief Falconer very high indeed.

> 'Of the twenty-four "Servants of the Court" that officer ranked fourth; it appears a slight on a great profession, but the Court Judge ranked fifth. How inferior hunting was held as compared with hawking we may measure by the fact that the Chief Huntsman was the tenth on this list.
>
> 'Not less informing is the exactness with which the value of hawks is prescribed – as was that of all domestic animals. For example, 'the eyrie of the King's hawk' was worth one pound; the value of a 'red eyess after mewing' (i.e. after moulting) was the same. This does not afford any definite idea of their worth, but we gain light thereon by comparing it with that attached to other livestock: the King's buckhound, also his greyhound, when trained, were worth each one pound, while a palfrey or a sumpter horse was appraised at 120 pence, and a working horse at sixty. The 'King's Hawk' and 'Red Eyess' were peregrine falcons; the latter term is . . . a bird of the year, whose plumage wears the reddish tint that gives place to the characteristic slate-colour after the first moult. A sparrowhawk was worth only twelve pence. Falcons – eyesses – taken from St David's Head were famous in old days. That promontory was a favourite breeding resort of these birds, and Giraldus Cambrensis [Gerald of Wales] says that Henry II preferred eyesses thence obtained to all others.'

8. *Queen Elizabeth I hawking (from Turbervile's* Booke of Falconrie, *1611 edition)*

Like all other forms of the chase, falconry was very much the pastime of the privileged classes, and throughout the Middle Ages each monarch maintained hawking establishments in various parts of his or her kingdom.

> '*The* royal "Mewse", as we learn from a map [of] 1585, was situated on what is now Trafalgar Square, and covering a greater space; behind it, on the site of the National Gallery and other buildings, was the "Mewse Close" where the hawks were flown at hack when their taming was sufficiently advanced.'

Henry III maintained mews in Lincolnshire, Northamptonshire and several other places too. Another king, Edward III, prescribed the death penalty in 1363 for anyone who stole a hawk: 'it shall be done of him as of a thief that stealeth a horse or other thing.' The Church, likewise, very keen on sport, supported such severe measures. In the reign of the same sovereign, the Bishop of Ely excommunicated someone who stole a hawk (the Bishop's own) from her perch in the cloisters of Bermondsey.

Henry VIII was renowned as an accomplished sportsman in many types of hunting while he retained his athletic figure, and as an enthusiastic one when his expanding girth replaced it. Though many old illustrations might suggest that persons of rank would normally ride on hawking expeditions, it was as usual to go on foot, carrying a pole for vaulting ditches and streams. The old chronicler Hall describes with suitably loyal concern how, on one such expedition, Henry's bulk nearly brought him to an untimely end in the sixteenth year of his reign (1525).

> 'In this year the King following of his hawk lept over a ditch beside Hychyn

9. *Falcon (from Turbervile's* Booke of Falconrie, *1611 edition)*

10. A 16th-century falconer, designed and engraved by J. Ammon

> [Hitchin] with a pole and the pole broke, so that if one Edmund Mody, a footman, had not lept into the water and lift up his head which was fast in the clay, he had been drowned; but God of his goodness, preserved him.'

Elizabeth continued the royal sporting tradition although, as perhaps befits the chief sponsor of the red-blooded traditions of the 'Golden Age', her tastes ran the whole gamut of blood-letting from hawking to the coarser spectacles of bull and bear baiting. Indeed in the matter of blood sports her tastes might truly be said to have been catholic. Cuming recalls how her wrath was provoked when she heard that her unfortunate prisoner, Mary, Queen of Scots, had been allowed by her keeper, Sir Ralph Sadler, who held the office of Grand Falconer, to accompany him on a hawking expedition, while she was confined at Tutbury in Staffordshire, in 1585. Sir Ralph had apparently taken every precaution against any escape or rescue attempt, but it is clear from his excuses that his conduct had greatly angered Elizabeth.

> 'I sent home for my hawks and falconers wherewith to pass this miserable life I lead here; and when they came hither, I took the commodity of them sometimes abroad, not far from this castle, whereof this queen, having earnestly entreated me that she might go abroad with me to see my hawks fly, a pastime indeed which she taketh singular delight in, and I, thinking it could not be ill taken, assented to her desire, and so she hath been abroad with me three or four times hawking upon the rivers here, sometimes a mile, sometimes two miles, but not past three miles when she was furthest from the castle.'
>
> (*Sadler State Papers*)

During the reigns of both Henry VIII and Elizabeth, the shot-gun, which was to contribute so much to the decline of falconry, was gaining in popularity and technical efficiency, and several laws were enacted against firearms by both Tudors and the succeeding Stuarts in attempts to protect their favourite sport.

It was not until the end of the Stuart period that the shot-gun was generally adopted, and because it was a more convenient method of taking game, it was hardly surprising that it should strongly rival the hawk. Hawks, according to Richard Blome and various other writers and compilers of works on falconry, need a vast deal of attention. It is not merely a matter of feeding them daily and regularly cleaning out their mews, but of handling them constantly to keep them accustomed to the fist, encouraging them to bathe themselves, watching every sign of change in their general condition, and being ready, should a bird fall ill, to tend to it according to the advice given in the hawking treatises (at great length). Of these, part of Blome's *The Gentleman's Recreation* was typical; it was a large folio dealing with such diverse interests as music, heraldry and chemistry, and it first appeared in 1686. It contained a substantial section on hawking, the combined work of several sportsmen supervised by Blome, who was no expert on the subject. It did, however, give precise information on the care and training of the birds, and much sound information on the intricate and precise classification system commonly used in the seventeenth century.

Both in Charles II's time and after, the number of people prepared to devote themselves to the care of their own falcons was very few; and among the more privileged classes, those who in more prosperous times could afford to employ professional falconers were in the main obliged, after the Civil War, to dismiss their falconers, close their mews, and take what sporting pleasures they could with shot-guns.

There was of course a notable exception, whom Cuming describes.

> 'Charles himself was devoted to falconry; he appears to have maintained the royal mews on a rather extravagant scale, for when, in 1667, a Committee of the Privy Council Board was appointed to advise on economies generally, they included in their schedule the following: – "Whereas your Majesty's falconry consisted formerly of these four branches, *viz*, the Brook, the Field, the Heron and the Crow; and your Majesty having thought fit that the charge of the two latter should cease, the expense of the other two, *viz*, the Brook and the Field, we have reduced with Sir Allen Apsley's consent to £1559 17s 6d. *per ann*, with which the Master of the Hawks is for the future to keep six cast of hawks for the Brook and so many for the Field, and to defray all other charges, fees and salaries relating thereunto according to an establishment thereof to be prepared." The Committee also recommended that "the Cormorant keeper be taken away, by which will be saved £84." Whether this was the official appointed by James I to care for his cormorants, ospreys and otters at Westminster, or another, we do not know.
>
> 'Sir Allen Apsley might consent to the reduction of the establishment he directed, with what grace we can imagine; but it was a blow when he himself

11. The hawk on the fist

> was retrenched, as happened soon after. Says Pepys, 22nd August 1667: – "it makes him mad and (he) swears we are doing that the Parliament would have done – that is we are endeavouring to destroy one another". Fortunately Sir Allen was not dependent on his office, for Lady Apsley "was an ugly pusse but brought him money". The post was afterwards revived, and granted by Charles to his son by Nell Gwynn, whose descendants, the Dukes of St Albans, have been hereditary Grand Falconers ever since.'

George II paid Charles Beauclerk, Duke of St Albans, £1,372 10s. per annum to maintain his mews, a job which demanded a good deal of attention, even though the king was not over-keen on falconry; his son Frederick, Prince of Wales, was a great enthusiast, however, and would fly his hawks on the downs whenever he was resident at the Palace of the Durdans at Epsom.

But in the reign of George III came what was virtually the death knell for the ancient sport, which Cuming describes.

> 'Until that period the old "common field" system of agriculture prevailed over the greater part of England: and in the absence of hedges, walls and fences, hawks could be flown nearly everywhere. When these obstructions, as the falconer would regard them, came into being the conditions were so radically changed in favour of the quarry that the sport became impossible. The hedge or wall afforded the game cover under which it could evade the stoop of the falcon and make good its escape. Open country is the only country in which the long-winged hawk can be flown with a chance of success. It was, for example, the conversion of the Yorkshire Wolds into cornland, with the indispensable enclosure of the fields, that led the famous Colonel Thomas Thornton to leave his native country and migrate to Wiltshire on whose still open downs he could continue his favourite sport.
>
> 'About the year 1770 we have evidence of effort to keep hawking alive in the formation of a club. This was founded by Colonel Thornton, and numbered between fifty and sixty members, with the Earl of Orford at its head. In 1783 the Club owned 32 peregrines, 13 goshawks, and seven Iceland falcons: and the members met each April for kite and crow hawking, Alconbury Hill in Huntingdonshire being a favourite venue, by reason of the plenty of kites which haunted the locality. From 1792 to 1838 the club, known as the High Ash, was under the control of Lord Berners; during this phase of its existence herons were the game principally flown. Heron and kite becoming rare in this country (a few pairs of the latter, jealously preserved, still [i.e. in 1929] exist in Wales) the High Ash Club came to an end, and the Loo was formed under the patronage of the King of Holland; to which country members resorted for a few years to hawk the heron. In 1853 the Loo Hawking Club came to an end to be succeeded after a short interval by the Old Hawking Club, which met every spring on Salisbury Plain and the Wiltshire Downs to fly rooks; birds which try the falcon to the utmost. This club was wound up in 1927 and is replaced by the British Falconers' Club

which, with an increasing number of members, keeps those interested in the sport in touch with one another, holding no annual meet.'

By the early nineteenth century hawking was sufficiently rare for a falconry exercise to have become an entertainment, staged for the diversion of an audience – sadly almost a 'side-show'. Pierce Egan, reporting a demonstration of the art in 1824, points up its curiosity.

'A very interesting exhibition of this species of amusement, which in olden times was so favourite a sport in England, took place, on Thursday, October 7, 1824, in the neighbourhood of Amesbury, and was witnessed by a numerous field of sporting gentlemen and others attracted by curiosity. The hawks, six in number, were remarkably large and fine young birds; and their proprietor, Colonel Thornhill [sic – elsewhere Egan refers to Colonel Thorn*ton*] directed the sport of the day, in the presence of Sir Hussey Vivian, Sir Francis Burdett, Mr. Mills, and numerous other gentlemen, who were invited on the occasion. The scene of action was an extensive field of turnips, in which it was known that there were partridges in sufficient number for the purpose, and the ground was graced by several carriages containing ladies. The hawks were brought to the field by the Colonel's falconer and assistant, perching, hooded, upon a frame; the sportsmen and spectators were ranged on the outside of the field; a fine bird was then taken from the perch by the falconer, unhooded, and permitted to fly. The hawk immediately towered, and hovered over the field, with his eyes intently bent towards the turnip plants in search of prey; he beat over the ground with evolutions similar to those of a pointer upon the ground. After a few minutes had elapsed, Colonel Thornton ordered some boys to enter the field, for the purpose of disturbing the birds; and a partridge at length arose, which was instantaneously seen by the hawk, though at a great distance. The hawk darted after it and struck it to the earth, but the partridge recovering, flew as it were for protection amongst the spectators; here it was pursued by the relentless hawk and killed. The other kawks [sic] were severally let loose, and all but one of them killed a partridge each; some of the latter were pursued and killed out of the sight of the spectators; and it is highly worthy of remark that the hawks had been so well trained that they invariably returned to the falconer at his call; and when out of sight and hearing, he attracted them by throwing into the air a lure (something resembling a stuffed partridge). The above exhibition afforded a most gratifying specimen of this ancient and very curious sport. Several excellent coursing matches took place previous to the hawking.'

(*Pierce Egan's Anecdotes*)

It is hard to believe that so short a time could have seen so dramatic a decline that even the language had been lost. Egan feels obliged to describe a 'lure' to his readers but he has already exposed his own ignorance by his reference to the hawk's flight and worse yet to its sex. D. H. Madden explains and laments the passing of the sport and its language in his book, *A Chapter of Mediaeval History*.

'Sudden and complete was the downfall of a sport which, though not a native growth, seemed to have struck its roots so deeply in the national life of England. In the early years of the seventeenth century falconry was a national sport; its language was adopted by men of letters, and the manner in which it was affected by the vulgar was a favourite topic with the satirist. In less than a century – in 1718 – a book entitled *The Compleat Sportsman* was published by Giles Jacob, in which he says that he took no notice of the diversion of hawking because it was so much disused in his time, "especially since sportsmen are arrived at such perfection in shooting".

'The use of the shot-gun was only one of the causes which led to the disuse of falconry; with other sports and pastimes it had declined during the years of the Civil War and the Commonwealth, and it never regained its former position. "Hedge-rows and enclosures have taken part with gun and dog in the extinction of falconry, and though there never has been a time when hawks were not flown by lovers of the sport in some part of the British Isles, it cannot be said to have ranked among our national sports during the last two centuries".

'I have written elsewhere: "Although the falcon and the gentle art to which she gave her name are too picturesque in their accessories and lend themselves too readily to poetic treatment to lose their place in literature, they hold it with a difference. Dryden is the latest English classic who writes the hawking language with the accuracy of Chaucer, Spenser, and Shakespeare . . . It is worth noting that the hawking language, once spoken by the card with absolute accuracy, is the only dead language of antiquity which it is considered allowable to write without any regard to the meaning of the words – an indulgence which authors are tempted to allow themselves, partly from consciousness of the ignorance of their readers, and partly by reason of the vague, pleasurable ideas of medieval sport and gallantry associated with its terminology, however recklessly misapplied" (*Diary of Master William Silence*).

'In the age of falconry a writer of the Elizabethan age would as soon have written of a bull as "she" as of a falcon as "he", but even the greatest of their successors have not hesitated to unsex the noble bird and to degrade her to the level of her tercel. Illustrious examples in letters, including Dr. Johnson, may be quoted for the solecism. Tennyson published a poem entitled "The Falcon", in which the noble bird is the central figure, and always a male. In a poem by William Morris bearing the same title the falcon is likewise unsexed.

'From Scott, a lover of nature, a sportsman, and an antiquary, more chivalrous treatment was her due, but to him in *The Abbot, Ivanhoe,* and *Rob Roy* the falcon is "he".

'Scott had, in common with Homer and with Shakespeare, an intense love of nature and of country life, a sentiment which is, according to him, a common feature of genius (*Life of Swift*). He was a sportsman, too, though less catholic in his tastes than Shakespeare. When, therefore, we find his goshawks soaring high and hovering, after the fashion of a long-winged falcon towering in her pride of place, and when we note that his "falcons" are often male, we need no further evidence that falconry was unknown in his day, and from this and other tokens we may learn that he was less attracted by the sports and pastimes of antiquity than by other features of those bygone times which he has reproduced with such life-like reality – a unique example of letters of an antiquary inspired by the creative genius of a poet.'

(*A Chapter of Mediaeval History*)

CHAPTER FOUR

Game and the Law

My Hoarse–Sounding horn
Invites thee to the chace, the sport of kings,
Image of war, without its guilt.

(William Somerville, *The Chace*, 1735)

ONLY SOME faint echoes of those formalities remain today, in the framework of the sport and the distribution of the *dramatis personae;* these are even now as stylised as if they were choreographed for performance by the Bolshoi; but it is difficult to imagine the following scene anywhere else but on the classical ballet stage . . .

> *The Monthly Chronicle,* 1728: 'August 17. Between 10 and 11 o'clock in the morning, their Majesties, together with his Royal Highness, the Duke, and their Royal Highnesses, the Princesses, came to New Park by Richmond, from Hampton Court, and diverted themselves with hunting a stag, which ran from Eleven to One, when he took to the great pond, and defended himself for about half an hour, when being killed and brought out by the help of a boat, the Huntsman sounded the French horns. The skin was taken off, and the carcass given to the dogs. His Majesty, the Duke, and the Princess Royal hunted on Horseback; Her Majesty and the Princess Amelia hunted in a Four-wheel'd chaise; and the Princess Carolina in a two-wheel'd chaise; and the Princesses Mary and Louise were in a coach. Several of the nobility attended, and among these Sir Robert Walpole, clothed in green, as a Ranger. When the diversion was over, their Majesties, the Duke, and the Princesses, refreshed themselves on the spot with a Cold Collation (as did the nobility at some distance of time after), and soon after two in the afternoon returned for Hampton Court.'

Horse-racing is no more than a young pretender. Hunting was always the true 'Sport of Kings'. It is not surprising, therefore, given the necessity for regulating pecking orders, that it should always have been attended by 'forms' of one kind or another. While it is certainly not a unique characteristic of the British to be concerned infinitely more with property and the appurtenances of rank than with people, it is interesting that our constitution is based on the historical complexities of laws evolved principally for the protection of carefully stratified privilege; while newer or more volatile societies tend to have written constitutions based on universal equality (which are bent with equal or even greater ease). It may be that this is one of the secrets of British stability, since where there is manifestly no constitutional nonsense about all men being equal, people may devote their energies to 'bettering themselves' within the established order of things, rather than to the dissipating process of overthrowing that order.

Rank order has, on this principle, more than a superficial role to play even in the most superficial of activities, and the prescribed list of falconry issued in Henry VII's reign, faintly ridiculous though it now appears, was more than an extravagant example of court fawning. It was a very real disposition of well understood orders – to every man according to his station. (It would be nice to go further and credit the compiler with a shrewd political sense – or at least a keen sense of humour – for his considered selection of the baron's bird. The Wars of the Roses had, after all, just come to their final conclusion!)

'To what Honour all Hawkes do belong, and firft to an Emporor.

Firft, there is an Eagle, a Bawter, and a Melowne, the worft of thefe three will kill an hinde calfe, a fawne, a roe, a kidde, an elde, a crane, a buzzard, a ftorke, a fwanne, a foxe in the plaine ground: and thefe are not elured neither reclaimed, becaufe they be fo exceeding ponderous to the pearch portative, and thefe three by their proper natures belong to an Emporor.

What to a King:

Vnto a King belongeth at his pleafure tributaries a Gerfalcon, and a tercall of a Gerfalcon which is moft commonly called a Gerkin.

To a Prince.

There is a Falcon gentle, and a Tercal gentle, and both of them belong every way to a Prince.

To a Duke:

There is a Falcon of the Rocke, and that belongeth (in the opinions of all Falconers) to a Duke.

To an Earle:

There is one other falcon, and that hawke is called a falcon peregrine, which by the beft iugements is bequeathed to an Earle.

To a Baron:

To a Baron and his degree belongeth a Hawke which is called a Baftard.

To a Knight:

There is a Sacre and also a Sacret and both the one and the other do belong vnto a knight.

To an Efquier:

The Lanar and the Lanret, hawks of exceeding hardneffe do both belong to an Efquier.

To a Ladie:

There is an Hawke called a Merlin, both Iacke and Formale, and they belong vnto a Lady.

To a Yongman:

To every Yongman is due the Hawke called the Hobbie, and thefe be all the long-winged haugs or hawkes of the tower, and all thefe are by lure both called and alfo reclaimed.

Of fhort winged Hawkes

Of fhort winged hawkes, which are hawkes of another kinde, there is firft a gofhawke the which is for a Yeoman.

There is a tercell of a Gofhawke which is for a poore man.

There is a Sparre-hawke which is for a prieft.

There is a Musket, which is (as olde Authours have entitled them) for a holy water clarke: and thefe be the fhort winged hawkes, of an other kind from the former, for they flee to the Querre, and to fere iuttie and iuttie ferry.'

(*The Boke of St Albans*)

It is difficult today to believe that such punctilio was not more honoured in the breach than in the observance, especially in view of the tortured contrivance of the order *Falconiformes.*

Except that this probably does as little justice to the court jester as the lawyers did to justice, for according to legend, the jester was ever the only member of the court whose writ to speak his mind, without first tasting every word to see if it would suit his sovereign's palate, ran freely at all times; whereas the lawyers, to quote Charles Richardson '. . . modelled their statutes to suit the views of country gentlemen. Their patrons, as justices of the peace, brought offenders to book. If necessary, they sent

12. Lady setting out hawking: facsimile of a miniature in the Ms. of Livre du Roy Modus *(14th century)*

some to lodge in the King's prison for twelve months'.

Richardson makes it clear that the spirit of the law concerning game was well expressed in the letter.

> 'In mediaeval days, the hare claimed the protection of the law no less than the red deer or the wild boar. In England, as also upon the Continent, the chase of the hare was held in high esteem. A special breed of fleet greyhounds, termed leoporarii, was maintained both in England and in France. King John, for example, kept a kennel of these dogs in the county of Cumberland.
>
> 'For centuries, the fortunes of the hare oscillated between her persecutors and the legal strategy which devised protection for this animal is curious to study. Richard II passed a statute prohibiting any layman from keeping greyhounds, or catching hares in nets or snares, unless he could prove that he possessed land or tenements to the annual value of 40 shillings.
>
> 'James I was a sport-loving sovereign. The lawyers of his reign framed no fewer than three Acts to repress poaching. Of these, the first enacted that from August 1, 1604 no one might keep a greyhound for coursing hares, unless he was either a man of good family, or enjoyed an income, in his own or his wife's right, of £10 a year . . .
>
> '. . . Charles II sanctioned a much more stringent Act, by which the property qualification was raised to £100 due half-yearly from landed property, or at least a lease of £150 for 99 years. Only gentlemen of such visible substance, their heirs, and keepers, were thenceforward to have or keep guns, bows, greyhounds, harepipes, or other sporting implements . . .
>
> '. . . Under William III we are informed that, "Whereas great mischiefs did ensue by inferior tradesmen, apprentices, and other dissolute persons neglecting their trades and employments, in order to follow hunting, fishing and other game, to the ruin of themselves and the damage of their neighbours", it was enacted that "if any such person as aforesaid should presume to hunt, hawk, fish or fowl on his own account, he should be sued for trespass and mulcted in damages".
>
> '. . . In the time of George II, first and second offences of night poaching were followed by mild fines. A third conviction was a very serious matter. The transgressor was required to pay a fine of 50/–. If he failed to meet this heavy liability, the culprit went to gaol for a course of penitentiary discipline, not exceeding a year. He was a lucky man if he obtained a discharge without the addition of a public whipping outside the gaol . . . This primitive discipline was also provided for by an Act of William III which struck at "the use of nets and harepipes, and other unhandsome devices for killing hares".'

Not all the laws, however, were so blatantly discriminatory and those governing the approved seasons were universal in their application and obviously framed for preservation.

Even the Middle Ages saw the need for some control of the times of the year when game might be taken and the appropriate periods are already set out in the *Boke of St Albans*, under the heading, 'The Season of all sorts of Venery'.

'The Time of Greace beginneth at Midsummer day, and lasteth till Holyroode day.
The Season of the Fox from the Nativity till the Annunciation of our Lady.
The season of the Roebuck lasteth from Easter till Michaelmass.
The season of the Roe beginneth at Michaelmass and lasteth till Midsummer.
The season of the Wolf is as the Fox.
The season of the Bore is from the Nativity to the Purification of our Lady.'

By the time of George III the seasons had begun to assume their modern shape and the *Sportsman's Dictionary* of 1778 quotes the law in some detail.

Of the contemporary Game Laws its editor says,

'I have inserted abstracts of three late Acts of Parliament relating to the game . . . whereby . . . sportsmen may know the respective times when they are to begin and when they are to leave off sporting, and also the penalties and punishments of infringing or breaking the above Acts.

'The aforesaid statute of the 2nd of George III for the better preservation of the game enacts that no person after the first day of June 1762, shall upon any pretence whatsoever, take, kill, destroy, carry, buy or have, in his, or their possession, or use any *partridge* between the 12th day of February and the 15th of September, or any *pheasant* between the 1st day of February and the 1st of October or any *heathfowl* (commonly called *blackgame*), between the 1st day of January and the 20th of August, or any *grouse* (commonly called *redgame*) between the 1st day of December and the 25th day of July in any year. Persons offending in any of the aforesaid cases, forfeit £5 per bird to the prosecutor . . .

'N.B. Hares are not included in the above Act, they may be killed all the year under the restriction of the following Act.

'The Statute of the 10th of George III for the better preservation of the game, enacts that after the 24th of June, 1770, if any person shall take, kill or destroy, any hare, pheasant, partridge, moorgame, heathgame, or grouse in the night, between one hour after sun setting, and one hour before sun rising, or use any gun, dog, snare, net, or other engine for taking, killing or destroying any such game in the night as aforesaid, every such person shall for the first offence be committed to gaol for any time not exceeding six months, nor less than three, and be publicly whipped. And for the second offence, to be imprisoned not exceeding 12 months, nor less than six, and be publicly whipped. And if any person shall upon a Sunday take, kill or destroy any hare, pheasant, partridge, moorgame, heathgame, or grouse, or shall upon a Sunday use any gun, dog, snare, net, or engine for taking, killing, or destroying any such game as aforesaid and be convicted thereof, upon the saith of one witness, shall forfeit and pay any sum not exceeding £30 nor less than £20, one moiety thereof to go to the informer, and the other to the poor of the parish . . .

'N.B. By the Act of the 13th of George III the sporting season was again altered:–
for Blackgame from the 20th August to 10th December
for Redgame from the 12th August to 10th December
for Bustards from the 1st December to 1st March.'

Except for the hare, the appointed seasons, like the language of the law, have changed very little since the days of George III. Officially, they now are—

Red Grouse, Ptarmigan	August 12–December 10
Blackgame	August 20–December 10
Partridge	September 1–February 1
Pheasant	October 1–February 1
Red Deer and Fallow Deer	May 1–July 31 (Stags/Bucks)
	March 1–October 31 (Hinds/Does)
Roe Deer	March 1–October 31

Hares – Open season all year round in England, Wales and Scotland.

As to the other provisions in these Acts, they mostly disappeared in the wholesale repeal of some twenty-seven statutes dating back as far as Richard II, embodied in the New Game Act of the 1st and 2nd of William IV, which became law on November 1st, 1831. This Act still provides the substance of our modern game laws. Some of its later amendments would surely have pleased the redoubtable Colonel Peter Hawker, who had some strong words to say on the subject.

'So little was the prospect of our ever getting rid of the diabolical old Game Laws, notwithstanding almost every Member in both Houses admitted their absurdity and inconsistency! that we are highly indebted to Lord Althorp for carrying, as a ministerial measure, anything like an amendment on them; and reducing them (as I expressed a hope that they would be) "into one Act of the present reign" . . .

'The General Qualification is good; but the Sporting Licence should have been increased to 5*l*; or, at all events, to this amount for those who use double guns.

'Every thing between Landlord and Tenant had better have been settled by themselves. The legislature will do more harm than good by this interference. And with regard to the tenant being liable not only to the penalty of 2*l* for allowing people to shoot, but also to that of 1*l* for every head of game killed! – the clause, to say the least of it, is not one calculated to put the farmers in good humour – and if they are in a bad humour, the poor game, I fear, will be in a bad way!

'The penalty for trespass is the best law that was ever enacted. But at present it is inefficient. The grand object that I had in recommending a penalty for trespass only, was to have the power of taking up a man whom you knew to be a poacher, but who was too well versed in his art to suffer himself to be detected in the "pursuit of game"; and also to have the means of trouncing a dandified marauder, to whom the paltry sum of 2*l* would be no more an object than a bottle of champagne or a bundle of cigars. But, on the other hand, giving fair play to both of these worthies, by making them subject to a penalty only as wilful trespassers; or, in other words, for continuing or repeating the trespass after they had been warned off by the proprietor or occupier of the land . . .

'In Dec. 1832, – I had the very best authority for saying that the ministers admitted several provisions (of which they entirely disapproved) to be introduced in the new Bill; and, in short, were obliged to compromise with their opponents, on the best terms they could for the sake of attaining two great objects – legalising the sale of game, and the general qualification. The one, to say the least of it, an act of common justice to all gentlemen who are not possessed of landed property, or sporting rights – the other the extinction of a law that subjected even the second sons of noblemen to the same penalty as the lowest tradesman, when shooting on the property of their own fathers – not to say a word of its gross absurdity and inconsistency! – What objections there are to these two clauses I am at a loss to know! But as to the other sections of the present Act – it becomes quite a mystery to learn from whence they emanated! Certain, however, it is that almost every one is exclaiming most violently against the new game laws; and swearing that unless they are altered, field sports will soon cease to be the amusement of gentlemen. But is there any such great difficulty in discovering the evil that now exists, and renders the new game laws (which might be made excellent) even worse than the old ones? See how the matter at present stands – we have, on the one hand, legalised the sale of game, and thereby opened the market an hundred fold; without, on the other hand, having taken any one additional step against the wholesale destroyer of it – the poacher. We may proceed against the fair sportsman, like a common felon, if, by chance or absolute mistake, he crosses one little strip of land, without a formal permission; while the poacher, unless you can prove him to be "in search or pursuit of game", is wholly exonerated from the penalty of the present Act. No man should be subject to a penalty unless he has received a notice, and then let the penalty be made even more severe than that in the new game laws. And, above all, let the penalty be for wilful trespass, whether in pursuit of game or not. How could the poacher then go to reconnoitre – or to set his wires – or to take the eggs of game? – But, as the law now stands, it destroys the sport of the gentleman, whose interest it is to preserve the game; and, by an enlarged market, affords additional facility to the wholesale destroyer. As the law was (except qualification), and still is, any man with a license and permission may catch game, in the day time!! Only refer back to my "Hints for the Preservation of Game", and see what may be done in this way by the day-poacher. Again – walk through the streets of London, or any other large town, and see how many hundred head of game are hanging in the poulterers' shops, without one feather being touched with shot! – Is it possible that we can do away with qualifications – keep an open market – and at the same time have no effectual remedy against the trespass of the secret poacher, or the murderous havoc of the net and snare? – But,

13. Poachers Caught *by Kilburne, engraved by Angerer & Gosch (1890s)*

following up the same bad policy, we make war with the very men of all others who have the power to be our best assistants – who are constantly on the ground, and about at all hours – and who have the lower classes under their immediate control – I mean the farmers. They, who feed the game, are to be subject to even a greater penalty than the unknown trespasser; and to pay 1*l* for every head of game, in addition to the 2*l*. penalty for trespass! Can any man of common sense imagine that, while such a law exists, a farmer will exert himself to prohibit his labourers from poaching, or feel the smallest interest in preserving the nests of a partridge? – Impossible! With a general qualification and an open market, a three and a half guinea license is not sufficient. Though the legal attainment of game, by fair purchase or otherwise, is the undoubted right of the subject, yet the shooting it is an amusement – a luxury; and, for this reason, there can be no hardship in raising the price of a certificate. Why not also make every one who shoots wildfowl, plover, wood-pigeons, &c., any where but on his own land, pay a small license for his diversion, similar to a French port-d'armes?

'In short, after all, there has been an immoderate deal said, and but very little done, with, this everlasting subject, the game laws. Let us however hope that, before the sports of country gentlemen are completely annihilated, something will be settled to the satisfaction of all fair and rational men: – and as to those who are not of this number – whether they are pleased or not – is a matter of very little consequence.'

(*Instructions to Young Sportsmen,* 1844 Edition)

From a distance of 140 years, one might think that the abolition of qualification and the substitution of a general licence, the legalising of the sale of game under licence, the revision of penalties and so on, albeit a long way from any conception of perfection, represented rather more than 'anything like an amendment' on the old laws. But the Colonel is a pragmatist, even if he does permit himself the occasional flight of fancy (like the imminent 'annihilation' of the sports of country gentlemen). Sir Ralph Payne-Gallwey described him thus:

'In figure Colonel Hawker was over six feet and strikingly handsome, and up to the end of his life was very erect. He was, no doubt, somewhat of an egotist, but it was in a good-natured way, and a confirmed but amusing grumbler against his personal ill-luck, and his constant enemy the weather; he was, however, an instructive and witty companion, and a conversationalist who always commanded attention . . .

'My idea of the Author of this Diary has always been that he was the "hardest" man, in regard to health, that could be imagined; but it will be seen that he was continually fighting against illness and frequently incapacitated by his severe Peninsular wound; and the way in which he was, to use the words, wont to "quack himself up", to enable him to take the field with his gun, is worthy of admiration as an example of British pluck. Colonel Hawker was, it may easily be seen, a man of vast energy, and a very shrewd observer. Nothing, apparently, could escape him, whether on his travels abroad or in pursuit of game and wild fowl at home. He was, besides, a most accomplished musician and musical critic, and was intimately acquainted with many of the celebrated pianists and operatic singers of his day.'

The contrast between Hawker, the great empiricist and man of action, and his near contemporary, the Rev. William Daniel, is interesting. Daniel, an enthusiastic if less robust sportsman, was also a scholarly naturalist and an assiduous researcher. Writing twenty or thirty years before Colonel Hawker, he chooses to pitch his argument against the old Game Laws on a more academic level. Indeed, taking on no less an authority than Sir William Blackstone, he appears to achieve an easy points decision.

'The Game Laws were introduced amongst us at an Era when property was not governed, either in the use or in the possession, by those enlightened maxims of justice which at present secure it. The aristocratic orders of that period consulted their own amusement and pleasure, without any very scrupulous regard to the rights, or very provident care for the comforts of the least opulent, but not least valuable classes of the community. They were strong, and they were not willing to weaken the foundation of their power, by a relaxation of their privileges. Their pride made them averse from sharing with the commonalty an amusement, which, by a small stretch of power, they might appropriate to themselves. The exercise of hunting, and the pursuit of the various sorts of Game, partaking somewhat of that spirit of enterprize in which they delighted, were recreations of all others congenial to their taste; it is not therefore wonderful that they should contrive to debar the lower orders from their participation.

'It is admitted by Sir W. Blackstone . . . "By the Law of Nature, every man, from the prince to the peasant, has an equal right of pursuing and taking to his own use, all such creatures as are *ferae naturae*". . . . This truth is granted as incontestible. "But", he adds, "it follows from the very end and constitution of society, that this natural right, as well as many others belonging to man as an individual may be restrained by positive laws, enacted for reasons of state, or for the supposed benefit of the Community." When the public welfare in any instance obviously demands that the natural right of an individual should be controlled in its exercise by regulations established by law, the justice of such regulations is indisputable; but surely nothing but reasons of manifest good policy, and the actual benefit of the state, can justify such restrictions. If they may be abridged or withheld, as the learned Writer here affirms they may, for reasons of state, and the supposed benefit of the Community, we hold them by a tenure of very uncertain duration. Nothing can be more vague than the terms on which we must submit, if not to their absolute surrender, at least to an indefinite encroachment upon them.

'It may be worth while separately to investigate the solidity of the reasons assigned by Sir W. Blackstone, as introductive of the Game Laws, previously to the examination of the basis of his doctrine respecting them. "Many reasons", says he, "have concurred for making these constitutions: as, 1. For the encouragement of agriculture and improvement of lands, by giving every man an exclusive dominion over his own soil". It is said in the passage immediately preceding, that the municipal laws, in virtue of their authority to restrain our natural rights, "have invested the prerogative of hunting and taking such animals, as are usually the object of pursuit, in the Sovereign of the State only, and such as he shall authorize". How the restriction of a natural right to kill such animals on his own grounds, or permissively on those of another; how the forbidding a freeholder, of less than one hundred pounds a year, to kill a partridge upon his own estate, gives every man an exclusive dominion over his own soil, is not easily comprehended. It is certainly not so obviously beneficial in this way, as to promote the encouragement of agriculture, and the improvement of lands.

'2. "For preservation of the several species of these animals, which would soon be extirpated by a general liberty. 3. For the prevention of idleness and dissipation in Husbandmen, Artificers, and others of lower rank, which would be the unavoidable consequence of universal licence". These reasons destroy each other. It is evident to reflection, that without any restrictive law upon the subject, the evil would have cured itself. It is admitted, that Game would soon be extirpated by a general licence; of course all idleness and dissipation arising from this cause must end with the cause itself, and would require no law for its prevention.

'The last reason assigned, and which is said to be a reason oftener meant than avowed by the makers of Forest or Game Laws, is "the prevention of popular insurrections and resistance to government, by disarming the bulk of the people": that they were actuated by this motive is an opinion which the history of the temper and manners of the times will hardly allow us to admit. Hawks were at this time chiefly used to kill birds; military weapons do not seem to have been much used in the pursuit of Game. . . . Also it is expressly said, that "forasmuch as divers artificers, &c. keep greyhounds and other dogs", and enacts that no person, unless qualified as there required, shall from thenceforth "keep any greyhound, hound, or other dog to hunt, nor shall they use ferrets, hays, nets, harepipes, nor cords, nor other engines to take or destroy Deer". We have here no mention of any instruments likely to be very serviceable in the hands of sedition; nor were the government in those days so extremely tender of the liberties of the people, as to take this indirect method of disarming them, and of reliving itself from the apprehensions of revolt. The habits, whatever they were, acquired in the pursuit of Game, could not much contribute to initiate the peasantry in the rudiments of military science.

'It would be superfluous to cite all the Statutes relating to Game, to prove that the right to pursue and destroy it was at no time, by the constitutional law of this kingdom, held to be solely and exclusively in the Sovereign. It was clearly a general right, and did subsist as such in fact and usage, until upon principles of public expediency it was judged fit to regulate and limit the enjoyment of it.

'Previously to the enactment of any restrictive Statutes respecting it, it stood upon the basis of the common law. Games are considered as *ferae naturae,* and of these (as we before remarked,) the learned Commentator has himself affirmed, "that by the law of nature, every man, from the Prince to the peasant, has an equal right of pursuing and taking them to his own use". Now, with deference to so great a Writer, I affirm, that every natural right is protected and confirmed by the common law, and makes a part of it. To allow that this is a natural and common right, and at the same time to affirm "that no person whatever, but he who has a derivative right, is, by the Common Law, entitled to take or kill any beast of chase, or other game whatsoever", is utterly repugnant and contradictory. If to kill game be a natural right, (as it is declared to be,) an equally common to all the King's subjects, it follows that it cannot be the sole and exclusive prerogative of the King; if, on the other hand, it is the sole and exclusive prerogative of the Crown, then it cannot be in its origin a natural and common right. Lord Coke says, "the common law is sometimes called, right, common right, and common justice". Thus common law and common right are convertible terms; and Sir William Blackstone's positions controvert each other.

'No admirer of a manly, liberal, well-regulated system of public freedom, will be forward to assert, that the Laws for the preservation of Game do not require to be very thoroughly revised. They certainly depart more widely from the line of genuine political justice, and expose the humble unqualified classes of the community more to the hazard of punishment, and the oppression of power, than any rational advocate of moral equality can consistently approve. They are greatly imperfect, in as much as their penalties are infinitely too severe. That the punishment of death should in any case be inflicted on an act which in itself violates no rule of religion, justice, or morality, is a reflection from which the mind revolts with pain and horror. Where is the wrong to individuals that demands such an atonement? Where is the injury to Society which requires such an example? That the act of destroying game is not *malum in se* is evident, for if it were, the Legislature could not license it.'

(*Rural Sports*)

Despite the contrast between William Daniel and Peter Hawker – or perhaps because of it – the similarity in their attitudes is even more interesting. Hawker takes for granted the privileges of property and in his matter of fact way, merely seeks to ensure that they are only extended to, and protected for the pleasure of, 'fair' sportsmen. Daniel admits a certain bias in the law, but finds no difficulty in justifying it as not only proper, but necessary (for a manly, liberal, well-regulated system etc.).

'If the Game Laws may be regarded as somewhat favouring the propensities of the upper ranks, their policy may not be in this respect greatly erroneous. There is a selfishness in insisting, that no laws ought to accommodate themselves to those propensities. The very station of such persons excludes them in great measure from such diversions as make part of the recreation of the lower classes. . . . If these laws answered only this one end, the inducing persons of rank and property to reside more on their estates, by securing them a local amusement suited to their inclination and taste, this alone ought to weigh much in conciliating our approbation towards them. A sensible modern Writer remarking on a district in Yorkshire, where the landed proprietors chiefly reside on their estates, observes, that "the good effects of this are every where visible in the improvement of agriculture, in the repair of the roads, in the administration of justice, and in the good order, comfort, and general happiness of the people".

'The true strength and greatness of a State is in proportion to the virtue of its subjects; the empire of virtue is extended by whatever weans the inclination from pursuits by which the mind is contaminated and debased. The sports of the field contribute to this effect, and more particularly among those whom such pursuits are most likely to solicit with effect, and to these therefore they are with reason more exclusively reserved.

'Those who reprobate the Game Laws as violating the equal right of every man to enjoy the common unappropriated bounty of nature, have perhaps not sufficiently reflected on the subject. A more attentive consideration will dispose them to withdraw the objection raised against them on this ground. With respect to the distinction between animals *ferae naturae;* and animals reclaimed or domesticated, it has been well observed by a very judicious Writer, that "in a highly cultivated, well peopled country, no animal can properly be considered as wild: all are supported by the property and labour of those who cultivate the soil. Some, from their peculiar instincts, are, indeed, less capable than others of being entirely appropriated, and therefore like lands uninclosed, are held as a joint property. But he who has no land, and consequently contributes nothing to their maintenance, is no more entitled to any use of them than the inhabitant of one parish is to a right of commonage on the waste lands of another; and he who chooses to reside in a town, and to keep his property in money, has no more a pretence to seize to his own use a hare, or a partridge, than a sheep or a goose, from him who has chosen to vest his property in land. In the former, as in the latter case, he ought to tempt the owner to sell what is wanted".'

(*Rural Sports*)

The central dilemma of the history of game and authority's attempt to control its taking is that nobody has so far successfully found a way of explaining to the animals concerned what the rules are, and many of them are not even prepared to acknowledge, for example, that they 'cannot properly be considered as wild'. Pheasants, even today, persist in using their wings to fly from place to place, unaware of the demarcation lines of private property. Even stags and foxes, those well-known lovers of a good chase, have but the most superficial knowledge of any boundaries other than those marking their own instinctive and somewhat transient territories.

A final comment on the Game Laws belongs indirectly to Colonel Hawker. In the copy of his *Instructions to Young Sportsmen,* – which the Game Conservancy were kind enough to lend me (the ninth edition, printed in 1844) – most of the pages in the chapter on Game Laws were still uncut 127 years after publication. A more eloquent comment might defy the greatest talent! Thomas Hood's was not quite equal to the task, as the following lines testify:

I'm fond of partridges, I'm fond of snipes.
I'm fond of black cocks, for they're very good cocks –
I'm fond of wild ducks, and I'm fond of woodcocks,
And grouse that set up such strange moorish pipes,
I'm fond of hares, whether from Whig or Tory –
I'm fond of capercailzies in their glory –
Teal, widgeons, plovers, birds in all their types:
All these are in your care, Law-giving Peer,
And when you next address your Lordly Babel,
Some clause put in your Bill, precise and clear,
With due and fit provision to enable
A man that holds all kinds of game so dear
To keep, like Crockford, a good Gaming Table.

(Sonnet 'To Lord Wharncliffe, on his Game Bill'. Thomas Hood, Boston, 1856)

CHAPTER FIVE

The Literature of the Chase

'We have practically no original literature of the chase until the eighteenth century, and it is idle to pretend we have'.

D. H. Madden (in his *Chapter of Mediaeval History*) quotes from the Hon. J. W. Fortescue's contribution to *Shakespeare's England* and finds no room for argument: 'These words cannot be gainsaid.' Since both Hon. gentlemen were apparently concerned with literary merit it seems surprising that they were prepared to draw the line at the eighteenth century. While admittedly the statement is not in fact as unequivocal as it first appears, it is perhaps arguably valid to read 'nineteenth' as well. Madden himself makes the case.

> 'There was no lack of books. Burton exclaims at the "world of bookes" not alone on arts and sciences, but on "riding of horses, fencing, swimming, gardening, planting, great tomes of husbandry, cookery, faulconry, hunting, fishing, fowling, and with exquisite pictures of all sports games, and what not?" a reference to the beauty of the illustrations of the books of sport of his day which suggests a hope that our good friend Burton knew nothing of them beyond the titles.
>
> 'In this crowd of books not one can be found of literary importance or interesting from the character of its author, and yet they have a historical value which is absent from works of the kind produced in other countries.
>
> 'Their woodcraft is borrowed from the great French classics, and the books on falconry are little more than translations of well-known French and Italian treatises . . .
>
> 'As Latin was the language of learned clerks, so Norman French was for centuries after the conquest the language of venery. Survivals of the ancient order are found in the use of the Latin language at the conferring of degrees in the old universities; and in the hunting-field, although the master of hounds may rebuke his field in the vulgar tongue, the terms of his art are borrowed from the French.
>
> 'Twici's little treatise, like many other ancient books on sport, is in the form of a dialogue between the master of hounds and a disciple. The language is more archaic than that of the [*Livre du*] *Roy Modus*, written at about the same time,

and it may represent an Anglo-Norman dialect, as spoken in the hunting-field. The terms of art proper to venery are explained, but as a treatise on woodcraft the work compares unfavourably with its French contemporary.

'Next in date is the Master of Game, the earliest book on hunting in the English language, written at some time between the years 1406 and 1413, by Edward, second duke of York, who fell in the battle of Agincourt (1415). It is a translation of the Livre de Chasse of Gaston Phoebus, adapted by the translator to the use of an English master of hounds. It remained in manuscript until the year 1904, when it was printed in a sumptuous volume, edited by Mr. and Mrs. Baillie-Grohman, with reproductions in photogravure of the fine illuminations and miniatures with which a famous MS. of the Livre de Chasse is adorned. The notes, and the bibliography appended to this volume, constitute a mine of interesting and accurate information on old-world sport to which the writer of these pages has often had recourse; for which, and for helpfulness shown to one interested in similar studies by the late Mr. Baillie-Grohman, he desires to record his gratitude.

'The neglect of the Master of Game in the age of printing was due to the popularity of the Book of St. Albans. Between the publication of this work in 1486 and the death of Shakespeare in 1616 it was reprinted in whole or in part, more or less altered, no fewer than twenty-two times. "Its circulation for a long time vied with, and perhaps exceeded that, of every other contemporary production of the press of lesser eminence than Holy Writ".

'Although the Master of Game did not find its way into print, it was an important and well-known work widely circulated in MS. No fewer than nineteen extant copies were found as the result of the individual researches of the editors.'

(*A Chapter of Mediaeval History*)

The reasons for the lack of original literature are in essence all there. Given the great French works on what, in any case, was a largely French culture, together with the English 'Vade Mecum', the need for manuals of instruction was certainly fulfilled; and if hunting is only 'The Image of War' then in an age when 'Hunting and War were the only employment of the great' (Daniel) there would be little reason to seek inspiration in the image. The ease with which men make enemies of each other has always provided a wealth of heroic material whether in glorious defeat or famous victory.

The triumphs and disappointments of the hunting field were nevertheless on a somewhat less epic scale than Agincourt or Crecy and the nature of the contest more uneven, whatever the odds on the battlefield. Most of the poets suffered the disability of being as much or more in sympathy with the quarry than with the hunter. Shakespeare's 'Poor sequester'd stag' whose 'big round tears Coursed one another down his innocent nose In piteous chase' is mated by Spenser's 'Faire hinde'.

'Being one day at my window all alone,
So manie strange things hapned me to see,
As much it grieveth me to think thereon,

THE NOBLE ART OF

VENERIE OR HVNTING.

Wherein is handled and ſet out the Vertues, Nature, and Properties of fifteene ſundry Chaces, together with the order and manner how to Hunt and kill euery one of them.

Tranſlated & collected for the pleaſure of all Noblemen and Gentlemen, out of the beſt approoued Authors, which haue written any thing concerning the ſame: And reduced into ſuch order and proper termes as are vſed here in this noble Realme of Great Britaine.

AT LONDON,

Printed by Thomas Purfoot.

An. Dom. 1611.

14. Title page of The Noble Art of Venerie or Hvnting *by George Turbervile (1611 edition)*

At my right hand a hinde appearde to me,
So faire as mought the greatest God delite;
Two egre dogs did her pursue in chase,
Of which the one was black, the other white:
With deadly force so in their cruell race
They pinchte the haunches of this gentle beast,
That at the last, and in shorte time, I spied,
Under a rocke, where she (alas) opprest,
Fell to the grounde, and untimely dide,
Cruell death vanquishing so noble beautie,
Oft makes me waile so hard a destenie.

(Edmund Spenser, 'The Visions of Petrarch', 1569)

So the sportsman poet faces much the same dilemma as the sportsman naturalist, with his instinctive enthusiasm for the chase at odds with his natural sympathy for living things. (It has been said that while it is possible to be a naturalist without being a sportsman, it is almost impossible for a sportsman not to become to some degree a naturalist.)

Not that the literature is lacking in allusions. Hunting and hawking are woven all through *The Canterbury Tales* and Chaucer takes the Monk to task for over-indulging them at the expense of his spiritual duties; and Shakespeare makes frequent use of the language and scenario of the chase.

He must certainly have known *The Boke of St Albans,* either by repute or through one of the many editions (upwards of a dozen more of less altered from the original, and several of them undated) issued since it first appeared in 1486.

This original edition consisted of four parts, the first of which concerned falconry, with particular note of 'the termys of plesure belongying to gentill men having delite therein', and contained much invaluable information on such matters as:

'How to make your hawke flee with a courage in the morning.

'If you have a determination that your Hawke fhall flee in the morning, then feede her the night before with hote meate, and wafh the fame meate in vrine and wring out the water cleane, and that fhall adde vnto her a luft and courage to flee in the next morning to your contentment.

'How to make a Hawke flee well which is fully gorged.

'If your hawke be full gorged, and yet notwithftanding you would faine have a flight, take three cornes of wheate, and put them in a morfell of flefh and give it vnto your hawke, and immediately fhee will caft all that is within her, which as foane as fhe hath caft, looke you have a bit or two of fome hote meate to give her, and then you may boldly flee her: this medcine alfo is excellent for a Hawke that is overgorged.'

The second part is a treatise of hunting which instructs 'such gentill persons the maner of huntyng for all maner of beestys'. Its language and style (it is written in rhyme) suggest that it may have been a schoolbook.

15. *Queen Elizabeth at a hunting picnic* (*Turbervile*)

It is curious however that the great Elizabethan writers have so little to say on their Queen's favourite sport (she is reported to have been still enjoying the chase at the age of sixty-four). But if Spenser, Marlowe, Ben Jonson and Beaumont and Fletcher chose to neglect 'the Noble Art', the little known George Turbervile repaired their deficiencies with his book of hunting and hawking, printed first in 1575 and again in 1611.

Much of the book is in verse and if some of it appears to have been shaped with a hammer rather than with a pen, more famous names than Turbervile have been known to resort to force in forging a rhyming couplet.

'I might at large expresse how earely huntsmen ryse,
And leave the sluggish sleepe for such, as leachers lust devyse.
How true they tread their steps, in exercises traine,
Which frisking flings and lightbraind leaps, may seeme always to staine,
How appetite is bred (with health) in homely cates,
While Surfet sits in vaine excesse, and Banquet breeds debates.
How cries of well mouthed hounds, do contervaile the cost,
Which many a man (beyond his reach) on instruments hath lost.
How setting of Relayes, may represent the skyll.
Which souldiours use in Embushes, their furious foes to kyll.
How Fox and Badgerd both, make patterns (in their Denne)
Of Plotformes, Loopes and Casamats, devised by warlike men,
How fighting out at Bay, of Harte, Bucke, Goate, or Bore,
Declares the valiant Romains Death, when might may do no more.
How sight of such delights, doth scorne all common showes,
Of Enterludes, of Tumblers tricks, of antikes, mocks and mowes,
And how the nimble Hare, by turning in his course,
Doth plainly prove that Pollicie, sometime surpasseth force.
The venson not forget, most meete for Princes dyshe:
All these with more could I rehearse, as much as wit could wyshe.
But let these few suffice, it is a Noble Sport,
To Recreate the Mindes of Men in Good and Godly Sort,
A Sport for Noble Peeres, A Sport for Gentle Bloods,
The paine I leave for servants such, as beate the bushie woods,
To make their masters sport. Then Let the Lords Reioyce,
Let Gentlemen Beholde the Glee, and Take Thereof the Choyce.
For my part (being one) I must needes say my minde,
That Hunting Was Ordeyned First, For Men of Noble Kinde,
And unto them therefore, I recommend the same,
As exercise that best becomes, their worthy noble name.'

(George Turbervile, *The Noble Art of Venerie or Hunting*, 1575)

The book was by no means without its admirers. Gervase Markham, in *Country Contentments* (1611) apologises for having little to say of any great novelty where hunting is concerned ('I know not well what to write, except I should in some sort repeat another man's tale'), and recommends that his readers should consult 'old *Tristram's* Book, translated by Mr. *Turbervile,* and such other Books, where they may find *compleat satisfaction*'.

Turbervile's double work may be seen as an early example of the English sporting book tradition – but it was by no means an isolated one. In the same year or thereabouts appeared *A Perfect Booke for Kepinge of Sparhawks or Goshawks,* and indeed, several other works on falconry were issued within the next few decades, notably *Latham's Falconry, or the Faulcon's Lure and Cure* in 1615, and *Latham's New and Second Booke of Faulconrie* which followed three years later. Edmund Bert's *Approved Treatise of Hawkes and Hawking* was published in 1619, though it was not originally intended for publication, but merely for circulation among the author's friends. Both Latham and Bert were practical men, who unlike some of their predecessors wrote from their own substantial experience in falconry, rather than relying upon 'the best authorities'. Experts claim that Simon Latham's *Falconry* is one of the best works of its kind. Bert's work is noted for its records of the achievements of hawks flown at game, the earliest details in existence. On the Suffolk Downs with an intermewed hawk (one which had moulted in the mews) Bert had killed as many as eight, nine and ten partridges in a day; and he states that on one occasion he sold a goshawk and a tercel trained by himself for a hundred marks (£33.6s.8d).

Hunting and hawking were of such general interest to the Elizabethans that books of far wider scope would often – indeed, usually, – contain sections of some length devoted to these subjects: Markham's *Country Contentments* is one example. Blome's *The Gentleman's Recreation,* a weighty folio volume covering heraldry, philosophy, music, chronology, horsemanship, algebra, astrology and geography, among a multitude of other topics, is another. Richard Blome, who lived and worked in the parish of St-Martin's-in-the-Fields was a compiler and editor of a number of books which he published himself. Not being himself a sportsman, he was accused of 'bold practices' because he employed people (notably members of the nobility) to write for him on the various sporting recreations represented in his book, though he presided over the whole operation himself.

Part Two of *The Gentleman's Recreation* professed to deal with 'Hawking, Hunting, Horsemanship, Fowling, Fishing and Cock-Fighting; in some of which sports his Majesty delighted'. 'His Majesty', Charles II, became in some sort Blome's patron for the second part of the book, which was prefaced with a Royal Announcement to the effect that the king's approval was conferred upon the enterprise due to his princely desire to promote all such useful and laudable works. In fact, all that followed this fanfare was a brief commendation to subscribers.

The basis of the second part was, according to Blome, a translation from a French work, *Le Ruises Innocent* [sic], which had been recommended to him in the highest terms. In addition to obtaining the translation, he had collected many English authors of the proposed subjects (Turbervile, Markham and many others) together, and had their work 'rectified by such Sports Men as were approved excellent'. During the four years of the book's compilation, the editor encountered numerous difficulties; some of the sportsmen employed by him were 'found expert in Hawking and deficient in the rest that their genius was not addicted to; as some were for short-winged hawks, as the Goshawk, etc., not regarding the long-winged ones, as the Gerfalcon, etc. which to others were in the highest esteem'. Blome seems not to have been aware of the differences between the birds, their ways of killing their prey, and the types of terrain for which each were suited, thus he could not understand the bias of his writers for one variety or the other. Nonetheless, the completed work was, in time, hailed as a classic. A second edition appeared in 1710, five years after Blome's death.

One of the most remarkable sporting writers of the eighteenth century was Peter Beckford, considered by Ralph Nevill to be the first English writer to describe minutely and accurately the whole order of the chase. Other commentators went further, as Nevill illustrates in his *Old English Sporting Books,* quoting a contemporary's praise:

> ' "Never had fox or hare the honour of being chased by so accomplished a hunter; never was huntsman's dinner graced by such urbanity and wit. He would bag a fox in Greek, find a hare in Latin, inspect his kennels in Italian and direct the economy of his stables in excellent French." '

Peter Beckford's *Thoughts on Hare and Fox Hunting* (1781) contained an introduction dealing with methods of hare-hunting in Greece, and a thorough, erudite account of the chase in general which must have impressed and surprised the fox-hunting country squires of the day.

It is probably also true that eighteenth-century hunting enthusiasts were more impressed by William Somervile than twentieth-century literary critics have been; but his long blank verse poem *The Chace* (1735) and its supplement *Field Sports* contain some vivid descriptions of the contemporary hunting scene. And it was Somervile who gave the phrase 'the Sport of Kings' to the language.

Colonel Peter Hawker's *Instructions to Young Sportsmen* first appeared in 1814 and fourteen subsequent editions were published between then and Hawker's death in 1852. The popularity of this book, quite apart from its excellence as an instruction manual and the Colonel's trenchant style, must surely have had something to do with its author's character and reputation. A notable soldier, wounded during the Peninsular War (and subsequently much at odds with the army authorities), he was one of the most renowned sportsmen of his day and certainly the finest shot. Among his other literary achievements were a journal of his experiences during the Peninsular War and *Instructions for best position on the Pianoforte*.

The end of the eighteenth century saw the emergence of special interest journals and various periodicals catering for the tastes of sportsmen began to appear. *The Sporting Magazine* was founded in 1783 with the intention of 'pleasing the man of Spirit, Enterprise and Pleasure' and keeping its readers *au courant* with the latest sporting news, including events at Newmarket and other racing centres, pugilistic contests and even cock-fighting and bull-baiting though these were regarded with editorial disapproval. Any reference to them was in fact subsequently banned by Robert Surtees (creator of the immortal 'Jorrocks') when he became editor of *The New Sporting Magazine*. Indeed he went so far as to refuse to employ Pierce Egan because of his known association with bull-baiting, cock-fighting and similar coarse pleasures.

Rather similar to the *Sporting Magazine,* which survived, in various forms, until 1870, was a publication entitled *The Annals of Sporting and Fancy Gazette* which contained fine plates by such renowned artists as Alken, Cruikshank and Landseer. Only thirteen volumes of the *Annals* appeared, but the *Sporting Review,* which was also noted for its illustrations, achieved sixty-four volumes over thirty years from 1839. The literary content of these magazines, however, rarely aspired to the standard of their illustrations, for although most of the bucks and bloods of the 1820s had had a thorough grounding in the classics, the majority left serious reading behind them when they left school. Light-hearted and gossipy accounts of the Ring, the Turf and the Chase were what appealed to them most and publications which provided this kind of material could depend upon a steady readership.

Pierce Egan wrote both articles and books for this market. His 'Tom and Jerry' books, the best known of which is *Life in London* (1821), recounted the adventures of two dashing young men-about-town, forever embarking upon 'Rambles and Sprees through the Metropolis' which brought them in contact with various currently popular sporting events. The books were written with much use of slang, italicization, capital letters and inverted commas, 'inserted', according to Ralph Nevill, 'to bring out the writer's wit'; but what probably contributed most to the extraordinary success of these books were the colour plates, two thirds of which are said to be by Robert Cruikshank. Despite Surtees' strictures on Egan's sporting proclivities these were never in breach of the conventions of the times and Egan's heroes never stepped outside the bounds of good manners, as Ralph Nevill observes:

> 'Though no Puritans, and frankly fond of unrestrained rollicking fun, "Tom, Jerry and Logic" always strictly conform to the standard of conduct which, at the beginning of the last century, was required of a gentleman fond of indulging in wild pranks and dissipation, sometimes of an unrestrained kind, the trio are pictured as ever having virtue before them as man's true and final goal.'
>
> (*Old English Sporting Books*)

The *Sporting Magazine* itself, prior to the age of 'Nimrod' (Charles James Apperley, Surtees' predecessor), had apparently left much to be desired in its general tone: Herbert Maxwell, in his introduction to *The Chase, the Road and the Turf* (1898) refers to a section entitled 'Matrimonial Sporting', consisting of detailed exposés of 'what were then known as *crim. con.* cases'. Maxwell also relates Apperley's first reaction to the suggestion that he should write for the *Sporting Magazine.*

> ' "*The Sporting Magazine!*" exclaimed Apperley, "that will never do: it is a mere Cockney concern, and no *gentleman* writes for it." '
>
> ' "Never mind," replied the friend. "Take my advice, and go to the proprietor of it. If you write for it, other gentlemen and sportsmen will do so also." '

He did. And they did. And the standard of sporting journalism was enormously enhanced.

Apperley's articles, written under the name of 'Nimrod', were phenomenally successful; his 'Letters upon Fox Hunting' in fact doubled the circulation of the magazine within a short space of time. Perhaps his amazing success was due to the fact that before him, those who understood hunting best were the least likely to make the effort to write about it. Nimrod's style, hints of individual criticism and localised description stimulated his readers and ensured their attention. Mr Pittman, the proprietor of the magazine, repaid his new contributor with a liberal salary, a stud of horses and expenses-paid sporting tours.

The name Nimrod became known everywhere. It was adopted by manufacturers for new products (including coaches, breeches and blacking) and even by parents for new children. But Nimrod's fame did not endure as well as that of his successor.

Robert Smith Surtees followed Apperley as leading writer on sporting subjects, and later became the first editor of *The New Sporting Magazine*. The difference between them is the breadth of Surtees' appeal. Apperley wrote essentially with sportsmen in mind while Surtees, in *Handley Cross* and *Jorrock's Jaunts and Jollities*, created an immortal character of universal charm – so universal that one writer commented, at the end of the last century, 'Who is there that has worn boots and breeches and not read that immortal memoir many times?'

Other names appear briefly on the literary scene, sometimes for a single work, like Charles Palk Collyns, sometimes for a contribution incidental to their main preoccupation, like Charles St John, sometimes for their dedication to one pursuit, like William Scrope, whose work on deer-stalking is the most comprehensive ever written.

But few of these names remain familiar today; the fame of the great sporting writers of the past, along with the inspiration behind their work, seems to have died with the passing of the last century.

CHAPTER SIX

Stag-Hunting and 'the Noblest Beast' of Venery

When Phoebus the tops of the hills do adorn,
How sweet is the sound of the echoing horn!
When the antling stag is rous'd by the sound,
Erecting his ears nimbly sweeps o'er the ground,
And thinks he has left us behind on the plain;
But still we pursue, and now come in view of the glorious game.
Oh! see how again he rears up his head,
And winged with fear he redoubles his speed;
But ah! 'tis in vain that he flies,
That his eyes lose the hunters, his ears lose their cries,
That now his strength fails he heavily sies,
And he pants, 'till with well-scented hounds surrounded he dies,
  Tantaron, Tantaron, he dies.

(Seventeenth-century hunting song)

THE CHASE of the stag, for both sport and sustenance, has long been the subject of literary discussion, not least in the seventeenth century. Hunting songs – of which there were hundreds – enjoyed a tremendous popularity, and books of an instructional nature, such as Blome's *Gentleman's Recreation* were eagerly consumed; both these archaic genres have helped to preserve for us some of the lost and ancient traditions of a formal hunt. The account of correct procedure in the hunting section of Blome's book is, for example, supported by a complete table of the phrases to be sounded on the hunting horn at various key moments of the hunt, and some such phrases are mentioned in the following account of the climax of the chase, when the stag is about to be taken.

'The Hart or Stag at Bay.

'As to the Land Bay, if the Hart be frayed and burnished, then the Place is well to be consider'd of; for if it be in a Hedge side, or Thicket, then whilst he is staring on the *Hounds,* you may come covertly amongst the Bushes behind him, and so kill him; but if you miss, and he turn Head up on you, it is convenient to take Refuge behind some Tree; or when he is at Bay, Couple up your *Hounds*; and when you see him turn Head to fly, *Gallop* in roundly, and kill him with your Sword or Gun, before he can have time to turn Head upon you; But if he be at Bay in a plain and open Place, where there is no Wood, Tree nor Covert, 'tis dangerous and difficult to come to him.

'The Death of the Stag, with the Ceremonies to be observed therein.

'He that gives the falling Blow, ought of Right to sound the Recheat, to assemble together the rest of the Company, as also the Dogs; also at the Death of a Stag, there are several Ceremonies that should be observed.

'When the Huntsmen come in to the Death of the Hart, they should cry Ware Haunch, that the *Hounds* may not break in to the Deer, which being secured, the next Business is to cut his Throat, and to Reward the young *Hounds* with the Blood, to make them in love with a Deer, and learn to keep at the Throat; then having sounded the Mot, or Morts, he that is to break him up (that is, to *Take Say,*) first slits the Skin from the cutting of the Throat downwards, making the Arber, so that the Ordure may not break forth; then he is to be Paunched, and the Hounds to be rewarded therewith. Another Ceremony is, the Huntsman presents the Person that took the Essay with a drawn Hanger, to have a Chop at his Head, and after him, every one hath a Chop if it is not cut off; and generally the Huntsman, or Keeper is provided with such a Hanger, that is not over sharp, that there may be the more Chops for the gaining more Fees, every one giving him a Shilling at least: Which done, the Huntsman takes up the Head, and shews it to the *Hounds* for their Encouragement, rewarding the Young Ones with the Blood. And the concluding Ceremony is to blow a Treble Mot by one, and then a whole Recheat in Confort by all that have Horns bare-headed, with a general Ho-up: Upon which they depart Home: the Hart is carried away in a Cart, together with the Head, and the *Hounds* coupled up, and carried Home by the Keeper.'

Of all the 'Noble arts of Venerie' the only ones which survive in anything like their original form are stag-hunting and fox-hunting. The hare is still coursed, despite innumerable private members' bills to outlaw coursing, and the Waterloo Cup (the 'Derby' of the sport) is now in its 138th year. But this is a far cry from the days of Edward II, when his huntsman, William Twici, considered the hare 'King of all beasts of Venery'. And the fox, although a beast of the chase, was never game: so strictly speaking all that remains is West country stag-hunting, a view held by Lord Ebrington as long as seventy-five years ago.

'The chase of the wild red deer, as practised in Devon and Somerset, is the only survival in England of a sport which was followed in earlier days in most countries in Europe, and which still has many devotees on the Continent.

'Originally, no doubt deer were hunted for food as much as for the pleasure of chasing them, so we find that for a considerable period nets and bows and arrows played as prominent a part in the chase as hounds. But these methods led to indiscriminate slaughter, and breeding hinds with young deer of both sexes were of necessity the most frequent victims of such attacks; the superior cunning of the old stags and hinds – the very animals whose death was most desired – enabling them to escape. So in the 14th century, if not before, men began to recognise that if they would hunt or capture the best stag rather than the first who should present himself, it was indispensible that he should be harboured' . . .

'. . . It is recorded (in the Calendar of State Papers of Henry VIII) that King Francis I and Sir Thomas Fitzwilliam, after a long discussion of the English and French methods of harbouring and hunting deer, agreed to differ as to the merits of the two systems. This looks as though there had been some recognised distinctions in the practice of the two countries, though of these there is no trace in the old English works on the subject. One of the joint authors of the first sporting book in our language was a Frenchman, and little is said about stag hunting. Its successors, from *The Mayster of Game,* written for Edmund Langley, fifth son of Edward III, till Dr Collyns published *The Chase of the Wild Red Deer* in 1862, are all practically translations from the French . . .'

Lord Ebrington later describes the far-reaching hunting traditions of Exmoor.

'There were forest officers in Saxon times, and the early Norman kings seem to have hunted over it occasionally, when it was a Royal Forest of some 80,000 acres, in which roebuck as well as red deer flourished. Hugh Pollard, Queen Elizabeth's ranger, kept staghounds at Simonsbath in 1598, and his successors probably did the same, the great landowners of the district not taking up the task till 1740, when Mr Dyke became master; he was followed by his kinsman, the first Sir Thomas Acland, and from that time the record is unbroken . . .

'. . . There is no one connected with a stag-hunting establishment whose duties are more important, or on whom more depends, than the harbourer. It is his task to ascertain by woodcraft the whereabouts of a deer, suitable for the day's sport, so accurately that the animal may be roused without difficulty or delay, and yet so cautiously that he may not be conscious that he is being tracked and observed. All of which is easier said than done.

'Horace Walpole, writing on January 31, 1750, says of Lord Sandwich: "He goes once or twice a week to hunt with the Duke (of Cumberland), and as the latter has taken a turn of gaming, Sandwich, to make his court – and fortune – carries a box and dice in his pocket; and so they throw a main, whenever the hounds are at fault, upon every green hill and under every green tree; and it is related of some sportsmen of the last generation, who were as fond of whist as they were of hunting, that they might occasionally, when the tufting was tedious, be seen enjoying a quiet rubber in a convenient spot, with a sentry on duty to warn them when it was time to take the field. Luncheon and love-making are the modern substitutes, especially luncheon." '

Lord Ebrington was master of the Devon and Somerset from 1881–7, inheriting hounds and kennels from the legendary Mr Mordaunt Fenwick Bisset, who first became master of a subscription pack in 1855. The great Bisset (in one sense of the word, at least – he 'sat' twenty-three stone!) together with Mr Froude Bellew and Parson Jack Russell, was responsible for the resurgence of the sport in the West country. As a result of their efforts the Devon and Somerset were again flourishing when in 1902 the second edition of Dr Charles Palk Collyns's classic *Chase of the Wild Red Deer* was published. When the book first appeared in 1862, two years before the author's death, the whole future of stag-hunting in the two counties was very much in the balance.

Dr Collyns's great passion for the hunt is written on every line – and between the lines – of his book and the whole work is clearly a labour of love. Not only does it faithfully chronicle the history of the Devon and Somerset up to 1860, it also records much of the Doctor's researches into the traditions of the sport and his observations of the natural history of the deer.

> 'It has been asserted by some writers that the red deer was introduced into this country from France. The animal, it is true, is found in that country, and in Germany and elsewhere; but after some enquiry and investigation of the subject, I can find no sufficient ground for assuming that it is not a native of this island.
>
> 'The male red deer is called, in common parlance, a stag or hart, the female is called a hind, and the young a calf. But if we use a term of art, the male deer is not called indifferently a stag or hart. Different names are applied by the foresters to the animal at different ages. These have altered and changed perhaps in some slight degree from time to time, and it may be that in different districts and countries names may vary. John Manwood* thus writes:– ". . . at the first year you shall call him a hind calf, or a calf; the second year you shall call him a broket; the third year you shall call him a spayad; the fourth year you shall call him a staggard; the fifth year you shall call him a stag; the sixth year you shall call him a hart. But here note, that some ancient writers do report that in times past the foresters and woodmen were wont to call him a stag at the fourth year, and not a staggard as we now do. And also at the fifth year they did call him a great stag. And so they were wont to give him a difference by this word stag, and great stag. And whereas some do think that a stag, of what age soever he be, shall not be called a hart until the king or queen do hunt him; that is not so, for they are all greatly deceived that so do think; for after the fifth year of his age he should no more be called a stag, but a hart. And as Budaeus saith, at six years of age then a hart you shall him call; so that if a stag come to be six years of age, then he is a hart. But if the king or queen do hunt or chase him and he escape alway alive, then after such a hunting or chasing, he is called a hart royall. But if the king or queen do hunt or chase a hart in the forest, so far that he is not likely to return to the forest again of himself, and the king giveth him over, either for that he leaveth off from hunting, as being weary, or for that he cannot recover him, and because that such a hart hath shewed the king pastime for his delight, and is also, as Budaeus saith, *eximius cervus*, – a goodly hart; and therefore the king would have him preserved to return to the forest

*Collyns quotes from John Manwood's *Treatise on the Lawes of the Forest*, 1592.

Hawking: the Fatal Stoop (F. G. Turner, 19th century)

Deer Stalkers, by E. Landseer, engraved by Finden

16. *From Venery to Venison:* The Gamekeeper's Larder, *by John E. Ferneley (1836)*

again, he doth cause open proclamation to be made in all towns and villages, near unto the place where the same hart is so remaining, that no manner of person or persons shall kill, hurt, hunt, or chase him, but that he shall safely return to such a forest again from whence he came; and for that cause the king doth appoint certain foresters to harbor the said hart there for a while, and by degrees to bring him into the forest againe; and then ever after, such a hart is called a hart royall proclaimed; so note that there are three sorts of harts:–

A Hart,
A Hart Royall,
A Hart Royall proclaimed.''

'. . . Generally speaking, the stag and hind are in colour upon the neck, back, sides, and flanks, of a reddish brown. The face is of the same colour, shaded off with a grey or ashen hue upon and about the jaws. A dark brown stripe of wiry hair extends from the top of the neck, between the ears, to the shoulders, and this was sometimes called the mane of the deer. About and around the short tail (or ''single'', as it is technically termed) the colour is light brown, fading into buff between the haunches and over the belly. This buff colour is generally of a lighter shade in the male than in the female deer. The throat of the stag is furnished with coarse hair, which at the end of the autumn increases in growth, and forms a thick ruff during the winter . . .

'The calves, at their birth, and up to the age of three or four months, are spotted with white, like fawns of the fallow or park deer; the female calf is not spotted so fully as the male. The calves of the Wapiti deer (*cervus* Canadensis), of which several specimens may be seen in the Zoological Gardens in London, are spotted in like manner . . .

'The surpassing glory and majesty of the stag lie mainly in the ''beamed frontlet'' which adorns his brow. . . .

'The horns of the red deer, unlike those of the fallow deer, consist of a large beam, with single spires or points projecting from it. Occasionally, however, we find a red deer, when advanced in years, with a palmated horn or ''cup'' at the top of the beam from which the points issue.

'By the appearance of the beam and the number of points on the horns, the age of the deer may, up to a certain period, be ascertained with tolerable accuracy; and in technical language, the horns, as the remarkable ornament of the animal, are termed the ''head'' . . .

'Until he is one year old, the male deer has no horns. In his second year he has a knob of bones, about two inches in height, thrown out at each side of the head. At the age of three, a spire or upright horn, about six to eight inches high, with a brow antler projecting from the spire close to the base of the horn, grace the deer's head. At four we find the animal bearing the spire about fourteen inches long, with the brow antler and another projection, called among us the ''tray''. At five the ''bay'' antlers are added to the points found on the four-year old deer (not invariably, however, as in some stags the "bay" is never thrown out; in others it will be found on one horn but not on the other), and two points or brockets on the top of one horn. At six, the stag has the points or "rights" before named, with two points on top of each horn. At seven years he has all his "rights", with three points on the top of one horn and two on the other; and at eight years old he has three points on top of each horn. He is then known to the sportsman as a stag with "three on top", and is frequently, though erroneously, called a royal hart. After the age of seven or eight years the alteration in the horns becomes less marked than it was before that age. Generally speaking, however, the "beam" or main horn increases in size and length as the stag grows older – the horn becomes wider in its spread and more serrated or gnarled on its surface, the points or rights become longer; and in some very old stags the top of the beam spreads so as to become, to a certain extent, palmated, and the points borne on the palm or cup increase in number . . . An old stag, long known as the Badgeworthy Deer, had seven on top of one horn, and six on the other, when killed . . . in the year 1786. It occasionally happens, too, that after a stag has passed his prime, and is becoming stricken in years, the horns, which formed the beauty of his majesty, decrease in size and form, until the horn gradually deteriorates, and nothing but an upright or single spire, like that appearing in the three-year-old deer, shows itself. The deer is then called a "bater" or "backer". A hart that is past his sixth year was in ancient times, and is now, from the number of his points and rights, generally called a stag of ten . . .

'These wonderful developments, the horns, are shed or mewed every year. From the time when the horn drops off to that when the new horn reaches its full growth, is a period of from sixteen to eighteen weeks . . . the annual renewing of the chiefest ornament and most powerful weapon of offence, of the monarch of the wilds, is succinctly and accurately described by Dr Bell:

' "The growth of the horn is an astonishing instance of the rapidity of production of bone under particular circumstances, and unparalleled in its extent in so short a period. During its growth the branches of the external carotid arteries, which lend their assistance in the formation, are considerably enlarged for the purpose of carrying the great flow of blood required for the production of bone. It extends by means of the velvet (a plexus of blood vessels) all over the external parts of the horn; it is quite soft and highly vascular, so that the slightest injury causes blood to flow freely, and the horn, when this occurs, to be imperfectly developed".'

'The period at which stags shed their horns is the spring, and generally about the middle or latter end of April. The exact time depends in some measure on the age of the stag and the temperature of the winter and early spring. Should the winter be cold and the spring protracted, I have known the stags shed their horns as late as May; the old stags in the beginning, and the young deer at the end of that month. It is very rarely, however, that an old stag is seen with his horns on after the beginning of May, but a two-year-old deer will carry his horns for a month or two later. Before the period arrives when the stag is about to cast or shed his horns, he retires to the deepest and thickest coverts, and there remains secluded until his new horns begin to sprout. He then leaves the tangled thickets and seeks the open moors and heaths, or if these be far distant from his usual haunts, he retreats to timber woods and grown-up plantations. Instinct teaches him to do this, as the extreme sensitiveness and tenderness of the velvet-covered substance destined to grow into a branching antler are such, that he cannot endure the touch of the coppice wood or furze brake in which he has hidden himself, as if for very shame, since his former coronet dropped from his brow. So vascular and delicate is the velvet, that the slightest abrasion is followed by blood; and the scar resulting from an injury during the infancy of the horn, may frequently be discovered on the hard substance when the "head" has come to maturity. The life which the animals lead during this period is by no means enviable. Flies irritate and plague them; the least contact with a hard substance causes pain or apprehension; and the fear in which they live, of suffering pain, is observable in all their motions and actions . . .

'The horns attain their full growth about the beginning of September, but still the velvet surrounds them, and continues to case the horn until the substance is perfectly hardened and matured; then the covering begins to dry and fall from the horn in strips, and by the second week in September the stag has disencumbered himself of the ignoble "panni" that disgraced his head, and appears in full majesty and vigour. When the velvet begins to peel, he rubs his horns against the trunks of trees to assist in ridding himself of the now useless envelope . . .

'. . . I am well aware that a deer kept in confinement will shed his horns earlier, and that they will be renewed sooner, than in the case of a wild deer. I may also remark, that a deer kept in a park, or stall fed, will often, at the age of three years, present the appearance, in the horns, of a stag of four or even six years old; and I attribute these things to the undisturbed life led by the animal, and the abundance of nutritious food with which he is supplied.'

Stall-fed deer were never much to the true sportsman's taste, however. Collyns himself believes there is no way of counterfeiting the natural chase:

'Until the ancient sport of the country ceases to exist by the complete extinction of the wild deer, the more modern expedient of turning out a "calf" will never acquire popularity with the sportsmen of Devon and Somerset. Without implying the least disrespect to those who enjoy a gallop after a stall-fed deer, I am quite sure every one will feel that there is a charm in the sport . . . which can never attach to that of following a chase after an animal bred in a park "enlarged" for the day's amusement, and carted back to his paddock at the conclusion of the run. . . . One of the most exciting and picturesque incidents in a day's sport is the rouse of the deer. Then follow the duties of stopping the

17. Queen Elizabeth presented with 'a sharpe knyfe' for taking 'assaye of the Deare' (*Turbervile*)

tufters and bringing up the pack, so as to lay on with all dispatch; and what music hath greater charms to the sportsman's ear than that of the full-mouthed pack, when every hound settles well upon the line, and races, and flings, and jostles, and struggles for the lead across the open?

'I have met with many who were sceptical as to the possibility of a wild stag running the same distances and at the same speed as the stall-fed deer. Oats and beans, carefully administered, no doubt form good and hard food for an animal upon whose wind and condition the sport depends. Still, the denizen of the forest, though he may at his own discretion drink his fill, and glut himself with turnips and oak sprouts, grass and mountain ash berries, unaware that he may be called upon at a moment's notice to trust to wind and endurance to save himself from destruction, has at least the advantage of roaming at large, of travelling from covert to covert and from hill to hill, of following his own instincts in preserving the strength, and fleetness, and all the resources with which he has been endowed by nature; while the knowledge of the country through which he passes, of the points at which he may avail himself of the refreshing bath, and his hope of baffling his pursuers by taking soil, or mixing with the friendly herd, must in a large degree contribute to keep his "courage to the sticking place" throughout the chances and dangers, the exertion and excitement of the chase.'

And William Daniel, fifty years before, was highly contemptuous of the practice:

'At the present day, as an object of Chase to the Sportsman, the Stag requires but cursory mention; those indeed who are fond of pomp and parade in hunting, will not accede to this opinion, but the only mode in which this Chase can recommend itself to the real Sportsman, is, when the Deer is looked for and found like other Game, which Hounds pursue; and it is not uncommon for an Out-lying Fallow Deer, tried for and unharboured in this way, to shew much sport with a pack of Harriers, especially where the country is enclosed.

'At present very few Hounds (except those of the Royal Establishment) are kept for this amusement exclusively; and were the King once to see a Fox well found and killed handsomely, he would in all probability give a decided preference in favour of Fox-hounds; for what a marked difference is there, between conveying in a covered Cart, an Animal nearly as big as the Horse that draws it, to a particular spot where he is liberated; and cheerly riding to the Cover side, with all the ecstacy of Hope and Expectation.

'The Scent of Deer is so welcome to Hounds, that those of every description will most eagerly run it, and the only excellence of the Stag Hound, is, the being more readily brought to stop, when headed by the Huntsman or his Assistants, altho' in the midst of his keenest pursuit. The Earl of Derby used Fox hounds for this Chase in Surrey, and the consequence was, that they frequently defied all stoppages, beat the Horsemen, tho' mounted upon the first Blood Horses in the country, and baffled every effort to restrain their Speed and Spirit. The

Stag hound is large, and gallops with none of the neatness and fire of the Fox hound; the Deer is carried to the place of starting, for which an open country is chosen, where, (if it be a satisfaction,) the pleasure of beholding the animal hunted, may be enjoyed at the distance of three miles a head. This so forcibly struck a Lieutenant of the Navy, who was upon a Stag-hunting Party, that when the Stag, after a considerable run over the Champaign, at length got a few minutes out of sight, he coolly pulled out his watch and remarked, he had lost sight of the Chase twenty minutes P.M.'

This degradation of the true chivalry of the hunt was lamented by the Baillie-Grohmans, whose devotion to 'the Noble Art' and its aesthetic were paramount:

'Mediaeval hunting had none of the steeple chase elements about it which are now a *sine qua non*. Men went hunting in a leisurely manner, and they were out to enjoy a long day's sport; if night overtook them far from home in the depths of the forest they knew how to make the best of an unpleasant incident. They knew much more than we moderns do of the "nature" of the beast they were hunting, of its habits and wiles, of its strategems and ruses. They studied wild nature with a keenness unblunted by intellectual occupations, and they loved her with unstinted devotion. To see the play of the sun's rays in the forest's foliage, or to hear the song of the birds in the dewy morn delighted their senses, and they loved to listen to the brave music of their deep-toned hounds as they gave tongue in wooded glades. The chief pleasure did not lie in the slaying of the hart, but rather in the incidents that led up to it. To watch their pack at work, to cheer them on with their voices, chiding them when they were hunting the change, these were the principal attractions. And when the great hart was at last at bay, or the fierce boar finally turned upon his relentless foes, the foam flecked steed was pushed to a last effort, so as to be at their side before antlers or tusks could work havoc. And the killing itself was a true test of nerve, skill and strength. It was done in knightly fashion, without the use of unchivalrous wiles or taking refuge to cross bow or long bow. For the death stroke had to be given with cold steel, and needless to say, to approach close enough to a cornered hart, standing with lowered head, his rear guarded by rocks or by a big tree, so as to give the deadly thrust with a short hunting sword, was a feat that required grit of the true sort; while in the case of a big boar, dealing out strokes of his deadly tusks with lightning rapidity, it was, if it was performed on horseback, a deed requiring not only the above qualities but perfect horsemanship. No one who deemed himself a veneur would dream of delegating the killing to a subordinate, as was done very generally later on when men grew soft, and the use of gunpowder removed many of the risks of the chase, until, finally, sport was degraded to mere slaughter and that by men securely ensconced in danger-proof stands, to which they were driven in chariots or carried in litters.'

(*Sport in Art,* 1913)

18. Stag Hounds *by H. Alken (19th century)*

The more robust, physical appeal of the 'steeplechase' is heartily depicted by 'Snaffle' (Robert Dunkin) in his book, *The Image of War* (1914). 'Snaffle' quotes from Surtees' *Handley Cross*, presumably feeling a close affinity to Mr Jorrocks' philosophy.

> ' 'unting is all that's worth living for – all time is lost wot is not spent in 'unting – it is like the hair we breathe – if we have it not we die – it's the sport of Kings, the image of war without its guilt, and only five and twenty per cent of its danger.'

North of the Border, Daniel tells the story of Sir William St Clair's wager with Robert Bruce which might be said to be a good deal more dangerous than any battle. He describes it as 'a stake, upon the capture of a Deer, that perhaps neither *ancient* nor *modern* History, can parallel'.

> '. . . The King, in following the Chase upon *Pentland Hills,* had often started a "White haunch Deer", which had always escaped from his *Hounds;* and he asked the NOBLES, who were assembled around him, whether any of them had *Dogs* which they thought might be more successful. No *Courtier* would affirm that his *Hounds* were *fleeter*, than those of the King, until Sir William St Clair, of *Rosline,* unceremoniously said, he would *wager* his HEAD, that his two favourite *Dogs*, "HELP and HOLD", would kill the *Deer*, before she could cross the *March-burn*. The King instantly caught at his unwary offer, and *betted* the *Forest* of PENTLAND MOOR, against the Life of SIR WILLIAM ST CLAIR. All the *Hounds* were tied up, except a few *Ratches* or slow *Hounds*, to rouse the *Deer;* whilst SIR WILLIAM ST CLAIR, posting himself in the best situation for slipping his *Dogs*, prayed devoutly to CHRIST, the blessed VIRGIN, and *St Katharine*. The *Deer* was shortly after roused, and the *Hounds* slipped; SIR WILLIAM following on a gallant steed, to cheer his *Dogs*. The *Hind*, however, reached the *middle* of the *Brook*, upon which the Hunter, threw himself from his Horse, in Despair. At this critical Moment, however, HOLD, stopped her in the *Brook;* and *HELP*, coming up, turned her back, and killed her on SIR WILLIAM'S Side. The KING descended from the Hill, embraced SIR WILLIAM, and bestowed on him, the Lands of *Kirkton, Lepan-House, Earncraig*, etc., in free Forestrie. Sir William, in Acknowledgement of St Katharine's Intercession, built the *Chapel* of St Katharine in the *Hopes,* the Chapel-yard of which, is still to be seen. The Hill from which *ROBERT BRUCE*, beheld this memorable Chase, is still called the KING'S HILL, and the place where SIR WILLIAM hunted, is called the Knight's Field.'
>
> (*Rural Sports*)

Writing in 1883, J. E. Harting gives a lucid account of a winter deer-shoot, preceded by an appraisal of some of the practical difficulties likely to be encountered by the sportsman.

> 'It may seem an easy matter to shoot a deer in a park, yet to select an animal from the herd, drive it out, and kill it with a bullet at any distance from fifty to a hundred and fifty yards, is more readily conceived than executed.

'Deer, when alarmed, keep very close together, and, if they do not actually go off at a good pace, are constantly in motion, passing and repassing one another in the most vexatious manner, and thus rendering it impossible to fire at any particular animal without risk of hitting, and perhaps maiming, two or three others. It is here that the patience of the sportsman is tested, as well as his skill, in taking immediate advantage of an opportunity to fire.

'Again, one is expected to hit the Deer in the head, for a large hole made by the rotatory motion of a bullet spoils both skin and meat; moreover, unless particularly well directed, a bullet in the body does not always prove fatal. If, in addition to these drawbacks, the day is cold, with a fresh wind blowing or snow falling, it will be readily understood that success is by no means to be predicted as a matter of course.

'I have been let to these reflections on turning over the leaves of an old note book, in which I find chronicled the result of day's deer shooting in January. The day having been fixed a week or more previously, and a long railway journey being necessary, it was not possible to make choice of a favourable day for shooting, and we had to take our chance of the weather. As it happened, the weather could scarcely have been worse or more unfavourable for our purpose. It was extremely cold, and, while a sharp wind materially affected our shooting, our tempers were not improved by having the snow in our faces all day. But such was our fate. The park, from its large extent and the undulating nature of the ground, planted here and there with clumps of trees, was well adapted to the sport, for not only were the Deer able to run out of sight, and obtain a temporary repose, but, after the first few shots, when they became wary and restless, we were enabled to practise both stalking and driving.

'Owing to the difficulty, before alluded to, of picking out a Deer from a large herd in close order and constant motion, it became necessary to disperse the ranks, and by means of beaters judiciously placed, we contrived to break up the herd and scatter small parties of ten or a dozen each in different directions. Having effected this, my host and I separated in opposite directions, not without certain misgivings as to the result, but bouyed up with that pleasant feeling of excitement and friendly rivalry which sportsmen so well know when competing for the heaviest bag on different beats.

'In one respect my host had the advantage, in being armed with a double rifle. Mine was a single, a miniature express by Holland, bore ·360 (called by Messrs. Holland the 'Climax'), and although a mere toy in appearance, with a barrel of 28 in. and weighing only 6 lb., it proved to be quite as effective as the larger and more formidable-looking weapon of my friend. With this rifle I use a drachm and a half of powder, and a hollow-pointed short-cone bullet. This charge gives a very flat trajectory, and only one standard sight is required from 40 to 150 yards.

'Following the direction of a small herd of seven, and peering cautiously over a brow, I found myself suddenly in closer proximity to them than I expected, and obtained my first shot at about sixty yards; but whether from nervousness or haste, or both, I contrived to miss, and had the mortification of seeing the herd trot slowly away. I soon got another chance, however, and by keeping a large oak between myself and the particular Deer which I selected, I was easily enabled to get within range again, and dropped a fine doe, the bullet going in at the base of the ear. As she rolled over in their midst, her companions, with a sudden start of surprise, fled in all directions, but, soon reuniting, disappeared in the distance, and by the time the keeper had cut her throat, they were nowhere to be seen.

'As we stood over the fallen Deer, a sudden exclamation from my companion caused me to look round, but only in time to see the antlers of a buck disappearing behind the brow which we had so recently crossed. This, apparently, was the leader of a small herd which my host had driven from the other side of the park, and which in haste must have come upon us unawares. Running back to the brow and kneeling down, I saw the herd going away diagonally in a straggling line, and, firing somewhat too hastily at the last doe, was vexed to find that I had only broken the near fore-leg. The animal fell, but, instantly recovering herself, joined her companions and got away, much to the chagrin of the keeper, who importuned me to keep her in view and kill her if possible, lest, by losing sight of her, she might escape and die. What a run we had across the open and over the crisp snow, slipping and sliding, now and then almost falling, and again recovering our feet as we held forward in the vain hope of a check that might give us a little breathing time, and enable us to come up with the quarry; but we were distanced, and, for the nonce, lost sight completely of the wounded doe. Whilst we were discussing the chances of finding her again, a herd came in view, though at some distance, and appeared to be heading towards a clump of trees that stood upon a ridge of the undulating park. They were on our right, and we were to the right of the ridge. By crossing over to the left of this, and keeping down in the valley on that side, we contrived to run forward and reach the clump before them. They came along at the moderate canter, evidently driven towards us by my host or his beaters. We stood up behind the trees and the keeper whispered that I should take a fine black doe, which appeared to be in splendid condition. Suddenly they caught sight of, or winded us, and, halting for a second, instantly dashed off at a good pace to our left front. They passed almost in Indian file about fifty yards off, the black doe running fifth. "Now, then, sir," said the keeper, "the black doe, take the black doe!" How I hate anyone to shout in my ear just as I am going to fire. It is bad enough when birds are rising out of turnips within easy shot of you to have a man bawling "Mark!" as if you were either deaf or blind. But it is ever so much worse with deer, when success depends entirely upon the absence of all flurry and flutter. How I wished I was alone; but there was not time for such reflection – the deer were off, and the thought was "now or never". Taking the line of the animal's head and holding well forward, I pulled at the fated doe, and, much to my satisfaction – and, I will admit, to my surprise, for I scarcely expected

19. Hunting scene (early 15th century)

to kill – she rolled over like a rabbit, and lay prefectly still. The keeper shouted with delight and as he ran to cut her throat; and on getting up to her we found that the ball had passed through the neck, dividing the cervical vertebrae, so that death must have been instantaneous.

'As she fell the herd divided, those in her rear bounding a little to the right, and then standing to gaze in our direction. An excellent chance here presented itself of taking a Deer at a stand-still, and sufficiently apart from the rest to avoid risk of hitting any other. I was at a nice distance, too, as nearly as I could judge about eighty yards. I must have aimed a little too high, however, for, although the animal fell, it immediately recovered its legs, ran a few yards, and fell again. Hastening up to within half the distance, loading as I ran, I got a second shot, and the bullet, going in at the ear, proved instantly fatal. The first bullet, I found, had struck the base of the skull behind the ears, slitting the right one, but without penetrating the skull, the animal standing broadside on. The blow, however, had stunned it for the moment, and produced an evident giddiness, which caused it to fall, and then to rise and fall again, when the second bullet killed it. I was standing over the prostrate animal examining the wound, when a distant shout attracted my attention, and I saw my host standing on a brow and signalling me to come to him. I wondered what had happened, but thought perhaps he had marked a small herd down in a convenient spot, or had planned a "drive". On reaching him, however, I found that he had left his bullet pouch behind in another part of the park, and had to send back for it. Meantime he had just fired at and wounded a doe, and had not a bullet left to go on with. He begged I would follow the animal up, and kill it if possible, for he had broken one of the forelegs, and he came with me to show me where it was. We found it limping slowly along under the park fence, against which it seemed every now and then to lean for support, but still keeping on as if in an endeavour to rejoin the herd. By pushing on quickly we contrived to head it, and the moment we stopped it halted too, throwing up its head, and presenting a capital shot at about sixty yards. I aimed at the head, and the animal fell, as we thought, dead; but no sooner had the keeper approached within ten yards, to cut its throat, than it bounded suddenly to its feet, and, much to our astonishment, continued its walk under the park fence. Where could it have been hit, we said, to fall so apparently dead, and rise again? It must have been struck on the top of the head, the bullet stunning it, glancing, but not penetrating, and we must try another shot. Repeating the same manoeuvre, and heading the deer to make it halt, I got a second chance at about the same distance as the first, and a very similar shot. The animal dropped again, but this time remained perfectly still. On walking up with the keeper to examine it, we found that the first bullet had entered the right cheek, and passed out on the other side, breaking the left jaw, while the second had entered the right eye, and, passing into the brain, had proved instantly fatal. We were astonished to find how much it takes to kill a Deer, and how much easier it is to wound or miss, even in a park, than to place a

20. Return from a stag-hunt (early 16th century)

bullet in the right spot. As the day progressed we got thoroughly warm with our work; running full speed to cut off a band of fugitives, or stalking some outlying ones that had been separated from the main herd; and as we got warmer, we got steadier, and shot better. I found my doe with the broken leg again, that the keeper was so anxious about, and, although she was very restless, I succeeded in stalking and killing her with a bullet through the upper part of the neck, just behind the cheek. Another deer which had been wounded and had got back to the herd, gave us a great deal of trouble before it was secured. Three or four times it was driven out with ten or a dozen others, and as many times did I essay to get a favourable shot; but it invariably abstained from showing itself outside the herd, and there was always a risk of hitting one if not more of its companions. At length I climbed into a tree, and the keeper once more driving the little herd past me, I got a favourable chance at about fifty yards, the wounded doe fell to rise no more, and the startled herd were again soon lost to view. My friend had killed two more deer than I had, and when, as daylight waned, we walked across the park to the keeper's lodge, we found sixteen beauties stretched upon the grass. How pleasant the walk home was, over the crisp snow, as we compared notes, and recounted every shot; and how pleasant, too, was that after-dinner cigar in that old-fashioned chimney corner, where we discussed the prospect of the weather holding up . . .'

(*Essays on Sport and Natural History*)

J. E. Harting's deer-shoot, with keeper, beaters and one sporting friend for company, could hardly differ more radically from the pantomime described by the ubiquitous Pierce Egan earlier in the nineteenth century. Where Harting makes a serious and balanced appreciation of the problems of the sportsman and the tactics employed to overcome them, Egan presents a society report interspersed with a few details of the physical geography of the setting. The actual recounting of the hunt takes but few words. Here, then, from *Pierce Egan's Anecdotes* (*Original and Selected*) *of The Turf, The Chase, the Ring and the Stage; The Whole Forming a Complete Panorama of the Sporting World; uniting with it A Book of Reference and Entertaining Companion to the Lovers of British Sport*, is 'Stag-Hunting in Honour of Mr Plunkett, at Killarney, May 25, 1825'.

'A stag-hunt on the lakes of Killarney is a kind of jubilee; it is seldom given but on remarkable occasions, or in honour of some distinguished or popular individual; it never fails to attract people from all parts of the country, so that Killarney is literally crammed with strangers on the eve of the celebrated fete . . . Mr John O'Connell . . . shortly after the arrival of Mr Plunkett . . . expressed a hope that he would accept the amusement of a stag-hunt; Mr Plunkett accepted of the invitation. Thursday was fixed for the hunt. At an early hour on that day numerous parties, in all manner of vehicles, were seen moving from Killarney to the Quay of Ross, the usual place of embarkation. Amongst those I noticed the Attorney-General; he was accompanied by two of his sons, his son-in-law, and three daughters. Ross Island, which is by far the largest on the lakes, is separated on one side from the main land merely by a small stream; on the other side it looks

Partridge Shooting near Windsor, engraved by B. Howell, Jr.

Pheasant (*Phasianus colchicus*) by C. Whymper

directly on the Lower Lakes, the spreading branches of the arbutus and other trees of evergreen invade, as it were, the solitude of those waters. A little further on to the right rises the Island of Innisvallen (the most beautiful isle of the lakes, and travellers say one of the most delightful spots in the world); one side of this island falls into the waters; on the other it has what is called an ironbound coast, but out of its steep and rugged rocks springs the arbutus. This rare tree abounds in every island on the Lakes of Killarney . . . On the Lower Lake, studded with islands, hundreds of barges, of various description, laden with elegant and fashionable people, were seen making way to the Upper Lake, the appointed scene of the expected hunt.

'We now arrived at the upper extremity of the Lakes, right opposite the seat of Lord Brandon. The Upper Lake is joined to the Lower Lake by what is called the Long Range, a river of about from twelve to twenty feet in breadth, which winds round the Eagle's Nest. As you advance on the Upper Lake, the mountains present themselves. Behind these, in the distant ground, M'Gillicuddy's Reekes raises its towering front . . . A great number of islands spring, as it were, from the waters and are scattered over the Lakes.

'More than one hundred barges pressed to the upper extremity of the lake; Mr O'Connell's was the first, though heavily laden. It seemed to move over the waters with the elasticity and ease of the eagle that soared above it. It was rowed by eight men, dressed in checked jackets, and trousers of the same. Mr O'Connell was cheered, and stood up to return the numerous salutations from persons in the neighbouring boats.

'On the arrival of Mr Plunkett's barge the hunt commenced. The stag, which was of an amazingly large size, had been found on the mountains several days before, and was constantly watched by a number of men. He made his lair in a wood on one of the mountains that hang immediately over the lake. Here, as he lay in supposed security and repose, he was disturbed by the heavy bay of the hounds, the sound of the horn, and the shout of the huntsmen; he arose from his couch, and looked around him. I was curious to learn the particulars of this scene from one of the gentlemen who was on the mountains. He soon appeared, dashing on the brow of the mountains, where, extended, far beneath him, lay the beautiful scenery of Lough Lean. We had now a splendid view of the hunt, and nothing in the world could be finer. After the chase of more than two Irish miles, he plunged, exhausted, in the water in that part of the Upper Lake called the Bay of Derucunnihy. The noble animal, severely pressed on by the dogs, was not able to make way to the opposite shore. Twenty hounds, as least, plunged in after him; they would have bitten him severely, were it not for O'Sullivan of Tomies, the Lord of the Chase, a man of extraordinary strength and activity of the body. This gentleman dashed into the waters in order to rescue the stag; he succeeded in a work of considerable difficulty and danger. The stag, now brought on shore, though exhausted, still retained much of its energy; it required many men to hold him until a handkerchief was placed on his eyes. He was presented to Mr O'Connell, and kept for a considerable time, until the arrival of the barge of the Attorney-General. Mr John O'Connell [etc.] presented the stag to the Attorney-General. The Attorney-General returned thanks in a marked manner.

'The stag was now taken into Mr O'Sullivan's boat, and rowed to the Eagle's Nest. Here we determined to give this fine animal his liberty: accordingly, the bandage was taken from his eyes, and he was gently pushed out of the boat. He gave a look expressive of deep apprehension, fearing, no doubt, that the hunt was again about to commence. He made way in beautiful style through the water, and having reached the shore, he stopped for a moment, and looked to see if he were pursued; fresh vigour and hope returned to him, and he made to the mountains in full speed, pursued only by the shouts of a thousand voices. Thus terminated a scene which Shakespeare might have described, but which can be but feebly painted by a rude and ordinary hand.'

Something of the chequered history of the deer in Scotland and its greater dependence on the economic climate than the natural one is apparent from the conditions described by Cameron of Lochiel in 1896.

'The fact that large areas should be known by the name of forests serves to confirm the opinion that vast regions of the Highlands were in former times covered with indigenous forests of the various species of trees, whose descendants, in sadly diminished numbers, are found at the present day scattered among the valleys and on the hillsides of most of our northern counties . . .

'In those early periods of history, there existed certain royal forests set apart for the diversion of kings and nobles, while there were others, consisting of lands not belonging to the sovereign, but to great barons, to whom a sole right of forestry often conferred a right of servitude in his favour, that extended in some instances over lands belonging to other proprietors . . . such a system was not conducive to peace or good relations between the baron and his neighbours, and thus retaliation, feuds, and bloodshed were its necessary accompaniments . . . neighbouring proprietors gradually obtained charters or grants of forestry over their own estates and as the numbers of these charters increased, the few remaining rights of the great barons discontinued and were no longer exercised.

'Towards the end of the 18th and the beginning of the 19th century, a "revolution" took place in the economy of the Highlands by the introduction of "intensive" sheep farming. "Under this system, many deer forests were stocked with sheep . . . and as they no longer presented to those deer that were in the habit of frequenting them the attraction of 'clean' ground, the numbers of these must have also diminished", so that there was at this time a slump in the numbers of red deer in the northern parts of Scotland.

'The process of re-clearing the sheep runs and re-stocking with deer came twenty-thirty years later, caused perhaps by a newly developed taste for sport, the alleviation of the difficulties of travel through the invention of steam-

> powered engines. From 1860–74 the process of clearing ground for deer slowed down, and during that period sheep farming was profitable. After the Franco-German war, the economic factors reduced this profitability and, once more, land was converted into deer forests.'

Where the hunting of deer is concerned, Scotland is not just another country: it's another world. Although there are records of great hunts with as many as fifteen hundred clansmen present and the full panoply of the tribal gathering, it is the solitary hunter, in the 'Man against Nature' contest, that captures the imagination. The contrast could scarcely be greater than between the noise and speed and numbers of the hunt and the silent solitude of the stalk, which may take a whole day or two or more, and even then prove unsuccessful. Perhaps no-one better describes the discomfort, the frustration, the tension, the excitement, the skill, the luck, and the satisfaction of stalking and taking a big stag, than Charles St John in his *Wild Sports of the Highlands*.

> '*Sunday* – This evening, Malcolm, the shepherd of the shealing at the foot of Benmore, returning from church, reported his having crossed on the hill a track of a hart of extraordinary size; and he guessed it must be "the muckle stag of Benmore". This was an animal seldom seen, but which had long been the talk and marvel of the shepherds for its wonderful size and cunning. They love the marvellous, and in their report "the muckle stag" bore a charmed life; he was unapproachable and invulnerable. I had heard of him too, and, having got the necessary information, resolved to try to break the charm though it should cost me a day or two.
>
> '*Monday* – This morning at sunrise, I with my rifle, Donald carrying my double-barrel, and Bran, took our way up the glen to the shealing at the foot of Benmore. Donald had no heart for this expedition. He is not addicted to superfluous conversation, but I heard him mutter something of a "feckless errand – as good deer nearer hame". Bran had already been the victor in many a bloody tussle with hart and fox. We held for the most part up the glen, but turning and crossing to seek every likely corrie and burn on both sides. I shot a wild cat stealing home to its cairn in the early morning; and we several times in the day came on deer, but they were hinds with their calves, and I was bent on higher game. As night fell, we turned down to the shealing rather disheartened; but the shepherd cheered me by assuring me the hart was still in that district, and describing his track, which he said was like that of a good-sized heifer. Our spirits were quite restored by a meal of fresh-caught trout, oatcake and milk, with a modicum of whisky, which certainly was of unusual flavour and potency.
>
> '*Tuesday* – We were off again by daybreak. I will pass by several minor adventures, but one cannot be omitted. Malcolm went with us to show us where he had last seen the track. As we crossed a long reach of black and broken ground, the first ascent from the valley, two golden eagles rose out of a hollow at some distance. Their flight was lazy and heavy, as if gorged with food, and

on examining the place we found the carcass of a sheep half eaten, one of Malcolm's flock. He vowed vengeance; and, merely pointing out to us our route, returned for a spade to dig a place of hiding near enough the carcass to enable him to have a shot at the eagles if they should return. We held on our way, and the greater part of the day without any luck to cheer us, my resolution "not to be beat" being, however, a good deal strengthened by the occasional grumbling of Donald. Towards the afternoon, when we had tired ourselves with looking with our glasses at every corrie in that side of the hill, at length, in crossing a bare and boggy piece of ground, Donald suddenly stopped, with a Gaelic exclamation, and pointed – and there, to be sure, was a full fresh foot-print, the largest mark of a deer either of us had ever seen. There was no more grumbling. Both of us were instantly as much on the alert as when we started on our adventure. We traced the track as long as the ground would allow. Where we lost it, it seemed to point down the little burn, which soon lost itself to our view in a gorge of bare rocks. We proceeded now very cautiously and taking up our station on a concealed ledge of one of the rocks, began to search the valley below with our telescopes. It was a large flat, strewed with huge slabs of stone, and surrounded on all sides but one with dark rocks. At the farther end were two black lochs, connected by a sluggish stream; beside the larger loch a bit of coarse grass and rushes, where we could distinguish a brood of wild ducks swimming in and out. It was difficult ground to see a deer in, if lying; and I had almost given up seeking, when Donald's glass became motion-less, and he gave a sort of grunt as he changed his posture, but without taking the glass from his eye. "Ugh! I'm thinking yon's him, sir: I'm seeing his horns". I was at first incredulous. What he showed me close to the long grass I have mentioned looked for all the world like some withered sticks; but the doubt was short. While we gazed the stag rose and commenced feeding; and at last I saw the great hart of Benmore! He was a long way off, perhaps a mile and a half, but in excellent ground for getting at him. Our plan was soon arranged. I was to stalk him with the rifle, while Donald, with my gun and Bran, was to get round, out of sight, to the pass by which the deer was likely to leave the valley. My task was apparently very easy. After getting down behind the rock I had scarcely to stoop my head, but to walk up within shot, so favourable was the ground and the wind. I walked cautiously, however, and slowly, to give Donald time to reach the pass. I was now within three hundred yards of him, when, as I leant against a slab of stone, all hid below my eyes, I saw him give a sudden start, stop feeding, and look round suspiciously. What a noble beast! what a stretch of antler! with a mane like a lion! He stood for a minute or two, snuffing every breath. I could not guess the cause of his alarm; it was not myself – the light wind blew fair down from him upon me; and I knew Donald would give him no inkling of his whereabouts. He presently began to move, and came at a slow trot directly towards me. My pulse beat high. Another hundred yards forward and he is mine! But it was not so to be. He took the top of a steep bank which commanded our position, saw me in an instant, and was off, at the speed of twenty miles an hour, to a pass wide from that where Donald was hid. While clattering up the hill, scattering the loose stones behind him, two other stags joined him, which had evidently been put up by Donald, and had given the alarm to my quarry. It was then that his great size was conspicuous. I could see with my glass they were full-grown stags, and with good heads, but they looked like fallow-deer as they followed him up the crag. I saw down, disappointed for the moment, and Donald soon joined me, much crestfallen, and cursing the stag in a curious variety of Gaelic oaths. Still it was something to have seen "the muckle stag", and *nil desperandum* was my motto. We had a long and weary walk to Malcolm's shealing; and I was glad to get to my heather bed, after arranging that I should occupy the hiding-place Malcolm had prepared near the dead sheep next morning.

'*Wednesday* – We were up an hour before daylight . . . Our line of march to-day was over ground so high that we came repeatedly into the midst of ptarmigan. On the very summit, Bran had a rencontre with an old mountain fox, toothless, yet very fat, whom he made to bite the dust. We struck at one place the tracks of the three deer, but of the animals themselves we saw nothing. We kept exploring corrie after corrie till night fell; and as it was in vain to think of returning to the shealing, which yet was the nearest roof, we were content to find a sort of niche in the rock, tolerably screened from all winds; and having almost filled it with long heather, flower upwards, we wrapped our plaids round us, and slept pretty comfortably.

'*Thursday* – A dip in the burn below our bivouac renovated me. I did not observe that Donald followed my example in that; but he joined me in a hearty attack on the viands which still remained in our bag; and we started with renewed courage. About mid-day we came on a shealing beside a long narrow loch, fringed with beautiful weeping-birches, and there we found means to cook some grouse which I had shot to supply our exhausted larder. The shepherd, who had "no Sassenach", cheered us by his report of "the deer" being lately seen, and describing his usual haunts. Donald was plainly getting disgusted and home-sick. For myself, I looked upon it as my fate that I must have that hart; so on we trudged. Repeatedly, that afternoon, we came on the fresh tracks of our chase, but still he remained invisible.

'*Friday* – . . . "Benna-skiach" was my object to-day, and the corries which lay beyond it, where at this season the large harts were said to resort. My way at first was dreary enough, over a long slope of boggy ground, enlivened, however, by a few traces of deer having crossed, though none of my "chase". I at length passed the slope, and soon topped the ridge, and was repaid for my labour by a view so beautiful, that I sat down to gaze at it, though anxious to get forward. Looking down into the valley before me, the foreground was a confusion of rocks of most fantastic shape, shelving rapidly to the edge of a small blue lake, the opposite shore of which was a beach of white pebbles, and beyond, a stretch of the greenest pasture, dotted with drooping white-stemmed birches. This little level was hemmed in on all sides by mountains, ridge above ridge, the lowest closely covered with purple heath, the next more green and broken by ravines, and the highest ending in sharp serrated peaks tipped with snow. Nothing moved within range of my vision, and nothing was to be seen that bespoke life but a solitary heron standing on one leg in the shallow water at the upper end of the lake. From hence I took in a good range, but could see no deer. While I lay above the lake, the day suddenly changed, and heavy wreaths of mist came down the mountain-sides in rapid succession. They reached me soon, and I was enclosed in an atmosphere through which I could not see twenty yards. It was very cold, too, and I was obliged to move, though scarcely well knowing whither. I followed the course of the lake, and afterwards of the stream which flowed from it, for some time. Now and then a grouse would rise close to me, and, flying a few yards, alight again on a hillock, crowing and croaking at the intruder. The heron, in the darkness, came flapping his great wings close past me; I almost fancied I could feel the movement they caused in the air. Nothing could be done in such weather, and I was not sure that I might not be going away from my object. It was getting late too, and I made up my mind that my most prudent plan was to arrange a bivouac before it became quite dark. My wallet was empty, except a few crumbs, the remains of my morning's baking. It was necessary to provide food: and just as the necessity occurred to me, I heard, through the mist, the call of a cock grouse as he alighted close to me. I contrived to get his head between me and the sky as he was strutting and croaking on a hillock close at hand; and aiming at where his body ought to be, I fired my rifle. On going up to the place, I found I had not only killed him, but also his mate, whom I had not seen. It was a commencement of good luck. Sitting down I speedily skinned my birds, and took them down to the burn to wash them before cooking. In crossing a sandy spot beside the burn, I came upon – could I believe my eyes? – "the Track". Like Robinson Crusoe in the same circumstances, I started back; but was speedily at work taking my information. There were prints enough to show the hart had crossed at a walk leisurely. It must have been lately, for it was since the burn had returned to its natural size, after the last night's flood. But nothing could be done till morning, so I set about my cooking; and having after some time succeeded in lighting a fire, while my grouse were slowly broiling, I pulled a quantity of heather, which I spread in a corner a little protected by an over-hanging rock; I spread my plaid upon it, and over the plaid built another layer of heather. My supper ended, which was not epicurean, I crawled into my nest under my plaid, and was soon sound asleep . . .

'*Saturday* – Need I say my first object was to go down and examine the track anew. There was no mistake. It was impossible to doubt that "the muckle hart of Benmore" had actually walked through that burn a few hours before me, and in the same direction. I followed the track, and breasted the opposite hill. Looking round from its summit, it appeared to me a familiar scene, and on considering a moment, I found I overlooked from a different quarter the very same rocky plain and the two black lochs where I had seen my chase three days before. I had not gazed many minutes when I saw a deer lying on a black hillock which was quite open. I lay down immediately, and with my glass made out at once the object of all my wanderings. My joy was somewhat abated by his position, which was not easily approachable. My first object, however, was to withdraw myself out of his sight, which I did by crawling backwards down a little bank till only the tops of his horns were visible, and they served to show me that he continued still. As he lay looking towards me, he commanded with his eye three-fourths of the circle, and the other quarter, where one might have got in upon him under cover of the little hillock, was unsafe from the wind blowing in that direction. A burn ran between him and me, one turn of which seemed to come within two hundred yards of him. It was my only chance; so, retreating about half a mile, I got into the burn in hidden ground, and then crept up its channel with such caution that I never allowed myself a sight of more than the tips of his horns, till I had reached the nearest bend to him. There, looking through a tuft of rushes, I had a perfect view of the noble animal, lying on the open hillock, lazily stretched out at length, and only moving now and then to scratch his flank with his horn. I watched him for fully an hour, the water up to my knees all the time. At length he stirred, gathered his legs together, and rose; and arching his back, he stretched himself just as a bullock does when rising from his night's lair. My heart throbbed, as turning all round he seemed to try the wind for his security, and then walked straight to the burn, at a point about one hundred and fifty yards from me. I was much tempted, but had resolution to reserve my fire, reflecting that I had but one barrel. He went into the burn at a deep pool, and standing in it up to his knees, took a long drink. I stooped to put on a new copper cap and prick the nipple of my rifle; and – on looking up again, he was gone! I was in despair; and was on the point of moving rashly, when I saw his horns again appear a little farther off, but not more than fifty yards from the burn. By and by they lowered, and I judged he was lying down. "You are mine at last", I said; and I crept cautiously up the bed of the burn till I was opposite where he had lain down. I carefully and inch by inch placed my rifle over the bank, and then ventured to look along it. I could see only his horns, but within an easy shot. I was afraid to move higher up the bed of the burn, where I could have seen his body; the direction of the wind made that dangerous. I took breath for a moment, and screwed up my nerves; and then with my cocked rifle at my shoulder and my finger on the trigger, I kicked a stone, which splashed into the water. He started up instantly, but exposed only his front towards me. Still he was very near, scarcely fifty yards, and I fired at his throat just where it joins the head. He dropped on his knees to my shot; but was up again in a moment, and went staggering up the hill . . . Although he kept on at a mad pace, I saw he was becoming too weak for the hill. He swerved and turned back to the burn; and came headlong down within ten yards of me, tumbling into it apparently dead. Feeling confident, from the place where my ball had taken effect, that he was dead, I threw down my rifle, and went up to him with my hunting-knife. I found him stretched out, and as I thought dying; and I laid hold of his horns to raise his head to bleed him. I had scarcely touched him when he sprang up, flinging me backwards on the stones. It was an awkward position. I was stunned by the violent fall; behind me was a steep bank seven or eight feet high; before me the bleeding stag with his horns levelled at me, and cutting me off from my rifle. In desperation I moved; when he instantly charged, but fortunately tumbled ere he quite reached me. He drew back again like a ram about to butt, and then stood still with his head lowered, and his eyes bloody and swelled, glaring upon me. His mane and all his coat were dripping with water and blood; and as he now and then tossed his head with an angry snort, he looked like some savage beast of prey. We stood mutually at bay for some time, till recovering myself, I jumped out of the burn so suddenly, that he had not time to run at me, and from the bank above, I dashed my plaid over his head and eyes, and threw myself upon him. I cannot account for my folly, and it had nearly cost me dear. The poor beast struggled desperately, and his remaining strength foiled me in every attempt to stab him in front; and he at length made off, tumbling me down, but carrying with him a stab in the leg which lamed him. I ran and picked up my rifle, and then kept him in view as he rushed down the burn on three legs towards the loch. He took the water and stood at bay up to his chest in it. As soon as he halted, I commenced loading my rifle, when to my dismay I found that all the balls I had remaining were for my double-barrel, and were a size too large for my rifle. I sat down and commenced scraping one to the right size, an operation that seemed interminable. At last I succeeded; and, having loaded, the poor stag remaining perfectly still, I went up within twenty yards of him and shot him through the head. He turned over and floated, perfectly dead. I waded in and towed him ashore, and then had leisure to look at my wounds and bruises, which were not serious, except my shin-bone, which was scraped from ankle to knee by his horn. I soon had cleaned my quarry and stowed him away as safely as I could, and then turned down the glen at a gay pace. I found Donald with Bran . . . and . . . was satisfied with sending him to bring home the "muckle hart of Benmore", a duty which he performed before nightfall.'

(*Wild Sports of the Highlands*)

If St John's is the best description of an actual deer-stalk, John Buchan's may be the best known fiction. In *John McNab* (1925), Lord Lamancha draws the task of taking a stag from Lord Claybody's Haripol estate, having forewarned him of the attempt:

'The ascent of the ridge was a slow business, and toilful. Wattie was clearly following an elaborate plan, for he zigzagged preposterously, and would wait long for no apparent reason in places where Lamancha was held precariously by half a foothold and the pressure of his nails. Anxious glances were cast over his shoulder at the post where Macqueen was presumably on duty. The stalker's ears seemed of an uncanny keenness, for he would listen hard, hear something, and then utterly change his course. To Lamancha it was all inexplicable, for there appeared to be no deer on the ridge, and the place was so much in the lee that not a breath of wind seemed to be abroad to carry their scent. Hard as his condition was, he grew furiously warm and thirsty, and perhaps a little careless, for once or twice he let earth and stones slip under his feet.

'Wattie turned on him fiercely. "Gang as if ye was growin' ", he whispered. "There's beasts on a' sides".

'Sobered thereby, Lamancha mended his ways, and kept his thoughts rigidly on the job before him. He crept docilely in Wattie's prints, wondering why on a little ridge they should go through exertions that must be equivalent to the ascent of the Matterhorn. At last his guide stopped. "Put your head between thae rashes", he enjoined. "Ye'll see her".

' "See what?" Lamancha gasped.

' "That dour deevil o' a hind".

'There she was, a grey elderly beldame, with her wicked puck-like ears, aware and suspicious, not five yards off.

' "We canna wait", Wattie hissed. "It's over dangerous. Bide you here like a stone".

'He wriggled away to his right, while Lamancha hanging on a heather root, watched the twitching ears and wrinkled nozzle . . . Presently from farther up the hill came a sharp bark, which was almost a bleat. The hind flung up her head and gazed intently . . . Five minutes later the sound was repeated, this time from a lower altitude. The beast sniffed, shook herself, and stamped with her foot. Then she laid back her ears, and trotted quietly over the crest.

'Wattie was back again by Lamancha's side. "That puzzled the auld bitch", was his only comment. "We can gang faster now, and God kens we've nae time to loss".

'As Lamancha lay panting at last on the top of the ridge he looked down into the highest of the lesser corries, tucked right under the black cliffs of Sgurr Dearg. It was a little corrie, very steep, and threaded by a burn which after the rain was white like a snowdrift. Vast tumbled masses of stone, ancient rockfalls from the mountain, lay thick as the cottages in a hamlet. At first sight the place seemed to be without deer. Lamancha, scanning it with his glass, could detect no living thing among the debris.

'Wattie was calling fiercely on his Maker.

' "God, it's the auld hero", he muttered, his eyes glued to his telescope.

'At last Lamancha got his glasses adjusted, and saw what his companions saw. Far up the corrie, on a patch of herbage – the last before the desert of the rocks began – stood three stags. Two were ordinary beasts, shootable, for they must have weighed sixteen or seventeen stone, but with inconsiderable heads. The third was no heavier, but he had a head like a blasted pine – going back fast, for the beast was old, but still with thirteen clearly-marked points and a most noble spread of horn.

' "It's him", Wattie crooned. "It's the auld hero. Fine I ken him, for I seen him on Crask last back-end rivin' at the stacks. There's no a forest hereaways but they've had a try for him, but the deil's in him, for the grandest shots aye miss. What's your will, my lord? Dod, if John Macnab gets yon lad, he can cock his bonnet".

'Lamancha felt his heart beat faster.

' "I don't know, Wattie. Is it fair to kill the best beast in the forest?"

' "Keep your mind easy about that. Yon's no a Haripol beast. He's oftener on Crask than on Haripol. He's a traiveller, and in one season will cover the feck o' the Hielands. I've heard that oreeginally he cam oot o' Kintail. He's terrible auld – some says a hundred year – and if ye dinna kill him he'll perish next winter, belike, in a snaw-wreath, and that's a puir death to dee".

' "It's a terrible pull on the Beallach".

' "It will be that, but there's the nicht afore us. If we don't take that beast – or one o' the three – I doubt we'll no get anither chance".

' "Push on then, Wattie. It looks like a clear coast".

' "I'm no so sure. There's that deevil o' a hind somewhere afore us".

'Down through the gaps of the Pinnacle Ridge blew fine streams of mist. They were the precursors of a new storm, for long before the two men had wormed their way into the corrie the mountain before them was blotted out with a curtain of rain, and the wind, which seemed for a time to have died away, was sounding a thousand notes in the Pan's-pipes of the crags.

' "Good", said Lamancha. "This will blanket the shot".

' "Ba-ad too", growled Wattie, "for we'll be duntin' against the auld bitch".

'Lamancha believed he had located the stags well enough to go to them in black darkness. You had only to follow the stream to its head, and they were on the left bank a hundred yards or so from the rocks. But when he reached the burn he found that his memory was useless. There was not one stream but dozens, and it was hard to say which was the main channel. It was a loud world again, very different from the first corrie, but when he would have hastened, Wattie insisted on circumspection. "There's the hind", he said, "and maybe some sma' stags. It's early in the day, man, and since we're out o' Macqueen's sicht there's nae need to hurry".

'His caution was justified. As they drew themselves up the side of a small cascade the tops of a pair of antlers were seen over the next rise. Lamancha thought they were those of one of the three stags, but Wattie disillusioned him. "We're no within six hundred yards o' yon beasts", he said.

'A long circuit was necessary, happily in good cover, and the stream was not rejoined till at a point where its channels bore to the south, so that their wind would not be carried to the beasts below the knoll. After that it seemed advisable to Wattie to keep to the water, which was flowing in a deep-cut bed. It was a job for a merman rather than breeched human beings, for Wattie would permit of no rising to a horizontal or even to a kneeling position. The burn entered at their collars and flowed steadily through their shirts on to an exit at their knees. Never had men been so comprehensively and continuously wet. Lamancha's right arm ached with pulling the rifle along the bank – he always insisted on carrying his weapon himself – while his body was submerged in the icy outflow of Spurr Dearg's springs.

'The pressure of Wattie's foot in his face halted him. Blinking through the spray, he saw his leader's head raised stiffly to the alert in the direction of a little knoll. Even in the thick weather he could detect a pair of bat-like ears, and he realised that these ears were twitching. It did not need Wattie's whisper of "the auld bitch" to reveal the enemy.

'The two lay in the current for what seemed to Lamancha at least half an hour. He had enough hillcraft to recognise that their one hope was to stick to the channel, for only thus was there a chance of their presence being unrevealed by the wind. But the channel led them very close to the hind. If the brute chose to turn her foolish head they would be within view.

'With desperate slowness, an inch at a time, Wattie moved upwards. He signed to Lamancha to wait while he traversed a pool where only his cap and nose showed above the water. Then came a peat wallow, when his face seemed to be ground into the moss, and his limbs to be splayed like a frog's and to move with frog-like jerks. After that was a little cascade, and, beyond, the shelter of a big boulder which would get him out of the hind's orbit. Lamancha watched this strange progress with one eye; the other was on the twitching ears. Mercifully all went well, and Wattie's stern disappeared round a corner of rock.

'He laboured to follow with the same precision. The pool was easy enough except for the trailing of the rifle. The peat was straightforward going, though in his desire to follow his leader's example he dipped his face so deep in the black slime that his nostrils were plugged with it, and some got into his eyes which he dared not try to remove. But the waterfall was a snag. It was no light task to draw himself up against the weight of descending water, and at the top he lay panting for a second, damming up the flow with his body . . . Then he moved on; but the mischief had been done.

'For the sound of the release of the pent-up stream had struck a foreign note on the hind's ear. It was an unfamiliar noise among the many familiar ones which at the moment filled the corrie. She turned her head sharply, and saw something in the burn which she did not quite understand. Lamancha, aware of her scrutiny, lay choking, with the water running into his nose; but the alarm had been given. The hind turned her head, and trotted off up-wind.

'The next he knew was Wattie at his elbow making wild signals to him to rise and follow. Cramped and staggering, he lumbered after him away from the stream into a moraine of great granite blocks. "We're no twa hundred yards from the stags", the guide whispered. "The auld bitch will move them, but please God we'll get a shot". As Lamancha ran he marvelled at Wattie's skill, for he himself had not a notion where in the wide world the beasts might be.

'They raced to a knoll, and Wattie flung himself flat on the top.

' "There", he cried. "Steady, man. Tak the nearest. A hundred yards. Nae mair".

'Lamancha saw through the drizzle three stags moving at a gentle trot to the south – up-wind, for in the corrie the eddies were coming oddly. They were not really startled, but the hind had stirred them. The big stag was in the centre of the three, and the proper shot was the last – a reasonable broadside.

'Wattie's advice had been due to his loyalty to John Macnab, and not to his own choice, and this Lamancha knew. The desire of the great stag was on him, as it was on the hunter in Homer, and he refused to be content with the second-best. It was not an easy shot in that bad light, and it is probable that he would have missed; but suddenly Wattie gave an unearthly bark, and for a second the three beasts slowed down and turned their heads towards the sound.

'In that second Lamancha fired. The great head seemed to bow itself, and then fling upwards, and all three disappeared at a gallop into the mist.

' "A damned poor tailoring shot!" Lamancha groaned.

' "He's deid for all that, but God kens how far he'll run afore he drops. He's hit in the neck, but a wee thing ower low . . . We can bide here a while and eat our piece. If he wasna John Macnab I could be wishin' we had brought a dog".

'Lamancha, cold, wet, and disgusted, wolfed his sandwiches, had a stiff dram from his flask, and smoked a pipe before he started again. He cursed his marksmanship, and Wattie forbore to contradict him; doubtless Jim Tarras had accustomed him to a standard of skill from which this was a woeful declension. Nor would he hold out much hope. "He'll gang into the first corrie and when he finds the wund different there he'll turn back for the Reascuill. If this was our ain forest and the weather wasna that thick, we might get another chance at him there . . . Oh, aye, he might gang for ten mile. The mist is a good thing, for Macqueen will no see what's happenin', but if it was to lift, and he saw a' the stags in the corrie movin', you and me wad hae to find a hidy-hole till the dark . . . Are ye ready, my lord?"

'They crossed the ridge which separated them from the first corrie, close to the point where it took off from the *massif* of Sgurr Dearg. It was a shorter road than the one they had come by, and they could take it safely, for they were now moving up wind to the curious eddy from the south. Over the edge would be a different matter, for there the wind would be easterly as before. But it was a stiff climb and a bad business, for they had to make sure that they were on the track of the stag.

'Wattie trailed the blood-marks like an Indian, noticing splashes on stones and rushes which Lamancha would have missed. "He's sair hit", he observed at one point. "See! He tried that steep bit and couldna manage it. There's the mark o'his feet turnin' . . . He's stoppit here . . . Aye, here's his trail, and it'll be the best for you and me. There's nothing like a wounded beast for pickin' the easiest road".

'On the crest the air stirred freely, and, as it seemed to Lamancha, with a new chill. Wattie gave a grunt of satisfaction, and sniffed it like a pointer dog. He moistened his finger and held it up; then he plucked some light grasses and tossed them into the air.

' "That's a mercifu' dispensation! Maybe that shot that ye think he bauchled was the most providential shot ye ever fired . . . The wund is shiftin'. I looked for it afore night, but no that early in the day. It's wearin' round to the south. D'ye see what that means?"

'Lamancha shook his head. Disgust had made his wits dull.

' "Yon beast, as I telled ye, was a traiveller. There's nothing to keep him in Haripol forest. But he'll no leave it unless the wund will let him. Now it looks as if Providence was kind to us. The wund's blawin' from the Beallach, and he's bound to gang up-wund".

'The next half-hour was a period of swift drama. Sure enough, the blood-marks turned up the first corrie in the direction from which the two had come in the morning. As the ravine narrowed the stag had seemingly taken to the burn, for there were splashes on the rocks and a tinge of red in the pools.

' "He's no far off", Wattie croaked. "See, man, he's verra near done. He's slippin' sair".

'And then, as they mounted, they came on a little pool where the water was dammed as if by a landslip. There, his body half under the cascade, lay the stag, stone dead, his great horns parting the fall like a pine swept down by a winter spate.

'The two regarded him in silence, till Wattie was moved to pronounce his epitaph.

' "It's yersel, ye auld hero, and ye've come by a grand end. Ye've had a braw life traivellin' the hills, and ye've been a braw beast, and the fame o' ye gaed through a' the country-side. Ye micht have dwined away in the cauld winter an dee'd in the wame o' a snaw-drift. Or ye micht have been massacred by ane o' thae Haripol sumphs wi' ten bullets in the big bag. But ye've been killed clean and straucht by John Macnab, and that is a gentleman's death, whatever''.'

The original idea for *John MacNab* came from a real wager between James Brander Dunbar and Lord Abinger made over dinner at Pitgaveney House, Lossiemouth, some time in 1897.

Dunbar, recently summoned home from Africa by his father to play his part in the management of the family estate, found the domestic life more than a little tedious. To relieve the boredom he bet £20 that he could poach a stag off Lord Abinger's Inverlochie estate with as many keepers deployed to catch him as Abinger could muster.

Alone, and barefoot, he stalked and took his stag in the early hours of the morning, removing it from the ground over his shoulders (he stood only 5 feet 4 inches). He presented himself at Abinger's door at breakfast time, handing the butler the traditional token to convey to his lordship's table. The framed cheque still hangs on the wall at Pitgaveney among the many other trophies of a lifetime's hunting.

'The Lairdie', as he became known after his father's death, was a prodigious sportsman. Whether or not he kept the head of everything he ever shot – apart from birds – is impossible to tell, but his somewhat bizarre collection ranged from the rhinoceros head over the main staircase to the skull of a German soldier (unmounted) in his study.

On his death at the age of 94, the estate passed to his nephew Alexander Dunbar, now Director of the Scottish Arts Council. The sporting rights over some 7,000 acres, including Loch Spynie, are leased to the Baxter company and Ian Baxter maintains some, at least, of the old laird's traditions when he entertains visitors from all parts of the world.

James Brander Dunbar was one of the last of the feudal barons, regarding himself as very much the lord and the law in his own domain. While he dealt summarily with poachers on his own land, he was not above sniggling a salmon or lifting a deer from somebody else's if the opportunity presented itself, though fully prepared to make recompense if he was caught.

From a modern point of view, his behaviour appears pretty outrageous, but in his place and time he was scarcely even seen as eccentric.

CHAPTER SEVEN

'The Last of the Free Foresters'

When I was bound apprentice in famous Lincolnshire,
Full well I served my master for more than seven year,
Till I took up to poaching, as you shall quickly hear:
  O! 'Tis my delight on a shining night
  In the season of the year!
As me and my companions were setting of a snare,
'Twas then we spied the gamekeeper – for him we did not care,
For we can wrestle and fight, my boys, and jump o'er anywhere,

As me and my companions were setting four or five,
And taking on 'em up again, we caught a hare alive,
We took the hare alive, my boys, and through the woods did steer,

I threw him on my shoulder, and then we trudgèd home,
We took him to a neighbour's house, and sold him for a crown,
We sold him for a crown, my boys, but I did not tell you where.

Success to every gentleman that lives in Lincolnshire,
Success to every poacher that wants to sell a hare,
Bad luck to every gamekeeper that will not sell his deer –
  O! 'Tis my delight on a shining night
  In the season of the year!

(*The Lincolnshire Poacher*, Old Song)

THE GREAT eccentrics in the world of game are surely the poachers, though whether they are more so than those gentlemen sportsmen of the last century whose passion seems to have been to kill as much as possible as quickly as possible, is debatable. Certainly their exploits are infinitely more romantic, if for no other reason than their illegality. There is a sort of Robin Hood air about them, despite the fact that they are usually their own beneficiaries. W. McCombie–Smith in his book *The Romance of Poaching in the Highlands of Scotland* illustrates the point from the lives of Alexander Davidson and John Farquharson, whom he described as 'the last of the Free Foresters'.

'Romance in this instance means that the poachers and poaching delineated are strangely and picturesquely different from the ordinary conception of both . . . There is no romance in prowling by night, covering coveys of partridges, or enveloping scores of rabbits in the meshes of a net. There is nothing romantic in the idle loafer who haunts low 'pubs' by day, and by night steals out to set across field-gates a net, into which his dog silently drives the timid hare. Not romance but brutal savagery marks the fierce, and not seldom fatal, encounters between lawless ruffians, bent on having a share of animals possessing a high market value protected in a semi-wild state, and those who are hired to protect them.

'The ordinary poacher lives a life apart from the more reputable portion of the community, even amongst the wage-earning classes. He is seldom seen by day, except when on his way to and from a court of justice, or the jail, in the hands of policemen. John Farquharson, at the time he was performing his most brilliant poaching exploits, proved himself the champion shot of the British Isles at long range shooting, could fire more shots in a minute than any man living; introduced a new position in rifle shooting, which was deemed worthy of mention in Punch, and was adopted by many of the best shots in Great Britain and America. He was the inventor and patentee of two valuable improvements on gun and rifle. . . He was on terms of intimacy with many of the nobility and gentry interested in shooting of all kinds, and for a long time his name was a household word amongst thousands of his countrymen. . .

'The reader will find in the life of Farquharson's prototype, Alexander Davidson, a man as far removed and superior to the ordinary run of poacher, as John Farquharson was. Davidson's poaching exploits were so transparently the outcome of an ineradicable love of the primitive man for the pursuit of beasts of chase, that many landed proprietors, the class to which we owe the enactment and enforcement of the game laws, gave him direct permission to shoot over their properties, or indirectly granted it by ignoring or winking at his presence and depredations. Of a man who at his death carried on his person an invitation from a future Duke of Richmond, to come as a welcome guest to Gordon Castle, and of whom two respected ministers of the Church of Scotland wrote with respect, and kindly appreciation, after he was gone, we cannot think or speak as we do of men who became poachers to shirk a life of toil, kill animals by unsportsmanlike methods, and sell them to afford the means of drunken debauches.

'John Farquharson and Alexander Davidson were men who could and did read their Bible, and found therein". . . and God said unto them . . . and have dominion over the fish of the sea, and over the fowl of the air, and over every living thing that moveth on the earth". They did not find it written that God said, "Let a few favoured individuals have dominion over fish, fowl and every living thing, with power to punish the many to whom such a dominion has not been given", but believed that all creatures living in a state of nature were for all mankind. In following that belief to its logical conclusion, they were called poachers; if so they were far from being common ones, and their lives had so many elements of romance in them that their infringements of the game laws were a veritable romance in poaching.'

John Watson, writing in 1891, says very much the same thing, although again it seems probable that he has just one individual in mind, the boyhood hero and life-long friend whose *Confessions* he had published the previous year.

'It need hardly be said that our poacher is a compound of many individuals – the type of a numerous class. The tinge of rustic romance to which we have already referred as exhibited in his character may have been detected in his goings. And we may at once say that he in nowise resembles the armed ruffian who, masked and with murderous intent, enters the covert at night. Although his life is one long protest against the game laws, he is not without a rude code of morality. He complains bitterly of the decrease of game, and that the profession is hardly now worth following. Endowed with marked intelligence, it has never been directed aright. His knowledge of woodcraft is superior to that of the gamekeeper, which personage he holds in contempt. He quietly boasts of having outwitted the keepers a hundred times. The "Otter" is chary as to those he takes into confidence, and knows that silence is essential to success. He points to the "Mole", – the mouldy *sobriquet* of a compatriot – as an instance of one who tells poaching secrets to village gossips. The "Mole" spends most of his time in the county gaol, and is now undergoing incarceration for the fifty-seventh time. Our "Otter" has certainly

21. The Poacher *by Britton-Rivière*

been caught, but the occasions of his capture form but a small percentage of the times he has been "out". He is a healthy example of pure animalism, and his rugged nature has much in common with the animals and birds. As an accurately detailed reflection of nature, his monograph of any one of our British game-birds would excel even those of Mr Jeffries himself; yet of culture he hasn't an idea. He admires the pencilled plumage of a dead woodcock, and notes how marvellously it conforms to the grey-brown herbage among which it lies. So, too, with the eggs of birds. He remarks on the conformation to environment – of partridge and pheasant, the olive colour to the dead oak leaves; of snipe and plover to the mottled marsh; of duck and water fowl to the pale green reeds.

'As to his morality with regard to the game laws, it would be difficult to detect exactly where he draws the line. He lives for these to be repealed, but his native philosophy tells him that when this time comes game will have become well nigh extinct. Upon the Ground Game Act he looks with mingled feelings, for, after all, are not rabbits and hares the chief product of his nights? The farmers now get these, and the poacher's field is limited. They engage him, maybe, to stay the ravages upon clover and young wheat, or to thin the rabbits from out the pastures. He propitiates the farmer in many ways. Occasionally in the morning the farm lad finds half-a-dozen rabbits or a hare dropped behind the barn door. How these came there no one knows – nor asks. The country attorney is sometimes submitted to a like indignity. In crossing land the poacher is careful to close gates after him, and he never breaks down fences. He assists cattle and sheep which he finds in extremity, and leaves word of the mishap at the farm. Is it likely that the farmer will dog the steps of the man who protects his property, and pays tolls for doing it?

'And it frequently happens that the poacher is not less popular with the village community at large than with those whose interests he serves. It is even asserted that more than one of the county Justices have, in some sort, a sneaking affection for him. The same wild spirit and love of sport take him to the fields and woods as his more fortunate brethren to the moor and covert. It is untrue, as has been said, that the poacher is always a mercenary wretch who invariably sells his game; he as frequently sends in a brace of birds or a hare to a poor or sick neighbour. He comes in contact with the law just sufficient to make him know something of its bearings. When charged with being in possession of "game", he reiterates the old argument that rabbits are vermin. Being committed for four months "for night poaching", he respectfully informs the presiding Justice that at the time of his capture the sun had risen two hours, and that the law does not allow more than half the sentence just passed upon him. The old clerk fumbles for his horn spectacles, and, after turning over *Stone's Justices' Manual* solemnly informs the Bench that defendant in his interpretation is right. He remembers this little episode and chuckles over it.'

(*Poachers and Poaching*)

Not surprisingly, the day of the anti-hero being a long way off, the poachers who found their way into print were the local counterpart of the 'noble savage', as near to being gentlemen as men could come without the necessary pedigree.

'Nature', says Watson, 'made old "Phil" a poacher, but she made him a Sportsman and a Naturalist at the same time. I never met any man who was in closer sympathy with the wild creatures about him; and never dog or child came within his influence but was permanently attracted by his personality. Although eighty years of age, there is still some of the old erectness in his carriage; some of the old fire in his eyes. As a young man he was handsome, though now his features are battered out of all original conception. His silvery hair still covers a lion-like head, and his tanned cheeks are hard and firm'.

St John's man is built on an even more heroic scale.

> 'I had a visit last week from a Highland poacher of some notoriety in his way. He is the possessor of a brace of the finest deer-hounds in Scotland, and he came down from his mountain home to show them to me, as I wanted some for a friend. A finer specimen of the genus Homo than Ronald I never saw. As he passes through the streets of a country-town, the men give him plenty of walking room; while not a girl in the street but stops to look after him, and says to her companions – "Eh, but yon's a bonnie lad". And indeed Ronald *is a "bonnie lad"* – about twenty-six years of age – his height more than six feet, and with limbs somewhat between those of a Hercules and an Apollo – he steps along the street with the good-natured, self-satisfied swagger of a man who knows all the women are admiring him. He is dressed in a plain grey kilt and jacket, with an otter-skin purse and a low skull-cap with a long peak, from below which his quick eye seems to take in at a glance everything which is passing around him. A man whose life is spent much in hunting and pursuit of wild animals, acquires unconsciously a peculiar restless and quick expression of eye, appearing to be always in search of something. When Ronald doffs his cap, and shows his handsome hair and short curling beard, which covers all the lower part of his face, and which he seems to be something of a dandy about, I do not know a finer-looking fellow amongst all my acquaintance – and his occupation, which affords him constant exercise without hard labour, gives him a degree of strength and activity seldom equalled. As he walked into my room followed by his two magnificent dogs, he would have made a subject worthy of Landseer in his best moments – and it would have been a picture which many a fair damsel of high, as well as low degree, would have looked upon with pleasure. Excepting when excited, this is the most quiet, good-natured fellow in the world; but I have heard some stories of his exploits, in defence of his liberty, when assailed by keepers, which proved his immense strength, though he has always used it most good-naturedly.'
>
> (*Wild Sports of the Highlands*)

Young Lochinvar himself could not have been said fairer than that!

There is also a distinctly partisan element in the defence of these 'natyre's gentlemen'.

St John is quite chauvinistic following the tradition of the true 'convert'.

> 'The life of the Highland poacher is a far different one from that of an Englishman following the same profession. Instead of a sneaking night-walking ruffian, a mixture of cowardice and ferocity, as most English poachers are, and ready to commit any crime that he hopes to perpetrate with impunity, the Highlander is a bold fearless fellow, shooting openly by daylight, taking his sport in the same manner as the Laird, or the Sassenach who rents the ground.'

Yet even within England, John Watson tells us, there are differences between one part of the country and another.

> 'Among southern woods and coverts, the pheasant poacher is usually a desperate character; not so in the north. Here the poachers are more skilled in woodcraft, and rarely surprised. If the worst comes to the worst it is a fair stand-up fight with fists, and is usually bloodless. There is little greed of gain in the night enterprise, and liberty by flight is the first thing resorted to.'

22. The Gamekeepers attacking the Poachers (*George Cruikshank, 1839*)

Perhaps the social standing of the poacher was in inverse proportion to the degree of protection authority could provide against his activities. The specific reference to pheasants seems to support this view. Watson's poacher himself admits the problems facing the pheasant poacher, though he has one or two solutions.

> 'Of all species of poaching, that which ensures a good haul of pheasants is most beset with difficulty. Nevertheless, there are silent ways and means which prove as successful in the end as the squire's guns, and these without breaking the woodland silence with a sound. The most successful of these I intend to set down, and only such as have stood me in good stead in actual night work. . . .
>
> 'It is well for the poacher, and well for his methods, that the pheasant is rather a stupid bird. There is no gainsaying its beauty, however, and a brace of birds, with all the old excitement thrown in, are well worth winning, even at considerable risk. In a long life of poaching I have noticed that the pheasant has one great characteristic. It is fond of wandering; and this cannot be prevented. Watch the birds; even when fed daily, and with the daintiest food, they wander off, singly or in pairs, far from the home coverts. This fact I knew well, and was not slow to use my knowledge. When October came round they were the very first birds to which I directed my attention. Every poacher observes, year by year (even leaving his own predaceous paws out of the question), that it by no means follows that the man who rears the pheasants will have the privilege of shooting them. There is a very certain time in the life of the bird when it disdains the scattered corn of the keeper, and begins to anticipate the fall of beech and oak mast. In search of this the pheasants make daily journeys, and consume great quantities. They feed principally in the morning; dust themselves in the roads or turnip-fields at mid-day, and ramble through the woods in the afternoon. And one thing is certain: That when wandered birds find themselves in outlying copses in the evening they are apt to roost there. As already stated, these were the birds to which I paid my best attention. When wholesale pheasant poaching is prosecuted by gangs, it is in winter, when the trees are bare. Guns, with the barrels filed down, are taken in sacks, and the pheasants are shot where they roost. Their bulky forms stand sharply outlined against the sky, and they are invariably on the lower branches. If the firing does not immediately bring up the keepers, the game is quickly deposited in bags, and the gang makes off. And it is generally arranged that a light cart is waiting at some remote lane end, so that possible pursuers may be quickly outpaced. The great risk incurred by this method will be seen, when it is stated that pheasants are generally reared close by the keeper's cottage, and that their coverts immediately surround it. It is mostly armed mouchers who enter these, and not the more gifted (save the mark!) country poacher. And there are reasons for this. Opposition must always be anticipated, for, speaking for the nonce from the game-keeper's standpoint, the covert never should be, and is, unwatched. Then there are the certain results of possible capture to be taken into account. This affected, and with birds in one's possession, the poacher is liable to

be indicted upon so many concurrent charges, each and all having heavy penalties. [Rather] than this I obtained my game in a different and quieter way. My custom was to carefully eschew the preserves, and look up all outlying birds. I never went abroad without a pocketful of corn, and day by day enticed the wandered birds further and further away. This accomplished, pheasants may be snared with hair nooses, or taken in spring traps. One of my commonest and most successful methods with wandered birds was to light brimstone beneath the trees in which they roosted. The powerful fumes soon overpowered them, and they came flopping down the trees one by one. . . .

'I have already spoken at some length of my education in field and woodcraft. An important (though at the time unconscious) part of this was minute observation of the haunts and habits of all kinds of game; and this knowledge was put to good use in my actual poaching raids. Here is an instance of what I mean; I had noticed the great pugnacity of the pheasant, and out of this made capital. After first finding out the whereabouts of the keeper, I fitted a trained game-cock with artificial spurs, and then took it to the covert side. The artificial spurs were fitted to the natural ones, were sharp as needles, and the plucky bird already knew how to use them. Upon his crowing, one or more cock pheasants would immediately respond, and advance to meet the adversary. A single blow usually sufficed to lay low the pride of the pheasant, and in this way half-a-dozen birds were bagged, whilst my own representative remained unhurt.

'I had another ingenious plan (if I may say so) in connection with pheasants, and, perhaps, the most successful. I may say at once that there is nothing sportsmanlike about it; but then that is in keeping with most of what I have set down. If time and opportunity offer there is hardly any limit to the depredation which it allows. Here it is: A number of dried peas are taken and steeped in boiling water; a hole is then made through the centre, and through this again a stiff bristle is threaded. The ends are then cut off short, leaving only about a quarter of an inch of bristle projecting on each side. With these the birds are fed, and they are greedily eaten. In passing down the gullet, however, a violent irritation is set up, and the pheasant is finally choked. In a dying condition the birds are picked up beneath the hedges, to the shelter of which they almost always run. The way is a quiet one; it may be adopted in roads and lanes where the birds dust themselves, and does not require trespass. . .

'Still another method of bagging "long-tails", though one somewhat similar to that already set down; It requires two persons, and the exact position of the birds must be known. A black night is necessary; a stiff bamboo rod, and a dark lantern. One man flashes the concentrated light upon the bare branches, when immediately half a dozen necks are stretched out to view the apparition. Just then the "angler" slips a wire nooze over the craned neck nearest him, and it is jerked down as quickly, though as silently as possible. Number two is served in like manner, then a third, a fourth, and a fifth.'

(*Confessions of a Poacher*)

The relationship between poachers and gamekeepers seems always to have a strangely ambivalent one of love-hate. Mutual respect and even interdependence, a sort of Jekyll and Hyde or Siamese twins bond existing between them. Charles Kingsley saw them as opposite sides of the same coin.

> 'Grimes rang at the gate and out came a keeper on the spot, and opened.
>
> ' "I was told to expect thee," he said. "Now thou'lt be so good as to keep to the main avenue, and not let me find a rabbit or a hare on thee when thou comst back. I shall look sharp for one, I tell thee."
>
> ' "Not if it's in the bottom of the soot-bag," quoth Grimes, and at that he laughed; and the keeper laughed and said:
>
> ' "If that's thy sort I may as well walk up with thee to the hall."
>
> ' "I think thou best had. It's thy business to see after thy game, man, and not mine."
>
> 'So the keeper went with them; and, to Tom's surprise, he and Grimes chatted together all the way quite pleasantly. He did not know that a keeper is only a poacher turned outside in, and a poacher a keeper turned inside out.
>
> 'They walked up a great lime avenue, a full mile long, and between their stems Tom peered trembling at the horns of the sleeping deer, which stood up among the

23. Game Keeper*: engraving by Henry Birche, after a painting by George Stubbs (late 18th century)*

ferns. Tom had never seen such enormous trees, and as he looked up he fancied that the blue sky rested on their heads.

' "I wish I were a keeper," said Tom, "to live in such a beautiful place, and wear green velveteens, and have a real dog-whistle at my button like you."

'The keeper laughed; he was a kind-hearted fellow enough.

' "Let well alone, lad, and ill too at times. Thy life's safer than mine at all events, eh, Mr Grimes?"

'And Grimes laughed again, and then the two men began talking quite low. Tom could hear, though, that it was about some poaching fight; and at last Grimes surlily said, "Hast thou anything against me?"

' "Not now."

' "Then don't ask me any questions till thou hast, for I am a man of honour."

'And at that they both laughed again.'

(*The Water Babies*)

By no means all poachers were romantic 'hero' figures, however. There are many accounts of bloody encounters and even pitched battles between gangs of well-armed poachers and gamekeepers and police in which men on both sides suffered serious, sometimes fatal, injuries.

Neither did the problem of poaching disappear with the nineteenth century, though the romance may have done.

Writing in 1920, the naturalist and sportsman Tom Speedy observed that poachers could be divided 'into three distinct classes, differing as widely in their several characters as in their mode of operations!'

'There are those who belong to the generally well-conducted and industrious section of the community, who would scorn to commit any offence against society other than an infraction of the game-laws. While clearly understanding the nature and provisions of the statutes for the preservation of game, they recognise no breach of morality in their non-observance. This class of poachers contrive quietly to transfer themselves into some thinly-populated district on the occasion of an autumn or winter holiday, and there devote the short time at their disposal in endeavouring to shoot such game as they may be able to fall in with during their wanderings. The quantity of game killed by this fraternity is so trifling, and their motive merely to have a day's enjoyment in the country so manifest, that few landed proprietors are disposed to deal hardly by them when reported by the keepers.

'There are those, again, who work the greater part of the year, but who never fail to turn to account any contingency which may arise in the way of dull trade or reduced wages as an excuse for indulging in poaching expeditions. One section of the community who contribute largely to this class of poachers is to be found among the mining population.'

But it was the hardened professionals, who made a trade as well as a sport of the illicit taking of game, whose activities were particularly difficult to combat, especially in sparsely populated districts (i.e. those areas most rich in the various species of game). Speedy instanced the islands off the western coast of Scotland, such as Mull, Islay, Jura and Scarba as a case in point:

> 'Sailing round the coast, – deer take little notice of boats, from seeing them daily, – and discovering some "beasts", the poachers push on till out of sight to leeward, get ashore, and commence a stalk. Should they be successful in killing one it is dragged downhill to the boat, when they sail away with it. A keeper on the north end of Jura one day from the top of a hill discovered a boat moored at the shore. Suspecting poachers, he made for the boat, but being seen by them, it became a race who was to reach it first. The poachers had the advantage, not having so far to run, and so escaped.'

It seems unlikely that poachers using such chancy methods in so remote a spot would have got very far on their trade, but even with fewer self-inflicted handicaps the poaching of deer appears to present too many problems of logistics to be a major attraction for organised crime.

> 'About that time it was no unusual thing for poachers resident in the district to obtain their meat-supplies for the winter from the forest. They generally contrived to find their way into the mountain solitudes by the light of the moon; and after daybreak, having stalked one or two deer, they dragged them into a narrow gorge or mountain stream, where they were gralloched and concealed. Their next concern was to remain in concealment until darkness had set in, when they proceeded homeward with their booty. Some of these hill poachers have been known to be sufficiently daring to take with them a small Highland pony to lighten their burden.'
>
> (*The Natural History of Sport in Scotland with Rod and Gun*)

Speedy himself reports a decline in the number of raids into the deer forests since the time of his youth. What would he have made of the news that beef farmers in Herefordshire in 1972 hired security guards to protect their herds from rustlers!

CHAPTER EIGHT

Histories of the Pheasant

SEE! FROM the brake the whirring Pheasant springs,
And mounts exulting on triumphant wings,
Short is his joy: he feels the fiery wound,
Flutters in blood, and panting beats the ground,
Ah! what avail his glossy, varying dyes,
His purple crest, and scarlet-circled eyes,
The vivid green his shining plumes unfold,
His painted wings, and breast that flames with gold?

(from 'Windsor Forest', Alexander Pope, 1713)

'Pheasants were brought into Europe by the Argonauts 1250 years before the Christian era, and are at present found in a state of nature in nearly the whole of the Old Continent.'

(*Rural Sports*, William Daniel, 1802)

'Pheasant: *Phasianus colchicus*. Geographical distribution: British. The pheasant was probably introduced into the British Islands by the Romans. It is resident throughout all parts of the country where it is preserved, even in some of the wildest districts of the Outer Hebrides, the presence of cover being all that is required in addition to artificial feeding during severe weather.'

(*Game Birds and Wild Fowl*, Charles Dixon, 1900)

'The Pheasant appears to have been especially invented in order to provide not only the best of shooting, but one of the finest table birds.'

(*Game Birds and Game Bird Shooting*, Hugh Pollard, 1936)

Whatever debate there may be concerning the comparative merits of different sporting birds, there can be no doubt that Hugh Pollard has distilled into this sentence the essence of the meaning of 'game'.

The pheasant is clearly the premier bird, in Pollard's opinion, and he deals at some length with its history.

'The history of the coming of the pheasant to Britain is still obscure. Actually the native habitat of our original black-necked pheasant, *Phasianus colchicus*, was the river Rion, then called the river Phasis, in the district of Colchis near the Black

Sea, hence the generic and specific names. The bird, however, occurs in a wild state as far west as Dalmatia, and there is abundant literary evidence, mainly gastronomic in trend, which shows that he was well known to the ancient Romans. On the strength of these classic associations rather than on any sound evidence as yet forthcoming, we have been taught to believe that the Romans introduced the pheasant to Great Britain.

'If they did, the motive is obscure. You cannot get the best of pheasant shooting with a bow and arrow or a sling. The country in Roman times was infested with every kind of vermin in the shape of wolves and predatory beasts, and the only logical conclusion is that if the pheasant did come over with the Romans he was brought in at great expense, not in the interests of our local avi-fauna or from any idea of aesthetic pleasure, but simply to put the game strain into cock-fighting.

'This notorious and degrading form of sport was highly popular with the garrison, and though my interest in matters archaeological is slight, and my *joie de vivre* is not accentuated by old brickbats in museums, I have an idea that somewhere or other, probably near Newcastle-on-Tyne, there is a brickbat or a mortuary tablet of some cheery old pagan with a native gamecock under his arm. It remained in memory because of its human interest. If you ever spend a winter in Northumbria you will sympathise with the garrison of Hadrian's Wall.

'As a matter of fact, I still doubt the success of the Roman introduction. When the natives rose and wiped out the Italian settlements they did not bother much about the goods and chattels, which remain to be dug up by archaeologists, but they almost certainly collared all the livestock, and most probably ate it . . . Now the pheasant is a beautiful bird and a lovely design, and if he had been common it is pretty certain that he would have appealed to the eye of the Celtic draughtsman. He is so perfectly adapted to the job; but so far – and I have kept an open and inquisitive eye on the point for many years – I have never found a pheasant in early art. Peacocks, yes; eagles, yes; even hares; but no rabbits and no pheasants, in spite of their glorious suitability to the style . . .

'The pheasant, admittedly one of the best table birds there is, appears to have been associated with the Church. Judging by the little time it has taken to become successfully established in the United States and New Zealand, but making allowances for contemporary slowness in transport by human agency, we can assume that it must have been introduced at least half a century before it is first mentioned.

'The first accepted reference is a detail of the scale of rations allotted to a Canon's household by King Harold in 1059 . . . (but) the evidence adduced takes us back before the Norman Conquest of 1066, and . . . the bird was soundly established not only in England but in Ireland by Tudor times, and seems to have been introduced into Scotland prior to 1594. It still flourishes in Scotland, but is relatively rare in Ireland because of systematic poaching and disregard of the close season.

Grouse Driving: the Time of Peace, by C. Whymper

Red Grouse (*Lagopus scoticus*) by C. Whymper

'The original bird introduced to Britain was the type we now call the "Old English Blackneck". This bird is still called the Common Pheasant (*Phasianus colchicus* Linnaeus), but it is by no means the most common pheasant of our countryside, for it is mixed with other sub-species, and it is doubtful if a perfectly pure strain exists. Our usual pheasant is a hybrid between three or four species, and is denoted by game farmers as an "ordinary" pheasant in order to avoid confusion with the scientific name Common Pheasant, which applies solely to the "Blackneck".

'The next introduction was the Chinese or Ringnecked Pheasant. The exact date of its introduction is unknown, but it probably came in with the development of the tea trade with China during the first half of the eighteenth century about 1740. The introduction was slow, but here and there colonies of ringnecked pheasants were in existence as wild game birds by the close of the eighteenth century. The extension of the bird to the North and Scotland came a good deal later, and despite the influence of eggs from game farms and the influence of our cross-bred ordinaries, I believe that many wild Scotch birds still show far more of the original old Blackneck strain than is common among birds in the South of England. The mixing of the blood between Blacknecks and Ringnecks does not appear to have resulted in a Ringneck dominance until relatively late in the nineteenth century. Amid a wealth of sporting illustration the Ringneck is not usually portrayed as the conventional bird of the time, and only emerges definitely about the late seventies and early eighties. We shall not, I think, be far wrong if we date the general effect of hybridisation at about the period of the introduction of the earlier sporting breech-loaders some sixty to seventy years ago.

'There was, however, a third sub-species, the Japanese or Versicolour Pheasant, which was introduced in 1840, a gift of a pair from the King of Italy to the Earl of Derby being the foundation of the stock. Within a few years of its establishment as an aviary bird, it was developed into perhaps the most usual of the pheasants to be found in parts of East Anglia. These cross-bred Versicolours did not, however, breed true, and at the end of a relatively short period of years the Versicolour strain bred out, and the Ringneck type dominated. The fact that the plumage change did not prove resistant does not preclude the possibility that some other genes or factors from the Versicolour strain may not persist in our ordinaries of today, and are probably responsible for the dark or melanistic mutant variety of pheasant.

'From time to time the Versicolour has been reintroduced, but it is doubtful if it has exercised such a powerful influence on our birds as the last strain which has been added to our admirable mongrel. This is the Mongolian (*Phasianus c. mongolicus*), introduced by the late Carl Hagenbeck, and then intensively reared by Mr C. E. Russell at his game farm in the first years of the present century. The Mongolian is a fine bird, but the first cross Mongolian is far better, and I believe that the influence of the strain during the last thirty years has added valuable factors of resistance to climate and disease to our ordinary birds.

'Of late years the influence of the Mongolian blood has been more in evidence in the plumage of birds shot, but it is not by any means as unmistakable as the Chinese strain. Pure, or perhaps, it would be preferable to say nearly pure, Mongolian stock is carried by nearly every game farm of importance, and the admixture occurs in most game farm eggs, for the Chinese x Mongolian or Blackneck x Mongolian first cross cock is a favourite with breeders.

'These four strains have contributed to our bird, but within the last few years we have developed a sub-species which is a new type. It is a dark-plumaged bird known for the moment as a melanistic mutant (*Phasianus mut. tenebrosus*), and it is claimed by some authorities to breed true, though this is doubted by others who hold that it has appeared and disappeared before . . .

'The elements in our ordinary English pheasant are, as we have seen, Colchicus, Torquatus, Versicolour and Mongolicus. Later perhaps we shall have to add Mut. Tenebrosus, or Darkie, to coin a less ponderous title. If you go to a pheasant farm you will see a few pens of segregated aristocrats – almost pure lines – and a larger proportion of cross-bred gentry "first cross", and a herded democracy of ordinaries. A wealth of personal experience is necessary before you can even guess at a hen's parentage, but the distinctive features of the pure cocks are fairly easily determined.

'Colchicus [colour plate IV] has a purple-black neck shading to green, with *no white ring at all*. Torquatus has a white ring which should go *all round,* Mongolicus has the white ring *broken* at the front collar-stud where the gold chestnut of the upper breast joins the iridescent neck, and is much broader, and Versicolour is a metallic green, not gold-bronze, bird, with no neck ring at all. The mutant has not the indented Japanese flank feathers. Seen pure it is easy, but when we come to look at the serried rows which mark the bag of the last stand, identification, as they say in the police reports, is not so easy. The ring basis no longer holds good, for the blood is mixed.

'The eye and the rump are perhaps the next best points. Colchicus has a yellow-brown eye in keeping with his neat uniform, and a dark maroon rump. Torquatus has a white eyebrow and a grey-blue, almost lavender-coloured rump, and the same kind of colour on the wings, where those of Colchicus are bronze-brown. Mongolicus has a very light pale yellow eye, white patched wings, and is a larger bird than the others. Versicolour crosses are still dark metallic in the overlay of ordinary feathering, and the flank feathers bear an indented bar like a Japanese war fan in place of the straight bar or lancet of the others. No mutant cross is known; they appear to breed clean, normal, or mutant.

'The very light hens are usually Mongolian or first cross Mongolian, and have very light yellow eyes; very dark hens are either Versicolour or mutant; in the case of the latter the rump is usually grouse plumaged. In the past, very light bleached-looking birds, either cocks or hens, were often called Bohemian pheasants. They are, in fact, albinistic mutants and not a true sub-species, but simply sports.

'The importance of these cross breedings is the different sporting characteristics of the birds in their pure state. The Blackneck is a smallish bird of good sporting qualities and able to resist climate well. He is, however, rather more pugnacious than the ordinary.

'The Ringneck or Chinaman is slightly larger, rather more lethargic, and, according to some authorities, rather more difficult to rear when pure. Believed to be a more prolific layer, the Mongolian is a much larger and lighter-coloured bird, and more peacefully inclined than either of the foregoing. To this we owe his reputation for straying, for he is easier noticed, and often feeds well away from covert, whence he has been driven by older and more pugnacious cocks of the other varieties. He is extremely weather resistant. The Versicolour is a very fast, rather small, and very sporting bird, but a poor layer, and suffers badly from cold winds rather than wet.

'In their crosses many of the disadvantages of the pure strains entirely disappear. First cross Chinese and Mongolians are splendid birds, and far the best for the table. First cross Blackneck x Mongolian are rather lighter, but give a quicker rise. So far as driving is concerned, in a well laid out shoot there is, I think, little to choose between them. First crosses between either Mongolian or Blackneck and Versicolour are also excellent sporting birds and prolific. The cross between "ordinary" hens and a Versicolour cock is perhaps the best combination for the private owner who wishes new strains in his stock without any sacrifice of sporting capacity.

'There are a few other pheasants which have been tried as sporting birds but which have for some reason or other never made headway. It is probable that these might do well in the U.S.A., where a wider range of climatic conditions and a higher degree of freedom from disturbance prevail. They are birds which might do well on wild range, where they fail under the slightly more artificial conditions inseparable from a thickly populated country.

'First is the Prince of Wales Pheasant (*P.c. principalis*), a bird rather like Colchicus, but with white wing coverts. It is wilder and shyer than our birds, but has never succeeded here. Lord Fisher tried a pair in the pen at Kilverstone, but wild cock pheasants attacked them (they were wing brailed), and nearly plucked them bald. It is supposed to do well in damp, swampy places, is prolific and a markedly strong flier, a point which needs caution when it is brailed for the pen.

'Next the Reeves Pheasant (*P. Reevesii*), which has a splendid tail and is often over six feet in total length. It has done fairly well where introduced, but is a hill bird, and though it will cross with other pheasants the hybrids are infertile. It is not a prolific layer, but gives very sporting shooting.

'The Golden Pheasant (*Chrysolophus pictus*) is mainly an aviary bird and

24. Pheasant Making its Spring Call
by J. G. Millais

quarrelsome, but might be established and thrive on its own. There are a few wild at Kilverstone and they fly moderately well. Lastly, there is the Monaul (*Lophophorus refulgens*), which looks like a cross between a peacock and a turkey, and its related Impeyan (*Lophophorus l'Puysii*), which is even gaudier. I have seen them as aviary birds in England, but never heard of their breeding or being really successfully set out in semi-wild state. They are, however, good, hardy sporting birds in their native countries, and might some day be adapted in a suitable environment.

'So far as my experience goes, I have not been able in over twenty years to detect any appreciable difference between the sporting qualities of the hybrid "ordinary" and selected strains of first cross birds. It all depends on how they are shown, and provided the birds are handled properly, an equally good result should be obtained.'

(*Game Birds and Game Bird Shooting,* 1936)

Hugh Gladstone also gives a fairly detailed account of the introduction of the pheasant into Britain, and of the sport, which developed much later. However, his real study is numbers, and these he records meticulously.

'There must surely be a sense of modesty which precludes the proprietors of big Pheasant shoots from proclaiming the results of their battues among this "terror of mangel-wurzels". One of the first occasions, if not the first, on which 1,000 Pheasants were bagged in one day was in 1845, when something over that number were killed on Lord Ashburton's estate at Buckenham (Norfolk) by a party of nine guns . . .

'That upwards of 3,000 Pheasants have been obtained in one day on more than one estate in England is common knowledge but no exact figures have, as far as is known, been published . . .

'The record bag for Great Britain is believed to have been got at Hall Barn, Beaconsfield (Buckinghamshire) on the Burtley beat. Here on 18th December 1913 seven guns:– His Majesty the Prince of Wales, Lord Charles Fitzmaurice, Lord Ilchester, Lord Dalhousie, Lord Herbert Vane-Tempest and the Hon H. Stonor, shot 3,937 Pheasants, 3 Partridges, 4 Rabbits and 1 Various, a total of 3,945 head . . .

'It is but seldom that two Pheasants are killed at one shot: it may therefore be worthy of record that the Duke of York is said, about 1826, to have killed three at a shot at Chippenham (Cambridgeshire). On 6th November 1912, I saw three Pheasants killed at one shot by Maj. T. Ranken at Capenoch (Dumfriesshire) from a not very large "flush": a similar shot, resulting in the deaths of one white cock, one pied cock and an ordinary hen Pheasant, has been recorded. To kill two cock Pheasants with one's first barrel and two more with one's second must surely be a very rare achievement. A curious "record" is that out of 630 Pheasants killed in one day in 1826 at Chippenham (Cambridgeshire) over 300 were white or pied.'

(*Record Bags and Shooting Records,* 1930)

As Pollard says, 'you cannot get the best out of pheasant shooting with a bow and arrow or with a sling', but there is no doubt that they were shot in this way. An Act passed by James I in 1630 prohibited the shooting of partridges, pheasants, grouse, and hares with any gun, crossbow or other weapon, although it is probable that this was directed more against the 'occasional sportsman' than the organized hunting party, which would have been more likely in any case to have hawked (or netted).

Gladstone remarks on the marvellous accuracy of 'the Old-Time Bow-Men', instancing the Emperor Maximilian of Austria (1459–1519) 'who is alleged to have killed 100 wild duck with 104 shots and to have bagged with one and the same cross-bow bolt 26 hares, without missing'.

The modern sport was born in the late eighteenth century and brought up in the nineteenth. The two greatest influences on its development were the technical advances in the design and manufacture of firearms and the introduction of domestic breeding and rearing for the purpose of stocking coverts.

Pheasants have always been reared for the table in the same way as poultry, but it was not until the turn of the century (about 1800) that any large-scale breeding for sport began. By 1820 there were already several large estates noted for breeding, among them Lord Braybrook's at Audley End, Essex, and the Earl of Jersey's at Osterley Park, Middlesex. The Suffolk manors of Mr Thellusson were also providing sport to the tune of 2,000 brace of cock pheasants in a season, and by 1845 it was possible to record the first '1,000' day, on Lord Ashburton's estate in Norfolk (Gladstone).

Alexander J. Napier, writing in 1903 about the Holkham Estate in Norfolk, graphically illustrates the beginnings of the planned pheasant shoot and how it is worked.

> 'The arrangement of the home coverts is simple enough; its claim to distinction is the immense scale on which it is planned. The park contains about 1,500 acres, or $2\frac{1}{4}$ square miles. Round this runs a great wood, protected on the outer side by a wall, but having on the inner side this picturesque feature – that in parts the park runs right in among the tree trunks, and one sees hundreds of pheasants feeding in this semi-open space. The depth of this belt varies, but its general form, and the position of the woods and clumps, within the park, may be judged from the plan [which appears on page 137]. On the side furthest from the sea the land rises gradually, and on these heights is Scarborough Wood and the famous Scarborough Clump, towards which the pheasants are driven half-way round the park, starting from the western front.
>
> 'Inside the park is the model farm. This has arable fields, yielding abundance of ground suitable both for partridges and pheasants to scratch and feed on, and some other detached arable fields draw the pheasants *inside*. Along the whole north front is a great fringe of marsh, down the dykes of which the pheasants love to wander. Outside, on the east and south, are wide stubble, turnip, and clover fields, and in the centre of the northern side is the lake sanctuary, crowded

with duck and wild-fowl. The park itself is full of oak and ilex. Scotch fir is also abundant in the woods, and gives a warm and beautiful look to the lines of covert. These are also famous for woodcock, though their times and seasons are rather uncertain . . . the ground to be beaten forms one continuous covert, and the object of the first day's shooting is to drive every pheasant, if possible, into Scarborough Clump, at the south-east corner of Scarborough Wood. It is a long business, and there is always a fear that the pheasants may not run forward; but a master hand is in charge of affairs. No one in England knows better than Lord Leicester how to make pheasants do what he wants them to. His knowledge of the birds and how to persuade them is so great that it is quite possible that he might be able to achieve what has always been credited to his powers by a figure of speech, and drive them into his billiard-room . . .

'Through the covert runs a broad drive, and here the guns may amuse themselves knocking over the hares and an occasional rabbit as they endeavour to cross the ride. No pheasants are allowed to be shot until just before reaching the Clump. It must be rather tantalising to the guns to have fine rocketing pheasants turn back over them and not be able to shoot. This, we believe, has sometimes been allowed, but occasions a great loss of time, and also the searching of the whole beat for lost game the next day, which is not desirable. On reaching the Fox Covert – a spinney of thick hazel bushes – a favourite ground for woodcock – some pheasants generally break back over the beaters, and are lost for the day. Going on now slowly, Scarborough Wood is reached at length, and a little further on lunch is taken, the guns, however, keeping their places and eating their lunch standing, the beaters the same . . . Not much time is lost over lunch. And now comes the critical time of the day. In front of the guns, within a space of perhaps four or five acres, are at least a thousand pheasants. Will they be kind and go into the 'stop' over the road, or will they be perverse and come back over guns and beaters? During lunch-time the pheasants have had a much-needed rest, for it does not do to hurry them too much, for in that case they are very likely to break back. The great object is to get them to run into the 'stop', if possible. If once they get on the wing there is no telling exactly where they will go.

'The order is now given, "Shoot cocks going back", and "Make plenty of noise". Scarborough Wood is divided by a road. That part on the left has now to be beaten, but no guns are drawn from the right for this purpose. The pheasants are to be seen crossing the road, running and flying like a swarm of bees going into a hive. It is a pretty sight, and not the least interesting from the spectators' point of view. At length all are in the Clump, obeying Lord Leicester's compelling hand; the last pheasant has disappeared beneath its trees, and the keeper of the beat, to whom this is *the* great day of the year, feels a sense of relief and exultation.

'A few years ago a fox was seen to go right through the middle of the pheasants at the end of Scarborough Wood, and straight away into the Clump. The state of consternation into which this threw every one, from the keepers to the pheasants themselves, may be imagined. But Reynard did not cause a disaster. There was a great commotion. Many pheasants took to the trees when he entered the Clump, and some remained there during the whole of the shooting, complacently looking on while their brothers and sisters were being knocked over outside.

'The great artistic triumph, from the beating point of view, is now complete; it remains only to put the birds out over the guns by a single keeper flushing them as gradually as possible out of the Clump, which, of course, has been stopped on the far side from a very early stage of the operations, and then the

25. *Early picture of a pheasant: 'Showing how to catch pheasants', from the* Livre du Roy Modus (14th century)

real sport of the shooting begins. The guns are posted three deep here, and if the last line is not exactly the *place d'honneur,* it is at least the line in which the shooting is most difficult. The birds, as a rule, have passed the apex of their flight and are beginning that downward glide which is so difficult to "get on terms with". After a period of this gradual flushing of the birds, by a single man, or one or two, in the Clump, the order is given – "All hands to the back of the Clump", and the beaters, forming a line, drive the whole Clump through to the guns, and put out what pheasants remain there. This brings a day's sport to a close, and though there are larger bags made elsewhere, it is doubtful whether there is any place in England where pheasants can be shown better or brought in a more ideal fashion over the guns.'

Today, with most estates being run as commercial enterprises, the economics of pheasant shooting loom larger than ever before. Charles Coles, Director of the Game Conservancy, has recently commented upon the practical problems of running such estates.

'Pheasant husbandry at the present time is not as efficient as it was 10 years ago. Too many tailless birds go to covert, for instance; quality is sacrificed for quantity. And not surprisingly the average recovery rate of first-year reared birds shot has declined over this period from 38 per cent to 34 per cent. This sample is taken from the one million acres of our National Game Census.

'In an effort to find out what it does cost to shoot a pheasant – and thereby to have a yardstick against which different estates can check their own figures – the Game Conservancy have started a cost-analysis scheme . . .

'In accountant's language there can only be one cost – the true cost. This means that an owner who grows his own corn, has a rent-free rearing field, employs casual labour from the farm and so on, should really put these items in at what they would cost, if he bought them over the counter. Nevertheless, as it may be useful to show the differential between the actual costs of the landowner and the tenant, we shall keep two sets of figures.

'There will also be other variations. The shoot which produces all – or a high proportion of – wild pheasants, compared with the estate which has a heavy rearing programme, is but one. On the mixed shoot, good partridge bags are another economic factor to be considered. They share the keeper's time amongst other things.

'At present, the returns from the National Game Census suggest that two pheasants in three are wild-bred. This vast area, however, probably includes shoots which – though representative regionally and from a farming point of view – are probably better managed than a true cross section of the country. The average for the country, omitting the bog-and-bramble acres, would probably be nearer four wild birds in five.

'For this reason we shall try to draw a distinction between the cost of the wild and the reared bird . . . It is clear to us that the most inefficient part of the business, where birds are mainly reared, is concerned with the recovery rate in the bag. This varies from over 60 per cent to under 25 per cent. . . . The majority of shoots waste two-thirds of the birds they release. At least, they do not shoot them, and for the most part nor do their neighbours.

'On one of our own study areas, 45 per cent were accounted for – including birds caught up for the laying pens – by 1 February. But instead of 55 per cent of the released birds surviving to breed, a maximum of only 20 per cent was recorded.

'The main mortality occurs during the acclimatization period, though exactly when these losses occur or what are the precise causes we do not as yet know. Obviously they vary from shoot to shoot – unsuitable release points, unsympathetic coverts, incorrect feeding, predation, disturbance, disease and farming pressures all contribute. We are concerned with correcting the main ones.

'Sometimes there is much wastage before the birds go to covert, and this naturally puts up the cost of the bird in the bag. It can start with the egg. Everyone ought to be able to hatch 65 per cent of all eggs set in an incubator – early

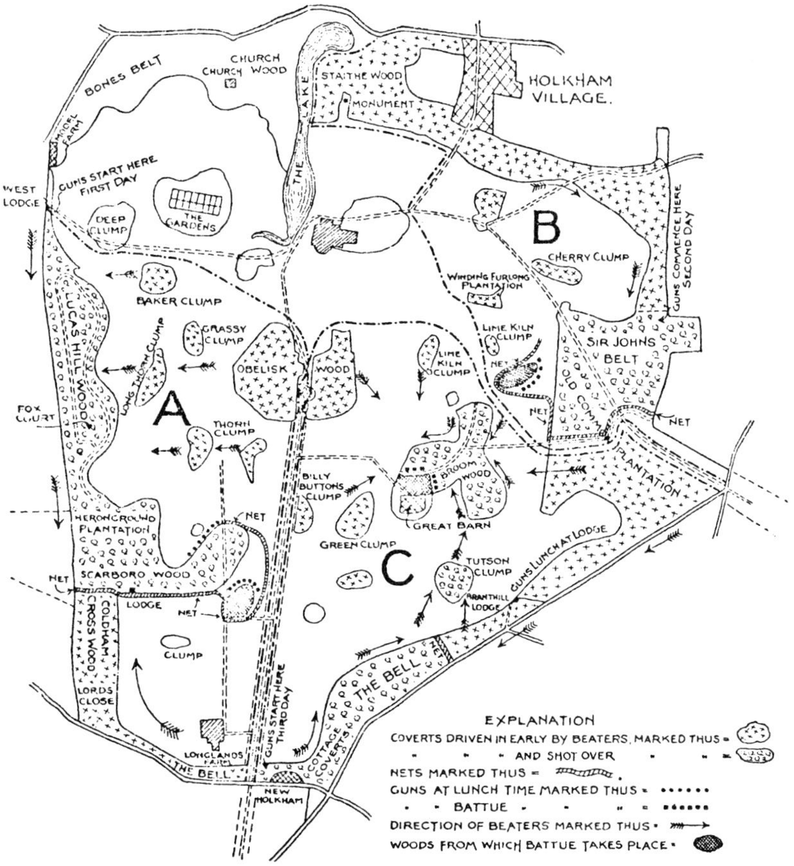

26. Plan of Holkham estate in Norfolk

season to late – and then rear 90 per cent of his day-old chicks, using modern foods and equipment.

'After release the outlay on covert feeding can be another item which will bump up the cost of the pheasant harvest. One of our study areas in Sussex – shooting around 2,000 pheasants a year – recently saved £400 annually by going over to hoppers which dispense grain when pecked at from underneath, as opposed to those that provide the food at the sides, thereby profiting sparrows, finches, squirrels, crows and pigeons as well.

'Transport costs seem to vary enormously – according to whether a tractor, a van or a four-wheel drive vehicle is suitable for the keeper's rounds. Many ways of saving money, or shooting a higher proportion of the birds released, will emerge as we know what every phase, from egg to game cart, costs and as our research develops.

'Occasionally the fault lies not with the game management but with the shooting plans. Too few beaters and dogs in thick coverts, or a team that cannot hold their guns straight, can obviously make an appreciable difference to the bag.

'On Brownsea Island we are learning much about the wild unmanaged pheasant. Facts are emerging which we can relate to ordinary shoots and which can teach us how to make much more of the less expensive wild bird. The key to wild pheasant production lies in a better understanding of its food and habitat requirements. For example, it has always seemed to us that, where there are extensive woodlands, the central areas are largely wasted from the pheasant's point of view.

'A different pattern of rides and a new approach to ride-cropping might more than offset the loss of a few rows of trees by producing many more wild birds.

'Followers of the sport of ocean racing often say: "If you know what it costs, you won't be able to afford it". Shooting – except in certain limited circles – is unlikely to provoke the same response. But if a high pheasant falls out of the sky and crumps down on the grass, and represents to the shooter nothing but the actual cash value involved, I believe the man who pulled the trigger should take up another sport.

'In this respect most of us have our heads cosily buried in the sand, but if it permits us to go on enjoying shooting, a little ostrich-like behaviour is allowable. The Bank Manager and the Game Conservancy can do most of the worrying.'

Seventy years ago Horace Hutchinson expressed a specific view of the 'science' of pheasant shooting.

'A great part of the second half of the nineteenth century was occupied with the discussion whether it were better to post guns ahead and beat pheasants towards them, or to let the guns come along through the covert and flush the birds either for themselves or with the use of dogs. Virtually it was a discussion whether it was better to shoot the pheasant in the head or in the tail. Incidentally there were other points of difference. The pheasant rising out of the covert and shot as he rose was a very much easier bird to kill, or at all events to hit, than when he came to the gun after being flushed by the beaters far back, and going at his "full speed ahead".

'It is a discussion, however, which the twentieth century has left behind. No one, it may now be said, proposes shooting his pheasants in the tail. It still is done, here and there, where the covert is very thick and the pheasants are very few; it is done, for instance, by the man who takes out a licence to shoot in the New Forest. But this sort of thing hardly is pheasant shooting, in the modern acceptance of the term. It is more to be called "a walk with a gun"; and a very delightful pursuit it is, with a small but varied bag in prospect, and perhaps a nice dog for your intelligent assistant and companion; but it is not "pheasant shooting". There is nothing to be said about it, except in the line of description. There is little science.

'The chief science connected with pheasant shooting, in the modern sense, is the science of beating your coverts in such a way as to make your pheasants give the best possible shots to your guns. There is no sport that presents so great differences as the sport of pheasant shooting – differences that depend wholly on the manner in which the pheasants are brought to the gun. Keepers, speaking generally, are a race of butchers. They like to post the guns within thirty or forty yards at most of a covert, and bring the birds out to them in such a manner that a bird passing ten or fifteen yards over the shooter's head is about the most elevated thing he will have to shoot at. Practically speaking it is impossible to miss these birds. No properly constituted person ought to find the slightest satisfaction in killing them. In two words, it is "not sport".'

(*Pheasant Shooting*)

Horace Hutchinson's criticism of keepers as a 'race of butchers' appears, on the face of it, a bit harsh. The *battue* is, by definition, 'driving game out of cover towards the guns' and although it is obviously the usage implication of 'indiscriminate slaughter' that outrages Hutchinson, the blame can scarcely be laid at the door of the keepers. Sportsmen, like people with governments, presumably get the sport they deserve. Fifty years before J. H. Walsh had already disposed of the *battue* in round terms.

'The Battue:– It is for the purpose of the *battue* that pheasants are now reserved and preserved with all the formidable retinue of head-keepers, under-keepers, day-watchers and night-watchers. None but men of large means, and in possession of extensive coverts, can indulge in this amusement, except by the invitation of those who have at their command these pleasant auxiliaries to sport; but in this instance power has been abused, and instead of promoting sport, it has totally destroyed it. No one can deny the fitness of the pheasant for affording gratification to the good sportsman, if the bird is fairly found, put up and shot; but as well might "mobbing" a fox be called fox-hunting, as a *battue* be considered genuine pheasant-shooting; and this I will endeavour to show in the following description of this amusement:– In the *battue* nothing short of hundreds, or if possible thousands, of killed, to say nothing of wounded, will constitute a successful day. The pseudo-sportsman who should be tempted from his fireside and his *Times* after breakfast by anything short of five brace an hour to his gun, would be strongly inclined to complain, and would think, if he did not say, that his presence had been obtained under false pretences. The mode usually adopted is as follows:—

'First, get together eight or ten crack shots, who may, many of them, be in wheeled-chairs or on shooting-ponies, but should be capable of killing, without spoiling, this beautiful bird; then, having breakfasted the party, proceed to post them at certain stations where the game must cross a piece of open ground commanded by the shooters' guns. Thus, in wide coverts, the guns are arranged along the edges of the open springs at about 40 or 50 yards apart so as to command every head of game which passes, whether pheasant or hare, or sometimes rabbit &c., each shooter having two or three guns, and a man to load them; for even now, when breech-loaders are indispensable, one gun would become too hot for use. As soon as these are posted the beaters are sent to the other end of the portion of wood which is to be driven, and they proceed to drive the game through it, often with the aid of a steady dog or two, but as often without any such assistance. For some time nothing is heard but the men calling to each other to keep the line, or their taps on the trees &c., which may be distinguished at a long distance; presently a hare canters quietly out of the edge of the covert, and, putting up her head to observe what is going on is knocked over – as easy a shot as a farm-yard cock tied to a tree. Next, perhaps, a rabbit shares the same fate; she, however, seldom waits to look about her, but goes at a flying pace, and is a fair mark for a good shot. By and by, another and another shot is heard, with the squeal of a hare or two following them; then the beaters may be distinguished approaching, and their blows and cries are very loud and audible. The shooters are now collected to the spot to which all the beaters congregate, termed *the bouquet*. Here expectation is on tiptoe, every moment being the one at which the slaughter is supposed to be about to begin. Suddenly a loud "whir-r-r" is heard, followed by the peculiar "cock-cock-cock-cockle" of the cock-pheasant, of which some one, two or three rise from the edge of the high wood, to be as certainly brought down; as fast as one falls another shares his fate, and in five minutes or less the ground is covered with the slain. In many instances, low nets are fixed along the edge of the wood, which compel the pheasants to get off their legs and rise, as they are so very tame, and so much inclined to run, as to escape in that way but for the nets. In this manner, the whole of the pheasants in a portion of wood, or a great part of them – that is all those which have neither doubled back nor escaped the guns – are brought to bag, and the keepers' retrievers are set to work to recover those which are not artistically disposed of. As soon as this part of the work is accomplished, another portion of wood is driven in a similar way; and this is repeated, till the whole of the preserves are exhausted, or the sporting(!) propensities of the guests fully gratified.

'Now it will be observed that in this description nothing whatever has been said of finding the game, or of the use of the instinct of the dog, or of the gratification of the desire for exercise or even of the benefits derived from it; on the contrary, the admirers of this sport are generally wholly ignorant of the art of finding game, or of the hunting of the dogs, or unwilling or incapable of using their legs; they only long for blood – which may really be said to form the positive, comparative, and superlative degrees of their ideas on the subject. There may be some excuse for the boy feeling gratification and pride in obtaining the mastery over a fine pheasant by this kind of butchery; but I never could see the grounds for these feelings in a full-grown man, with all his faculties about him. For a gouty valetudinarian also, who still clings to his old associations, I can find some excuse; but these form only a small proportion of those who habitually delight in the *battue*.

'Excuse for the Battue – The excuse made for this abuse of sport is, that where pheasants are thick, no one gun, or even two or three, can pursue them in the old sportsmanlike way without losing a great many, which are driven off into an enemy's country. Now, this I admit fully. It *is* impossible to enter a covert abounding with pheasants and hunt them with spaniels, without nine-tenths of the birds running off out of shot, and escaping to a distance; and if pheasants are wanted for the table, and must be killed for it, and, by consequence, must also be reared and preserved for it, then kill them in this way; but let paid hands do the butchery, and do not gloat over your victims, and dignify their slaughter with the name of sport. Domestic poultry must be reared and killed; but who would admit the pleasure of wringing their necks or cutting their throats? Yet where lies the difference? The pheasant is not even a difficult shot. On first rising from covert, his flight is slow and hurried, though when in full swing it is often fast enough and the man who can be sure of a fast "rocketer" must have a good eye and hand; but the shots presented in a *battue* are almost always easy ones, and the practice afforded is so great that those who indulge in it are almost sure of their mark. The only excuse I could ever make for myself or others who have partaken of the *battue*, is that as it is a rare and expensive amusement, people are apt to value it by the general estimate – namely, its cost. Everyone knows that pheasant-preserving causes a most extravagant outlay, and he also knows that he cannot indulge in the sport many times a year. This may perhaps account for the high rate at which it is estimated, but is only a lame apology at the best.'

(*Manual of British Rural Sports*)

Examples of the kind of wholesale destruction to which both Walsh and Hutchinson took such exception are legion in Gladstone. He quotes William Daniel as his authority for the largest bag of game ever made in one day.

> 'During the month of October 1797, Prince Lichenstein and eleven other gentlemen killed in one day, in Germany, during fourteen hours shooting, 39,000 pieces of game; it was of all sorts, but chiefly Hares and Partridges . . . it is perhaps worthy of note that in 1753, twenty-three shooters – among whom the Emperor of Austria and Her Imperial Highness the Princess Charlotte were included – killed, in the course of twenty days shooting in Bohemia, 47,950 head, of which 18,273 were Hares, 19,545 Partridges and 9,499 Pheasants.'

A subsequent reference to the standard of marksmanship reveals that this royal party fired 116,231 shots – a rather mediocre average of 41 per cent.

It is of course as pointless in shooting as in any other sport to compare the outstanding performers of different times. There is no doubt, however, that Peter Hawker would find a place in any list of the best of all ages. Gladstone notes that he once killed 77 partridges out of 78 and Payne-Gallwey says of him: 'that the Colonel was a marvellous shot there can be no doubt whatever, and in the style of game shooting he pursued has probably no equal in these days [1893]; as a snipe shot he has never been, and perhaps never will be, equalled – fourteen to fifteen snipe without a miss in as many single shots, and with a flint gun, speaks volumes as to his skill.'

Colonel Hawker's style of shooting was certainly vastly different from the *battue* and although his reputation is principally as a wild-fowler ('the father of wild-fowling', Payne-Gallwey calls him) he has some useful tips to offer on taking pheasants, in his book *Instructions to Young Sportsmen.*

> 'For shooting pheasants it often becomes necessary to start very early in the morning, as they are apt to lie, during the day, in high covert, where it is almost impossible to shoot them till the leaf has fallen from the trees. We can never be at a loss in knowing where to go for pheasants, as we have only to send some one the previous evening, for the last hour before sunset, to watch the different barley or oat stubbles of a woodland country, and on these will be regularly displayed the whole contents of the neighbouring coverts. It then remains to be chosen which woods are the best calculated to shoot in; and, when we begin beating them, it must be remembered to draw the springs, so as to intercept the birds from the old wood. If the coverts are wet, the hedge-rows will be an excellent beginning, provided we here also attend well to getting between the birds and their places of security. If pheasants, when feeding, are approached by a man, they generally run into covert; but if they see a dog, they are apt to fly up.
>
> 'If a person holds land, over which keepers have a reservation, and therefore drive it in the morning to spoil his sport, he should sprinkle it well with buck-wheat, barley, and white pease, for which the pheasants would most likely come back again in the evening, and he has then only to begin beating with his back to the extreme point of his liberty, and the birds, being cut off in their retreat, will either fly to him or lie very close. If the wind should blow strong from the preserves, or if the foxhounds should happen to run through them, he would then, by this means, be still more sure of having retaliation on those who

Partridge (*Perdix cinerea*) by C. Whymper

Capercaillie (*Tetrao urogallus*) by C. Whymper

had been taking pains to defeat him in the fair and lawful amusement of sporting on his own ground.

'This plan, however, would be followed with little success, if the person adopting it should take out a cry of noisy spaniels, or a set of wild pointers. He should recollect, that in order to intercept the birds, he may be obliged to work down the wind; and it therefore becomes necessary that he should have only one steady old pointer, or setter, who will keep within gunshot, and quarter his ground with cunning and caution, so as to work round every stem of underwood, instead of hastily ranging forward; and, above all, be well broke, either to fall to the gun, or lie down when he has brought a bird.

'For one alone to get shots in a thick underwood, a brace or two of very well-broke spaniels would, of course, be the best. But were I obliged to stake a considerable bet, (taking one beat with another, where game was plentiful,) I should back, against the sportsman using them, one who took out a very high-couraged old pointer, that would keep near him, and would, on being told, break his point to dash in, and put the pheasants to flight before they could run out of shot. This office may be also performed by a Newfoundland dog; but, as first getting a point would direct the shooter where to place himself for a fair shot, the Newfoundland dog would always do best kept close to his heels, and only made use of to assist in this; and particularly for bringing the game; as we rarely see a pointer, however expert in fetching his birds, that will follow up the scent of, and find the wounded ones half so well as the real St John's Newfoundland dog.

'It will, of course, be recollected, that the pointer kept for *this* purpose should never be taken with regular-broke dogs. He will, however, before the season for pheasant shooting, be as well worth his keep as spaniels, by the service he will render his master (single-handed) among potatoes and bean-fields; the beating in which (and particularly if there are land-rails, or red-legged partridges,) is by no means a good practice for thorough-broke pointers or setters.

'It often happens that the boundary of a liberty ends with a broad hedgerow, which may be too high to shoot in, and may have land on the other side belonging to some one who is not on terms with the owner, and for whose property all his game fly out on the wrong side of this little covert. He has then only to sow buck-wheat, sunflower-seeds, and plant Jerusalem artichokes for the pheasants; and Swedish turnips, Dutch clover, or parsley, for the hares, on his own side, and cut down a space broad enough to shoot, on the enemy's side, in the hedgerow, which will soon induce him to compromise on equitable terms; because, should his competitor even do the same, he will most probably still have his share; and, if not, he will get away a great part of his game.

'If the hedgerow is hollow at the bottom, he should send some one to the end of it, as many of the old hares would probably run forward rather than cross him, or take away from home.

'If a rival shooter (some stranger) races to get before you, push him hard for a long time, always letting him have rather the advantage, and then give him the double without his seeing you. Having done this, go quietly round (supposing you have been beating up wind); and on reaching the place where you began, work closely and steadily the whole of the ground or covert that you have both been racing over, and you will be sure to kill more game than he, who is beating and shooting in haste, through fear of your getting up to him; and (if the wind should rise) driving the dispersed, and, consequently, closest-lying birds to your beat, as fast as he finds them.

'When staying in a town, take care not to let every one know where you shoot, by pompously riding through it with a display of guns and dogs; but either send on the latter in the dark, or take them closely shut up in your dog-cart. If driving, cover your shooting-dress with a macintosh or a box-coat; if on horseback, ride out of the town on some road diametrically opposite to where your sport lies, and then double back again on other roads, or by crossing the country. If you return by daylight, enter the town again by this means, or at all events in the most quiet and private manner, otherwise you will soon have your beat (if on a neutral place) worked by every townsman who can muster a dog and gun.

'If there is one month worse than another for the amusement of shooting, I should be apt to consider that it is November. The warmer weather of September and October is then gone by, and the birds become wild and cunning. The fall of the leaf, with the sports of rabbit, woodcock, and wildfowl shooting, are not in general to be fully enjoyed till December and January; so that, in the event of a sportsman finding it necessary to leave the country during the shooting-season, on any business, the precise time for which might be at his own option, I should advise him to choose this, the middle month, for laying aside his gun.'

(*Instructions to Young Sportsmen*)

A final word on pheasants comes from Eric Parker, editor of *The Field*, who concerns himself in this extract with the almost addictive attractions of the sport, as he considered them.

'So we come to the typical day's covert shooting. Am I to write "typical" of the past? I have no prophetic vision; but I can think of days of covert-shooting which seem to me typical, too, of the best of English country life. I hope I may still write of covert-shooting – even if it has developed too uniformly into the ordered morning and afternoon, the known numbers, precise methods; the definite object either missed or attained: at its best a succession of difficult and sporting chances at high-flying birds; at its worst regular and monotonous – the set piece. That is, of course, the difference between covert-shooting and the wilder, more natural business of grouse-driving.

'If we know the coverts, we know exactly what the birds and the keepers and beaters should be doing. We know that it is the keeper's object to push his birds away from home until he has run them to a certain spot that he means to stop them there, and that he has chosen where he will flush them so as to send them home flying at their best and highest, as pheasants will fly going home and in no other direction. And since we know exactly what the keeper is trying to do, we can judge precisely the measure of his success; almost as certainly, indeed, as we may judge our own, counting the number of cartridges (if anybody ever wants to do such a thing) and the birds picked up.

'But is that to deny the attraction of such shooting? Who is to deny it? Not I. Pheasants flushed far back in the wood and coming over the trees like grouse over the brae; pheasants crossing, swerving, soaring, at the sight of the guns; pheasants swinging back, sailing down wind, across wind; a score in the air together, twos and threes following them, a dozen, another score; all of them high, many of them thirty yards up, a few of them more; it is difficult to think of better shooting than that.

'If any man proclaims himself tired of covert-shooting, if he believes himself proof against its spell, let him stand with a walking-stick in the line of guns when pheasants are crossing high and fast. Let him arrive, say, as a casual guest, passing in a car, perhaps, or anxious to see something in the garden and unaware that shooting is going on. Let him be offered a gun, let him stoutly wave such offers aside, let him take his stand when the best birds are coming, and let him observe all from a suitable position. I have seen men suffer in this wise.

'We test our shooting best, perhaps, in familiar coverts. But is there not a fascination in standing for the first time in a new place? I think it is the most exhilarating thing in pheasant-shooting. All the possibilities expand. You know hardly anything; you do hope for much. You know which way the birds are coming; you do not know how many are likely to come your way, what sort of birds they will be, at what height and what angle they will fly, whether they will be crossing or swerving or straight overhead; you do not know – and that is the most absorbing problem – where you will first catch sight of them.

'You look at the line of the tops of trees in front of you, or at the level of the low-cut edging the ride, and you find yourself guessing how you will take birds going this way and that. There is an oak opposite you which seems to divide the roof of the wood into halves; will the birds rise to the left or right, or will you get them flying right over? There is a gap a little further off between spruce and larch; will it be suddenly filled? In the distance beyond the corner of the wood, out in the field, you can see a gun standing who is evidently to deal with birds breaking back; is the line of beaters level with him, and where is the other flank?

'You guess at the position of the stops, at the time the beat is supposed to take, at what lies behind you; and you realise in a flash that what you have been waiting for has begun – and differently from what you had been imagining. Three partridges suddenly swerve straight in front of you, coming from you have not seen where; you drop one and turn to find the others vanishing behind a beech. A couple of wild duck set themselves as tiny specks above a far horizon; are they coming your way? They swing off and round again and disappear; then with a whicker of wings they are above you. A single pheasant gets up a long way off and sails steadily forward, rising high over the gun to your left; another soars almost at the same place and swings back to the gun out in the field.

'Your own first shot of the day; the highest of the high birds – do you ever remember them so vividly as when they belong to the first shooting of an unfamiliar covert? The good birds seem better; even the poorest gain a value from the freshness of their surroundings.

'I will add, to complete the perfect day, frost and a crackle of sparkling leaves; sunshine of the field, snow in the shadows, the clearest of winter weather. And yet – and yet . . . What are all these conditions and chances of covert-shooting at its best? Are they not just the accidents, the unexpected, the wilder, happier part of it all? I am back again to the old contrast; here are pheasants at their finest, shooting of the most exacting kind, every accessory that skill, experience, pains, money can supply. And there, three and four hundred miles away, are the moors and the heather, the Welsh hills within scent of the Atlantic; Irish peat, Irish bogs, rough lodging, snipe rising far out in wet and wind. The two memories remain; and it may be just because one of them is so far off that I find myself thinking again and again of wet boots, the joy of being utterly tired, and sunset lighting orange lamps in the mosses and the pools of the bog.'

(*Shooting Days*)

CHAPTER NINE

Artists in Firearms

WITH THE flood gates of the industrial revolution wide open its material benefits flowed over the nineteenth century like a tidal wave, catching up every aspect of life. Sport could scarcely remain untouched. It was the golden age of gunsmiths and the progress in the design of guns and ammunition had a dramatic effect on all forms of shooting. From the great list of illustrious craftsmen certain names stand out. Hawker's epitaph to Joe Manton duly honours the man who revolutionised the conventional weapon of his time, with his development of the 'detonator':

> 'In memory of Mr Joseph Manton, who died, universally regretted, on the 29th day of June 1835, aged 69. This humble tablet is placed here by his afflicted family, merely to mark where are deposited his mortal remains. But an everlasting monument to his unrivalled genius is already established in every quarter of the globe, by his celebrity as the greatest artist in fire-arms that ever the world produced, as the founder and father of the modern gun-trade, and as a most scientific inventor, in other departments, not only for the benefit of his friends and the sporting world, but for the good of his King and Country.'

Interestingly enough, although he put the detonator to good use in his own account, Hawker was contemptuous of the effect of its introduction on the art of gun-making and the science of shooting.

> 'When flint-guns were the order of the day, few sporting gentlemen of distinction ever thought of using anything but the gun of a first-rate maker for the simple reason that – on the goodness of the work depended the quickness in firing, and consequently the filling of the bag. But, now-a-days, every common fellow in a market town can detonate an old musket, and make it shoot as quick as can be wished; insomuch that all scientific calculations in shooting at moderate distances, are now so simplified, that we, every day, meet with jackanapes-apprentice-boys who can shoot flying, and knock down their eight birds out of ten. Formerly, shooting required art and nerve – now, for tolerable shooting (at all events for the use of *one* barrel) nerve alone is sufficient.'

What would have been his reaction to the breech-loader, introduced soon after he died? J. H. Walsh (in his *Manual of British Rural Sports*) provides a wealth of detail on what the colonel missed!

'Action of the Hammered Gun – In principle this gun remains as it was when first invented by Lefaucheux about the year 1852. Up to that time a great many attempts had been made to construct a gun loaded at the breech, but in all of them there was such an escape of gas as to forbid their use. Lefaucheux, however, not only invented an excellent and simple plan of opening and closing the breech, but he added to it a strong cartridge case made of paper and brass by which all escape was prevented, while a sure and rapid ignition was effected by lodging a small percussion cap in the brass base provided with a pin on which the blow of the hammer was received. This case is now called the "pin cartridge" case, to distinguish it from the more modern one now in use and called the "central fire" case . . . in this invention rather than in that of the action itself lies the real value of the modern breech-loader, for with it many other plans of closing the breech are available, but without it no breech-loader is of any use. In this case the cap is placed sideways in a little chamber constructed in the base, . . . there being no external opening, except through a great thickness of paper perforated by the pin. Still there was a slight escape by the side of the pin, which is one objection to its use, whereas in the central fire, though the cap is introduced from behind, if properly made there is little or often no escape. I shall, however, hereafter more fully describe cartridge cases as now made. . . .

'The Lefaucheux gun . . . is hinged to the body of the action about two inches from the breech, and that its barrels are held in their place by a bolt (single grip) turned sideways in a circular direction by the lever lying under the action. This was soon found to wear, and a second tooth was added, making what is called the "double grip" – a bolt which is still the strongest known and is used for heavy rifles with that view. As, however, it will not snap quite home when the breech is closed, it is not quick enough, according to modern taste, for battues, &c. Consequently, a bolt which would have this desired effect was soon brought out by Mr Purdey, and is still in general use, called the Purdey bolt. Mr C. Lancaster devised a plan by which the barrels were not only held down by the grip, but also a projection was drawn back under a slot cut in the break-off; but this plan being confined to himself, did not get into general use. The Purdey bolt was originally worked by an under-lever let into the trigger-guard, and depressed by the thumb; but in 1865 a top-lever was patented by Messrs. Scott of Birmingham, by which this bolt was actuated and also, if desired, one working in a top extension. By mutual arrangement Mr. Purdey and Messrs. Scott were enabled to combine the two, and this plan is now in very general use. In the meantime, Mr Westley-Richards of Birmingham and London, introduced his top connection-bolt, which he relied on without the assistance of a bottom bolt, and which is still in vogue for both hammered and hammerless guns. The only other plan of any great importance is the cross-bolt used by Mr Greener, and, driven horizontally, more or less through a steel projection, continued from the rib in the same way as in the Westley-Richards gun. This is strong enough to dispense, like the Westley-Richards, with any other bolt, but it cannot be made to snap, if sufficiently long to cross the tang into the opposite side, without which it is not strong enough. Recourse is therefore had to a snap bolt below, like that of Mr Purdey which is connected with the cross-bolt and compels the latter to follow its course. Mr Powell's and Mr Tolley's cross bolts are on similar lines, but not quite so strong as that of Mr Greener, inasmuch as they work through slots instead of holes . . .

'Such are the chief variations in the actions of modern hammered guns, but since the introduction of the hammerless form several attempts have been made to bring them up to the requirements of those who use the latter. Thus the same principle which will operate on the tumbler is brought to play through it on the hammers, which are thereby raised to full cock in the same way as in the hammerless gun – i.e. either by the fall of the barrels or the force of the lever; and with these alterations, of course, safety-bolts are also required. Again a modification of the two has lately been invented in which a gun made like one of the hammerless forms has an outside hammer with a projection working in a slot cut in the lock-plate, by which it is enabled to reach the striker. This gun, called semi-hammerless, has the advantage of excluding gas from the lock, and will no doubt be accepted as a compromise between the two kinds by many sportsmen; but as cartridge cases are now so well made as to retain the gas, the above advantage is anticipated and negatived, so that I fail to see in what respect it can be considered to be an improvement. Time alone will, however, settle this question, and I shall not venture to anticipate the verdict of the British public.

'HAMMERLESS GUNS – These are now made in such variety that almost every

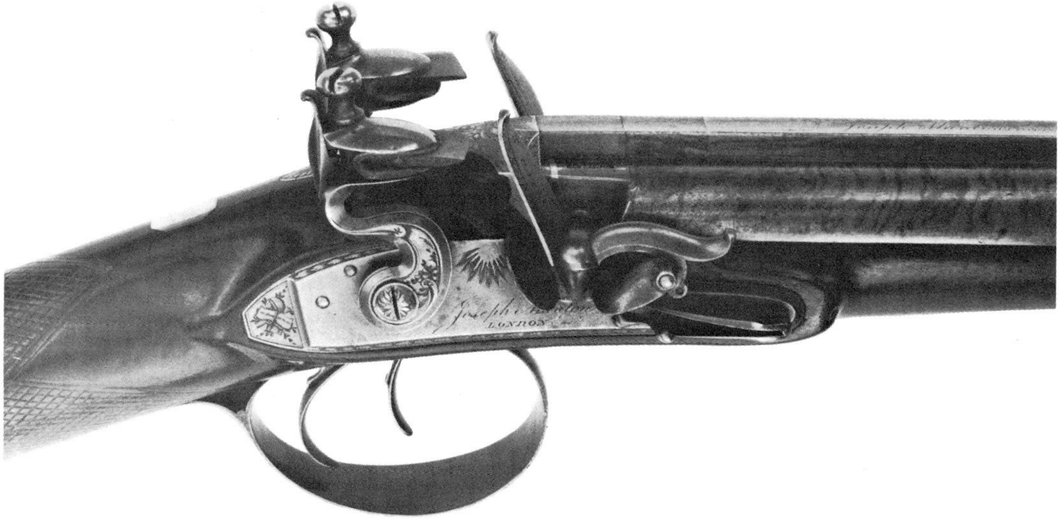

27. A double-barrel Manton flintlock (circa *1806*)

gunmaker has his special action. The principle is more than a quarter of a century old, but the first really useful plan was that of Mr Murcott, patented in 1871. They may be arranged in three leading divisions – first, those in which the gun is cocked by the power of the lever; second, those in which the fall of the barrels effects this object; and thirdly, those in which the cocking is divided between the opening and the closing of the breech, but in both cases through the agency of the barrels.

'LEVER COCKERS – The first action patented on this principle was that of Mr Murcott, above mentioned. Here a lever . . . lying under the guard has a projection or claw, which acts on the two tumbler-strikers . . . These tumbler-strikers are furnished with cross pieces which project from each tumbler sidewise, so that they react on each other. Thus the cocking is first done by the claw, which as it is taken forward in closing the lever, leaves the tumbler free to drive the striker on to the cap. The claw also brings back the bolt which keeps down the barrel and closes the breech. This gun was highly approved of in the infancy of hammerless guns, but is not now made. Three years afterwards Messrs. Gibbs and Pitt of Bristol, brought out their action, still much used, in which a double-grip lever drives back a bolt on to the face of the tumbler . . . which acts on a separate striker. When first brought out this action had an outside lever . . . by which the gun could be let down to half-cock, and cocked again, so that no safety bolt was absolutely necessary; but in a short time the outside hammer was voted an incumbrance, and then a trigger safety bolt was introduced. In 1877, Messrs Lang, of Cockspur Street, invented an action combining the two principles, and about the same time Messrs Woodward, of St James's Street, London, introduced another modification, with the substitution of a spiral spring for the flat one previously used. Lastly, in 1872, Mr Rigby of St James's Street, and Mr Bissell of Bermondsey, together patented a lever cocker which makes an excellent gun. An ordinary Purdey half locks the action below, while a perpendicular bolt is simultaneously driven up by the same action of the lever. This second bolt works in a projection from the barrels, but it is supported and greatly strengthened by a solid piece of the break-off lying in front of it, and so cut that the tang drops down over it when the bolt is depressed, but is securely locked as soon as the latter is raised.

'Objections are made to all these lever guns – First, that as they have to overcome the mainspring, this must be reduced in strength too much for perfect ignition; and secondly, that if the lever is not carried quite home the tumbler infallibly has to effect this before the striker can reach the cap, and hence it is said that they are more apt to miss fire than the barrel-cocker. Theoretically there is no doubt some truth in these objections, but practically they are not found to exist in any serious degree.

'BARREL COCKERS – In this plan a projection either from the barrels or the fore-end (which is practically a part of them) acts on a lever or levers or a rod, as the case may be. Whichever is employed, it bears on some part of each tumbler and raises it to full cock. The first of these brought before the public was the well-known action of Anson and Deely, which combined the Westley-Richards top-connection and bolt already described, with the new method of cocking the tumbler-striker. In this gun, the side lock usually capable of being removed, is replaced by a very simple lock contained within the body of the action, and consisting of four pieces only, besides the necessary scear spring and the pins used for working the parts. This lock consists of the mainspring . . . having a turn down on its shorter limb, which acts directly on the tumbler, without a hook and swivel.

'The tumbler-striker . . . is in one piece, as originally made; but sometimes an ordinary striker is let into the break-off and is acted on by a tumbler without the point . . . The scear . . . is usually wide and strong, which is alleged to be a great advantage in point of safety, while per contra its detractors say that this makes the pull-off unnecessarily coarse and unpleasant. Projecting about half an inch from the body is the round point of the cocking-lever . . . the end of which lifts the projecting front of the tumbler . . . This projection is received into a hole cut in the segmental face of the break-off, so that when this part is lowered in opening the gun it raises the front of the tumbler and of course throws back the striking pin to full cock. When first brought out this action was provided with a safety bolt, blocking the striker and also bolting the triggers; but it did not act well and was soon withdrawn, the gun being sold with trigger bolts only. At length under the pressure put upon the makers, by myself in the columns of the *Field,* the Westley-Richards Company, who have made this action in very large numbers gave in to my opinions, and an automatic safety bolt is combined with it as will be presently shown.

'Mr Greener has somewhat altered this plan by lengthening the forward limb of the tumbler and acting on it by a hook attached to the barrel lump, and having no connection with the fore-end. Various opinions are held on the

28. Lefaucheux breech-loading gun (circa *1855*)

comparative merits of these two actions, which I shall not attempt to decide; but I may state that, though legally Mr Greener is allowed to make this improved action without paying a royalty, the difference between the two is a matter of detail only.

'Messrs Scott of Birmingham, while using the principle, have made a more considerable alteration from the Anson and Deely. In the first place they replace the lever by a rod, drawn forward by a hook on the lump of the barrels, and itself hooking on to the bottom of the tumbler. To this gun a side lock furnished with an admirable safety bolt, to be hereafter described, is attached. The lock is in principle exactly like that of an ordinary back-action lock. This action and safety are combined in the well-known "Climax Safety" gun of Messrs. Holland and Holland, of New Bond Street.

'Lastly, Mr Henry Holland, of New Bond Street, has patented another modification of the barrel-cocker, in which the centres of the lever are so well arranged that the cocking is effected by the mere fall of the barrels without any jerk. In this action a lever is pivotted in the recess of a clip-lock about its middle, and is lifted by the fall of the barrels, through the agency of a hook . . . At the other end it is forged in a crane-neck form, the front of which bears on a projection . . . at the back of the tumbler, thereby raising it to full-cock.

'THOSE GUNS in which the cocking is divided between the opening and the closing of the breech, are few in number, the chief being Mr Purdey's which for the last three years has been extensively sold, and Mr C. Lancaster's only recently brought out. Of the former, I shall give no description, as it is against Mr Purdey's wishes, except that the barrels open extremely easily owing to pressure being exerted on them by the mainspring in this direction. On the other hand the closure is more difficult in proportion, because in the act of so doing the spring is again compressed.

'Mr C. Lancaster's new gun externally resembles the Purdey hammerless gun except in the shape of the lock-plate, which is not quite so neat. In mechanism it attempts to attain the object of Mr Purdey – viz. to divide the work between the opening and closing – and certainly, as it appears to me, it does this with greater advantage . . .

'EJECTOR GUNS – The ordinary plan of loading not being fast enough for some sportsmen, the ejector principle adopted for military rifles has been applied to shot guns first by Mr Needham of Birmingham, and subsequently by Mr Greener and Mr C. Lancaster. It is alleged by some sportsmen that with this gun a second together with its loader may be dispensed with at battues, but it does not prevent the heating of the barrels, which will take place even with ordinary loading, and on that account I do not see any great advantage in it to compensate for the extra complication of the working parts and the increased risk of admitting water to the locks. If desired the choice lies between the ejector gun of Mr Greener and that of Mr C. Lancaster, Needham's being withdrawn from sale.

'FOUR BARRELLED GUNS – Mr C. Lancaster has lately introduced a four-barrelled gun fired by one lock, but it is not generally approved of in this country. It is made either as a combined rifle and shot gun, or with four smooth barrels or four rifled barrels as may be desired. The lock is made to receive on much the same plan as the chamber turns in the revolver.

'Such are the varieties of the shot gun in common use. I must now consider how they can best be made safe.

'SAFETY-BOLTS – Hammered guns with rebounding locks are safe during loading because no jar can cause an explosion, the mainspring being at rest. All hammerless guns, however, are raised to full cock before reloading, and in closing the gun with the usual snap the scear is liable to be jarred out of bent. Both kinds of gun are intended, of course, to explode when the trigger is pulled (supposing no safety-bolt in action) and also liable to be jarred off when both barrels are fired at full cock, as we have known happen even in the Anson and Deely several times in one day, although the scear of that gun is of double breadth and strength as compared with others. Hence it is necessary to provide against all these contingencies as far as possible. I shall, therefore, consider these accidents in a reverse order – First, as to both barrels firing when one trigger only is pulled. This may occur in hammered as well as hammerless guns, and is not often attended with danger. When the pull-off is very light (in some cases I have known it to be purposely only 1 lb.) this accident is very common; but as the gun is always at the time it is fired pointed at the object aimed at or nearly so, it is chiefly as an annoyance to the shooter that it is to be regarded.'

What Pollard had to say about sporting guns in 1936 still holds good. The development of the immensely sophisticated weaponry of the atomic/electronic age has been confined to devices with which men may more easily exterminate each other. Sportsmen have not yet found it necessary to employ rocket-launchers or electronic guidance systems to enhance their enjoyment of a day's sport.

Pollard attributes the replacement of the old game gun by the twentieth-century short-barrelled type to the pioneering work of Robert Churchill, whom he compares to Joe Manton as an innovator. Of the modern gun, he says:–

'It represents a very perfect instrument for its particular purpose. It is fifty years since any radical change was made in its general design, but during those fifty years, it has been improved out of all knowledge in matters of detail. Many good old guns, made thirty or more years ago, are still in use today, and though we always say that modern work is not comparable with the older craftsmanship, this is not true of guns or scientific instruments. In general, modern design is far better than older design, material is decidedly better, and craftsmanship as good. Really first-class guns made today will last as long or longer, than their honoured predecessors, and a good pair of guns will give, with reasonable care, at least a lifetime's service.'

(*Game Birds and Game Bird Shooting*)

CHAPTER TEN

The Rise of the Grouse

SOME INDICATION of the impact of the breech-loader on grouse-shooting is given by Martin Stephens, writing in 1939.

'. . . In the long history of sport the story of the gun is a comparatively short one, and the history of grouse shooting is much shorter than that of the more pastoral pursuit of the partridge. The North of England and Scotland developed more leisurely and on more feudal lines than the south country. It is a truism to point out that until the 19th Century it was rare indeed for the laird or the chief to kill their game. "They left it to their retainers to do for them". This habit of mind was, no doubt, persisting to some extent in the early 1800's, when the first Englishmen, like Hawker and St John were beginning to go to the north in pursuit of game. Hawker had a day on Bowes Moor as long ago as 1812, and St John was exploring the terra incognita of Sutherland just a 100 years ago [1839].'

But the shooting of grouse by owners of moorland and their friends was general by the time Queen Victoria came to the throne, and must have been practised more or less regularly by a minority for fifty years before that.

'By the 1840s most people who had grouse wanted to shoot them. There then followed the next episode, the Anglo-Saxon invasion and the letting of shooting for sport. The most potent factor in this was, of course, the railway. As it crept northward to Inverness, the invading Sassenach came with it, wishing to enjoy the unrivalled sport of the Highlands. Moreover it included a new class, for besides the 18th Century aristocracy there came the wealthy founders of the Manchester tradition with the money let loose by the industrial revolution. In those days few moors were let, though, doubtless, fairly widespread permission was given to those who asked to shoot. Letting sporting rights was not considered either possible or gentlemanly. When rents were levied they were ridiculously low – Lord Malmesbury had the entire shooting rights for the Island of Lewis for £25 a year.

'Meanwhile another economic change was taking place. The years 1840–1870 may be said to have been those when grouse gradually began to take the place of sheep, and when proprietors of moors realised that they had in their grouse rents an economic asset. By this time letting was the custom.

'Two other factors greatly affected grouse shooting. The first was the invention of the breach loader in 1851 . . . Breach loaders were in common use by the early seventies. This allowed a much faster rate of shooting and called for more targets. The second was the grouse disease which was rampant in 1872. From those years date the beginning of efforts at scientific moor management, in the hopes of preventing fresh outbreaks. Both these factors caused the more widespread introduction of driving. It was felt to be less sporting to sit still and have a bird driven to you than to tramp after it on the moors and with this prejudice the acceptance of driving was slow. Driving proved to be beneficial to the sport. Firstly, in a year of plenty it is impossible to kill down the stock sufficiently and prevent disease by walking. A moor's capacity is gauged by the amount of grouse it can feed in the winter, and stock must be kept down to this level. Secondly, driving has the advantage of killing off the old birds which come first in the covey, and of splitting up the coveys and, therefore, making for more virile stock through change of blood. On every moor when driving was introduced there was an immediate beneficial result.

'Driving was in vogue on the Bolton Abbey Moors in the late "fifties": it was fairly common in Yorkshire and Durham by the "seventies", and Lord George Scott has recorded that driving blackgame was practised on the Buccleuch estates many years before 1866, and those drives, of course, included grouse. But driving was only practised at Cawdor and perhaps half a dozen other estates in Scotland by 1880. From that time onward, it began to be more and more the rule.

'The next stage in the history of grouse shooting comes between the 1880s and the Great [1914–1918] War. This was a period of luxury, and the old rough and ready methods of shooting began to go by the board, to the scandal of an elder generation.

'As grouse became more and more a source of profit to the Highland proprietor bringing to him his rents, to his retainers the money his tenant had spent up and down the glen, improvements began to be made in lodges and other arrangements.

'Things like "plenty of drying room and lots of hot water" and "comfortable beds" began to be insisted on in this period the end of which saw the introduction of the motor car, another not unimportant factor where lodges might be forty miles from a station.

'Very soon grouse shooting was a flourishing industry. Letting agencies sprang-up, keepers succeeded shepherds, the laird and his family moved out and the tenant and his family moved in.

'A bad letting year meant loss of considerable income and owners made moves to improve the value of their shooting.

'Moor management began to be systematically studied, heather burning was insisted on, vermin was kept down . . .

'In 1911 *The Grouse in Health and Disease* was published, as the result of the work of a committee under the chairmanship of Lord Lovat, after several years of careful research.'

The book remained the Charter of the Red Grouse and was the most complete record of the life of any one bird in existence. It exposed the cause of grouse disease and was a landmark in grouse-shooting history.

> 'Before the first war deer stalking represented the cream of Scottish sport. It was far luckier to get a stalking invitation than an invitation to shoot grouse. The cordon bleu deer stalker rather looked down on the grouse shooter. Today [1939] there can be no doubt the position is reversed . . . very many would prefer a day's grouse driving to a day's stalking.
>
> 'Also noticeable in this post-war period was the rise of the shooting syndicate. Many new shooters and others who wished to shoot with limited resources were saved by the formation of syndicates. Without syndicates hundreds of moors would have been unlet.'
>
> (*Grouse Shooting*)

However, important as individual factors may have been in themselves, it was the opportunity for potential profit in their coincidence that led to the improvements in husbandry (in Scotland particularly) in the second half of the nineteenth century. The supremacy of the sheep, whose introduction in the early 1800s had given rise to the misery and suffering of the highland clearances, was in many cases a fleeting one. John Guille Millais, fifty years before Martin Stephens, called the grouse 'a veritable golden goose'.

> 'Grouse have proved the greatest success of all birds of the chase, and their steady increase during the past fifty years is an achievement of which the game preserves may well be proud. A careful study of the bird's habits and requirements has shown the sportsman what may be done in the course of a few years to further the increase of his stock by good watching, vermin-trapping, and judicious heather-burning. The care bestowed on Highland moors during the last fifty years, with these necessary precautions, has made all the difference in changing desolate tracts of boggy moorland, on which a few stray birds contrived to eke out a precarious existence, surrounded as they were by Kites, Eagles and Foxes, into stretches of heathery moorlands, where heavy bags can now be obtained.
>
> 'Grouse then, may be said to be to the Highland laird the veritable golden goose, for such has become the esteem and pleasure with which grouse-shooting is looked upon by the "Sassenach", that immense tracts of country, the right to shoot over which could once have been had for a mere trifle, are now split up into several moors, each of which may perhaps command a rent of four figures.'

Millais' book, *Game Birds and Shooting Sketches,* contains more evidence of the author as a naturalist than a sportsman. The detailed descriptions of the behaviour of different species of birds suggest many patient hours of quiet observation and painstaking research. In his chapter on grouse, the only sporting reference is to flying kites!

> 'The flying-powers of Grouse, although at times extremely rapid, are far inferior in point of endurance to either Blackgame or Capercaillie. They seldom cover distances exceeding two miles at one stretch, unless unusually harassed in stormy weather, or scared from their ground by Hawks or the artificial Kite . . .
>
> 'Although shooting under the Kite has been much deprecated, it does not always follow that its use is ruination to a moor or in any degree unsportsmanlike. A shooting tenant will do more good than harm by the use of it for a couple of days at the end of the season, where driving is not practised and the birds are unapproachable. When only resorted to but once or twice during the shooting season it does not have any effect in driving the birds off the ground, as the continued practice of it would do, but only sends perhaps a few coveys of hens over the march: the latter, being far more terrified of the Kite than the cocks, take long flights and are all the better for having their lives spared; they remain away for the rest of the day on which they have been disturbed, but will return to their own moor the same evening to roost, or during the next day. It has, however, one drawback, which is, that if your neighbour happens to be shooting on that particular day, and comes across these coveys of hens, he can make great havoc amongst them. Should he be beating up towards the march over which the birds have lately come, they will then generally lie very close or rise before the guns and endeavour to break over the line rather than return to the moor from whence they have been scared.
>
> 'The best wind for working the Kite is one coming directly from behind the guns. The Kite should then be made to sail along in front of the centre of the line, about a hundred yards ahead, and when the birds rise, which they frequently do at a distance of about 70 or 80 yards, they come dashing back towards the guns at their greatest possible speed, affording some really pretty driven shots. Most birds will, however, sit close till the shooters are upon them, and then rise quickly behind or before, giving nice snipy shots and taking straight shooting.'

The great characteristic of the red grouse is that it behaves as if nature had bred it especially for the delight of British sportsmen – as if its evolution had been subject to some Pavlovian influence causing it to reproduce itself with the sport of the guns in mind. Charles Dixon calls it 'a thorough game bird and true sport-furnishing species'. He describes its habits in some detail.

> 'The Red Grouse (*Lagopus scoticus*) is confined to the British Islands where it inhabits the wild moorland districts throughout Great Britain and Ireland, except those counties of England that lie south and east of a line drawn from Bristol to Hull. Although inhabiting the Hebrides and the Orkneys, it is absent from the Shetlands . . .
>
> 'The Red Grouse is a thorough ground bird, although it may occasionally be seen sitting in the stunted willow, birch, and thorn trees, and is fond of perching on boulders or on the rough, "dry" walls that divide the moors from the highways

and upland pastures. In spite of the bird's abundance it does not make itself very conspicuous, and the inexperienced observer may wander over miles of moor without seeing many grouse. They skulk in the heather, and generally prefer to run out of harm's way instead of taking wing . . .

'At all times of the year the Red Grouse is socially inclined, and in autumn becomes to a great extent gregarious, "packing" towards the end of August, when it becomes more wary and wild. Previous to stormy weather these packs are found on the highest ground, but when the change arrives they seek the sheltered hillsides. During severe snowstorms the Red Grouse will burrow into the snow drifts for shelter.

'The note of the Red Grouse is very loud and highly characteristic, most frequently heard as the bird rises startled from the heather. It may best be expressed as a loud, clear, *go-bac go-bac bac-bac-bac*. Its crow, heard during the pairing season, and especially in the early morning, is slightly modified into a loud and clear *cok-ok-ok*. The cry of the female is a little more than a low croak.

'The food of the Red Grouse is chiefly composed of the green, tender tops of the ling (calluna) and the heather (erica); but various ground fruits are eagerly devoured in Autumn (the birds' droppings at this season staining the rocks dark purple) as well as the seeds of weeds; whilst during harvest and severe weather the birds will visit oat stubbles and even stack yards at some distance from their usual haunts. I have known Red Grouse to be taken in the streets of Sheffield during severe winters, and great numbers to be shot on farms and near dwelling houses several miles from the moorlands . . .

'The Red Grouse is singularly subject to what may well be termed a mysterious disease, seeing that its causes and nature are but imperfectly understood. This disease (which is said to have been traced to a parasitic worm, *Strongylus pergracilis*, breeding in the throat and rapidly spreading to the other organs), appears specially to attack the liver and the intestines; but whether the worm is the primary cause of the disorder seems by no means certain, for parasites of this character, if not of the same species, are often common in healthy birds.'

(*Game Birds and Wild Fowl*)

While the birds and beasts, *ferae naturae* are equipped to withstand all but the most severe conditions, civilised man is no longer so naturally well-endowed. It is in fact one of life's paradoxes that having one day complained bitterly about the inadequacy of the central heating he will the next voluntarily subject himself to extremes of discomfort, hardship and even danger in the name of sport.

J. H. Walsh's advice to grouse-shooters on the appropriate clothing for the moors, written a century ago, is interesting for the speculation it prompts about how little it might be changed if he were writing today.

'DRESS – For the purpose of grouse-shooting, with any prospect of a successful issue, the dress of the shooter is of great importance. None of the game birds in this country are so wary and so difficult to approach as the grouse; and an old

29. The Red Grouse (Lagopus scoticus, *white form*) *by Archibald Thorburn* (*1908*)

cock-bird will often defy the efforts of half a dozen sportsmen for many successive weeks, finally escaping to be the father of a future generation of clever ones. The colour of the clothes must therefore be attended to; but the most essential point is their suitability for preserving the health of the sportsman. In almost all cases, grouse frequent bleak and exposed moors, which are always cool, even in August, during windy and wet weather; mists and storms are constantly to be guarded against; and for these various reasons the material of the shooter's dress, throughout, should be woollen . . .

'Knickerbockers are found by experience to suit the walking over heather better than trousers by far, and are almost universal.

'Flannel should be worn next the skin as a precaution against the chill so often felt, when, on reaching the mountain-top, the skin reeking with the perspiration poured out on its ascent, is suddenly submitted to the searching powers of the wind prevailing there. I should therefore strongly advise flannel waistcoats and drawers however fine they may be, and, above all, worsted stockings. These last are not only necessary for the purpose of avoiding a chill to the feet, but they also are by far the best for walking purposes; cotton and thread, and even silk, are too hard for the skin, and will blister most feet in a very disagreeable manner. If the skin is very irritable, so as to render the woollen unpleasant to the sensations, a pair of silk socks may be worn under them; but the soft pad of the woollen material is necessary, to enable the shooter to wear the strong heavy shoe which is required, without suffering from it.

'For the feet there is nothing like the laced boot for those who are accustomed to have their ankles confined; the sole should be studded with nails; the heel, also, ought to be low, and resemble the ordinary walking shoe. All shooting-boots should be waterproof, as the dews or rains often compel the sportsman to submit his feet to a worse ordeal than a pail of water. In ordering shooting-boots, it is never desirable to procure them from a maker accustomed to consult appearances chiefly; on the contrary, a respectable cobbler is often the best man; but the leather is of more importance than any other point, and should be strong cow-calf, porpoise skin, or Russian leather . . .

'Let the shooter, some months before the season, provide himself with what will fit him, and let him wear them a little every day till they have taken the form of the feet; then let him put them carefully away, after having them dressed with a composition made of – boiled linseed oil, one pint; bee's wax and resin, of each, four ounces, melted together and stirred till cold.

'All shooting boots should have large-headed nails in the sole and heel, as both in greasy fallows and on bare rocks, the foot, without them, slips about in a disagreeable and even dangerous manner. It will insure their future fit, if the boots are wetted by walking into water before they are dressed with the composition; and in hot summer weather they may be suffered to dry on the feet, taking care to keep moving during that time, and to dry them thoroughly before dressing them. If the feet are very tender, and liable to excoriate, the best way is to soak them at night in hot alum and water, and in the morning to rub a little neats'-foot oil over them, before putting on the stocking.

'I have already said that the dress should be woollen; and any of the plain Scotch tweeds will answer the purpose, using the same material for trousers, waistcoat, and shooting-coat. The heather pattern is strongly recommended, from its resemblance to the general covet of the birds; but I believe that any plain and sombre colour will do, if neither too dark nor too light. Black and white alike strike the eye, by their contrast with the surrounding objects; but black and white check is as good a colour as any. The coat should have a strong patch of leather on each shoulder, for the gun to rest upon, and should be provided with pockets for cartridges; or if a belt is used for these, it is well to provide a flap to cover it, unless it is worn inside the coat. You will not require any game-pocket, because at the grouse-season, no game will bear the heat of the body without becoming speedily tainted.

'THE GUN should be of the breech-loading kind already described as suitable to every variety of open-shooting, but should be a hard-hitter, and the shot used No. 6 early in the season, followed by No. 5 later on. It is far better than the muzzle-loader, especially early in the season, as will be evident to those who have experienced the annoyance of waiting to load, while a scattered covey are rising one after another too fast to allow of more than two or three shots at them, and yet all within range.

'The other ACCESSORIES are, for your own person – merely the loaded cartridge-cases, with belt, dog-whistle, knife and dog-whip; and for your "gillie", as he is called in the North, a game-bag, dog-couples, some spare cartridges, gun-cover, and a Mackintosh coat.'

(*Manual of British Rural Sports*)

CHAPTER ELEVEN

The Partridge: Rearing and Shooting

There sprung a single Partridge – ha! she's gone!
Oh! Sir, you'd Time enough, you shot too soon;
Scarce twenty yards is open Sight! – for Shame!
Y'had shattered Her to Pieces with tight Aim!
Full forty Yards permit the Bird to go,
The spreading Gun will surer Mischief sow;
But, when too near the flying Object is,
You certainly will mangle it, or miss;
And if too far, you may so slightly wound,
To kill the Bird, and yet not bring to Ground.
(George Markland: *Pteryplegia, or The Art of Shooting Flying*, 1727)

IN HIS writings on the subject of partridge-shooting, J. H. Walsh, who is what Charles Dixon would describe as 'a sportsman of the old school', begins to offer some evidence for his choice of the *nom de plume* 'Stonehenge'.

'THE COMMON PARTRIDGE is too well known by appearance to need description. It is found nearly all over England, and in Scotland and Ireland, wherever there is inclosed land. In some counties, as, for instance, in Norfolk and Suffolk, it is so generally preserved as to be quite the pride of the locality, a good day's shooting being there considered the *beau idéal* of country pleasure. Nevertheless I never could see this beauty in Norfolk shooting; the birds are so tame and so plentiful, that nothing is required but the very moderate use of the legs and a good command over the gun; dogs are altogether at a discount, and are scarcely thought necessary to the sport except for retrieving and driving the stubbles. In my opinion, the expectation of true sport in partridge shooting is now for ever defeated, in consequence of the improved system of agriculture almost everywhere adopted. Formally, in every farm, during the month of September, nearly one-quarter was left with good (foul) stubbles, at least eight or ten inches high. Here there was a good cover as in turnips, or nearly so, and with the advantage that dogs were capable of finding their game without risk of running them up. Another very considerable proportion was left in rough fallow, undisturbed by the scuffle; and still another useful cover was met with in the shape of rough grass. But *nous avons changé tout cela:* the stubbles are now all "bagged", or mown, or machine-reaped, as bare as the back of your hand; the old stale fallow is no more; and the farm is so well stocked that in September no old feg containing grass-seeds is to be met with. Thus, however desirous we may be of finding our bird on the stubbles or fallows, we cannot succeed, for want of cover in the one and from the non-existence of the other. Besides, the science of farming is now carried to such a pitch, that no sooner is the corn off the ground than the plough is set to work; and, therefore, we often find our best stubbles, at the time of partridge-shooting, disturbed by three or four teams of horses with their attendant men, or, what is still worse, by the steam plough. No wonder, therefore, that the sportsman leaves the south, and betakes himself to a country equally full of game of even a superior quality to the partridge, and allowing the full beauties of the pointer and setter to be developed. There is, however, no more difficulty in preserving a good head of partridges now than there used to be; the increase of turnips and other green tops has more than counterbalanced the loss of the stubbles, if the mere facility of rearing and killing game only is considered; but to kill any number of partridges in the old style, with a brace of dogs finding them, is now out of the question. We often hear of more than 100 brace falling to one gun in one day; but how is this done? By using a lot of men to drive all the stubbles, and thus collecting the birds on a given number of acres of turnips, mangolds, or seed-clover, or some other green crop affording good lying for them. This is similar to the *battue* in principle, and, I think, more worthy of the butcher than the true sportsman. It is, in fact, the same spirit which leads to the use of the bagged fox or the trapped hare, though not, perhaps, quite so bad as those unmitigated Cockney tricks. It appears, to my limited capacity, that pigeon-trap shooting is quite as good a sport as this turnip-butchery, and it may be had much more easily, and at less expense; but, as General Hutchinson says, "every Englishman must have his prejudices", and whether this of mine is founded in truth or not is scarcely for me to say.

'THE RED-LEGGED PARTRIDGE, which is a species quite distinct from that just alluded to, and is even placed by some naturalists in a separate genus, is larger than the common bird; the bill, iris, and legs are of a bright vermilion; the back and top of the head are of a reddish-brown, approaching to a slate colour on the forehead and sides of the body; and of a pale ash colour on the breast and belly; the chin and throat are white, mottled with black; and there is a band of white over the eye. Various bars occur on the quill-feathers, of brown and grey, giving the bird a very party-coloured appearance. It is not so thick and plump as the common partridge, and differs in its habits. It is abundant on the Continent of Europe, and has been found as far off as Japan. It is more inclined to run than fly, and for that reason is a pest to the shooter, giving rise to unsteadiness in the dogs, and rarely leading to a good day's sport. It also often, by associating with the common partridge, teaches that bird its own bad manners. Unlike the common partridge, it perches on hedges and trees, but not so commonly as the pheasant, and always roosts on the ground. It was largely introduced into Suffolk in the last century on account of its hardihood and tendency to increase; but it runs too much even for the modern "walking-up" system, and is only now encouraged by those who confine their sport to "driving", for which purpose the "red-leg" is better adapted than the grey partridge.'

(*Manual of British Rural Sports*)

PERDIX CINEREA:

'Geographical distribution, British: the Partridge is a resident throughout the agricultural districts of the British Islands wherever it is preserved. It is absent from the Outer Hebrides, but has been introduced into the Orkneys.

'The great strongholds of the Partridge are the well-cultivated districts where the fields are not too large, the hedges dense and affording cover during the breeding season, and where grain is grown in abundance. It may aptly be described as a bird of the farm lands, although it is by no means rare in many moorland districts, and in some counties is fairly plentiful on commons and rougher ground.

'It shows no partiality for wooded districts, and is so thoroughly a ground bird that the known instances of its perching in trees are remarkably few. The Partridge lives on the ground, and at all times shows more or less reluctance to fly. Should danger threaten, it prefers to squat close to the earth or to run with great quickness to the shelter of standing crops or thick hedges, where its movements are so rapid as to enable it to elude pursuit with ease. When flushed, however, it not only rises quickly and suddenly but flies well and with no small speed, its rounded wings as they rapidly beat the air making a loud whirring noise. Sometimes the bird holds its wings stiff and arched and skims along for a short distance before alighting.

'The Partridge obtains its food on the ground, and is most active in search of it during morning and early evening . . . Its food consists of shoots and leaves of herbage, insects and their larvae, snails, grain and seeds, and various wild fruits.

'From the time the broods are grown until they are thinned down by the sportsman, the Partridge lives in coveys of varying size, which feed and sleep in company. At night each covey has a particular resort to which the birds retire to rest, usually sleeping in a circle on the ground, each with its head turned outwards so that approaching danger is readily observed.

'The note of the Partridge, which is uttered by both sexes, is a particularly shrill Kir-r-rrrick, most frequently uttered towards evening and in the pairing season.

'In the districts where the birds are not persistently chased by the sportsman the Partridges show gregarious tendencies during autumn and winter, several coveys joining into a flock. During severe weather the Partridge will visit the rick-yards, and is occasionally met with in very unusual localities, tempted thither by food. When fired at this bird has been known to fly out to sea for a considerable distance, returning to land in a very exhausted condition. Before the introduction of the modern reaping machine and turnip drill, when the weedy stubbles were left long by the sickle, and turnips were sown broadcast, Partridges were shot over pointers and setters; but now, when the straw is shaved off almost flush with the grounds, and the stubble ploughed as soon as the crop is harvested (unless sown with clover), and root crops are grown in rows or "ridges" dogs are of little service, and driving has been resorted to. This is regretted by some sportsmen of the old school chiefly, but certainly preferred by the more modern gunner; especially so as this method of Partridge shooting serves to prolong the season of sport and to furnish birds in prime condition.'

(*Game Birds and Wild Fowl*)

On the subject of partridge shooting, Peter Hawker has some characteristic things to say which, aside from the further fascinating glimpse they provide of the Colonel himself, paint a picture of what could as well be another planet as England a century and a half ago.

'Most young sportsmen, and many old ones, fancy that nothing great can be done on the first day, without they go out as soon as they can see to distinguish a bird from a dog. This may possibly be necessary for those who start from a *town*, where two or three unfortunate coveys are to be contended for by half the lawyers, doctors, schoolmasters, sporting parsons, and tradesmen in the place; but under other circumstances, this is the very *worst* method that can be adopted.

'In the first place, the birds being at this time on the feed, will very seldom lie well. By your springing them from the run, the covey are pretty sure to take wing altogether; and being once disturbed in this state, it becomes, afterwards, much more difficult to disperse them, than if they had been left quiet till the dew had dried on the stubble. Secondly, you throw off with long shots, instead of fair ones; which, to say the least of it, is not a favourable beginning, either for yourself or dogs. Thirdly, for one who may have no relay of pointers or setters, it should be recollected how much better bestowed would be the work which he takes out of them while slaving to little purpose in the dew of the morning, if he reserved it for the afternoon. This, from about three till six, is the time of day (in the early part of the season) that all the best shots are to be got. The birds are then scattered, and driven to the low grounds and meadows; where, with steady dogs, they may be found one or two at a time, and kicked up as fast as you can load and fire . . .

'Much game as I have seen killed in a September day, I do not recollect one solitary instance of anything extraordinary being done very early in the morning. Many people tell me about killing ten and even twenty brace before breakfast; but I never yet had the fortune to see the chance for such a performance; because the dew is seldom off before eight or nine o'clock. It would be bad manners to doubt their word; so I will conclude that they mean before some *déjeuner à la fourchette,* at 12; or perhaps before their breakfast on the following day. With regard to where and how we are to beat for game, &c., &c., it would now be unnecessary to inform even a schoolboy; and, indeed, others having mentioned all particulars, is a sufficient reason for my not imposing on the reader's patience with what he will have seen before, and what, to describe, would lead me into the very subject of other sporting-authors. Suffice it therefore to say, that the great object is, first to have good markers judiciously placed, and then to disperse the birds; the best way to do which, is to head your dogs, by taking an extensive circle. The second is, to make no more noise than what cannot absolutely be avoided, by doing as much by signal and whistling, and as little by hallooing as possible. Thirdly, go first on hills to find, and drive down from them, the birds, and then in vales to kill then. Fourthly, when distressed for partridges, in a scarce country; at the end of the season, take a horse, and gallop from one turnip-field to another, instead of regularly slaving after inaccessible coveys. After a storm, as soon as the ground is dry, or the next day, birds will lie in a calm; and, after a calm, they will lie in windy weather. Birds are frequently as much on the listen as on the watch; and this is why, towards the end of the season, we sometimes do best in boisterous weather.

30. Partridges: Pairing Time *by J. G. Millais* (*1908*)

'Many an excellent shot has come home with an empty bag, under the following circumstances. He has gone out in a cold raw day, and found that the birds were scarce and wild, and that even in turnips they would not lie. But had he then tried one kind of land, to which almost every man, as well as his dog, has a dislike – the fallows, he might possibly have got some good double shots; because the birds, finding it a misery to run here, particularly if he walked across the fallows, will sometimes lie till they are sprung the fairest possible shots.

'Let me conclude, under this head, with a few observations as to taking horses into the field. If birds are wild, a sportsman, who goes out with his man, and has no other attendant, will bring in more game if he contrives to mount that man, or rather a light boy, behind him; because, the moment the dog stands, he can then dismount, (by throwing his right leg over the horse's neck) and leave the man in full possession of the Rosinante, instead of being encumbered with a led horse, which frequently precludes the possibility of his galloping on to mark a covey, or follow up a towering bird. Moreover, it requires no conjurer to discover that two horses make more noise than one; and all noise, after the first few weeks, is the ruin of sport. The gentleman with his stud would say, – Why not have three horses? This, I admit, is a more dignified way of taking the field, than the subaltern turn-out of the Johnny Trot behind; but then we have the clatter of three horses, with the chatter of two servants' tongues, an increase of noise that would set the birds on the run; and it would be as vain to attempt the suppression of the one as the other. In short, I would back the double-mounted gent. against the great squire and his stud. Two on a horse, and the "cad" to be helmsman, is an excellent way of giving the shooter the liberty of his hands, the moment a covey springs unexpectedly. Recollect too, in wood about five feet high, a mounted man can shoot, where one on his legs cannot see; and again, if a hare runs straight away, she may be killed ten yards further, if you are well above her, and catch her head and pole clear of her high rump. All these little *et ceteras* are what we may call the finish: as to ordinary sporting, in the present day, we may as well tell a man how to eat his dinner. Double-mounted markers are always ready to act in any country. I took the hint from the French cavalry, who had frequently riflemen mounted up behind them, for the purpose of what, as a foxhunter, I should call "drawing the covers," . . .

'P.S., 1844 . . . within these few years, the shooting has so fallen off, that we can rarely get our ten brace even on the 1st of September. Many people say, "How do you account for this?" Why, the reason is obvious, from a combination of circumstances, all against the sportsman; viz. the "march of intellect" in poaching – a sale-of-game act without a summary proceeding against trespassers who are *without* guns – the increased demand for partridges' eggs – the facility of railway – the farmers cutting up the grass-banks for fuel, and thereby driving the birds to breed in open fields, at the mercy of hawks, wet weather, and scythes – putting among their seed-wheat vitriol (to prevent smut), which poisons many birds, that would otherwise be left to breed – and mowing their wheat, by which means they destroy all fine stubbles for shooting! – In short, the only wonder is that we have any birds at all; and the scarcity will, no doubt, increase every year, unless some alteration be made in the game-laws, and the landlords adopt certain restrictions in their leases, taking care, at the same time, to make amends to the farmer for any new clauses they may choose to introduce; or he will either destroy the game himself, or encourage his labourers to do so.'

(*Instructions to Young Sportsmen*)

The continuing story of the rescue of the partridge is now being scripted by the Game Conservancy under their 'Partridge Survival scheme', but it has had many previous authors, in whose work Hawker, although not much of a conservator himself, would have been keenly interested. C. J. Cornish, writing in 1903, describes the 'Assisted Nature' system:

'Where it is desired to get up a large head of partridges on ground suitable for their increase, some *via media* between artificial rearing and leaving the birds entirely alone is highly desirable. This will be found in the system, entirely on natural lines, but aided by human care and intervention, pursued for many years with extraordinary success on Lord Ashburton's famous Grange estate near Alresford, Hants . . .

'The first step is the guarantee that the sitting partridge shall be as secure from injury or disturbance as any bird possibly can be made by killing off its enemies. To the harmless partridge and to its eggs these are fatally destructive. A bird will leave the hedge where she has nested, if, when she has laid two or three eggs, one is sucked by a rat or a weasel, and move off into the grass to lay the rest, where the nest will be cut out. If put off its nest in the first day's sitting, it will probably forsake. Consequently at the Grange every hedgerow and bank is watched, and at the least sign of a rat or weasel about it is heavily trapped; and all the year round baited traps, perhaps thirty to every hundred acres, are set, and the vermin practically exterminated.

'Every sitting partridge then becomes practically a living incubator, ready to turn into an admirable mother later. The direct assistance to nature then begins in the following way. Eggs from very dangerous places, and all eggs cut out or left in nests accidentally disturbed, are taken up. These disturbances are reduced to a minimum, but when birds are so thick that there are perhaps twenty nests down one long hedge, some must inevitably meet with accidents. These eggs are placed in the nests of sitting birds, the number being made up to as many as twenty-two, of which the bird will often hatch every egg.

'It may well be asked, "How can you treat a wild partridge as if she were a hen, and why does she not forsake when put off her nest to place the other eggs in it?"

'It is on the answer to this that the success of the method depends, and that answer lies in a curious natural habit of the sitting partridge, for the discovery of which Marlow must be given the entire credit. When a partridge begins to sit she will probably forsake if disturbed in the first twenty-four hours. But after that time she undergoes a change in physical condition, and becomes "broody" just like a hen. If put off gently she will move about close by, trailing her wings and clucking; and often the birds will allow the eggs to be placed gently under them by hand, without leaving the nest at all.

'The use to which this fact is put has been stated above. But it is obvious that to succeed incessant vigilance on the part of the keepers is needed. They must find every nest if possible, and know exactly when the first eggs were laid, and when the bird ought to begin to sit. But when once that is done the complete absence of vermin will ensure astonishing results, unless the season should be exceptionally wet and cold. About 900 acres is the beat looked after by each partridge keeper at the Grange, and this takes him all his time. The head keeper rides from beat to beat, questions the men, and requires them to show him that any nests which he may ask news of are safe. What has been done on the Grange shooting is well known. The record bag of partridges killed in the county has been shot there.

'The ground is good, but not so good as much of the Norfolk land. It is lightish soil, with some red clay and chalk. It should be noted that when nests in the grass are cut out, the state of incubation must be roughly determined, in order to put the eggs into nests in which the bird has been sitting for a like period. This can be done by breaking an egg and seeing how far the embryo has developed, which to an experienced keeper is a fairly safe guide. I believe Marlow can tell by trying them in water, on some plan of his own. Or all the eggs can be placed under a sitting bird, and her eggs, the condition of which is known, can be transferred to other birds which have been sitting for the same time.'

(*Partridge Rearing*)

Debate about which is the best sport is as fruitless, though doubtless equally as entertaining over after-dinner drinks, as that about the sportsmen themselves. Dedicated grouse-shooters will scarcely give place to the 'softer' options, while dedicated shooters like Colonel Hawker are clearly more interested in the application of the science of ballistics to the art of shooting, whether the target be hares or Frenchmen.

Certainly, as a table delicacy, the partridge has always been very highly regarded, so perhaps Daniel should be left to sum up its place in sport.

' "PARTRIDGES," says Willoughby, "hold the principal place in the entertainment of Princes, without which their feasts are deemed ignoble and vulgar; the French are so fond of, and value them so highly, as utterly to despise the best spread table, if Partridges are wanting." However, it might be in the time of this Historian, Partridges are now too common in France, to have that consequence attached to them, and their former high station at the festive board, is supplied by luxuries of a more compound invention. In England, where the Partridge is both scarcer and dearer, it is a favourite delicacy. The old distich asserts,

If the Partridge had the Woodcock's thigh,
It would be the best bird that e'er did fly;

and the desire of appropriating it to certain classes of the community, has induced laws to be made for its preservation, no way harmonizing, in the judgement of many distinguished lawyers, with the general spirit of English legislation; were these birds solely nourished on those grounds that belong to the person whose entertainments they improve, the man who fed might claim them, with some show of justice, and like a peacock, or a Turkey, they might then be ranked as private property; however, the law has taken Partridges (wild as they are) under its preservation, and the only difference now is, that one is fed upon the farms, the other in the yards; that these are contented captives, those, servants that have the power to change their master, by changing their abode.

(*Rural Sports*)

CHAPTER TWELVE

Minor Game Birds: Capercaillie, Black Grouse, Ptarmigan and Woodcock

THE NATURAL wealth of Scotland is probably best seen in the continuing presence of the lesser members of game bird families. Ptarmigan, black grouse, and capercaillie are relatives of the red grouse and have all at one time been resident throughout Great Britain, and now almost exclusively Scottish sport (black grouse are still to be found in Wales and some remoter parts of England).

Their comparative rarity is evident from Hugh Gladstone's records.

> '[The Capercaillie] species, re-introduced and now confined to Scotland, became extinct there about 1762 and in Ireland about 1760. A stuffed cock Capercaillie, in the Hancock Museum, Newcastle-on-Tyne, would appear to be the only specimen now in existence of our indigenous Scottish Capercaillies. The species was re-introduced to Scotland from Sweden in 1827, or 1828, and in succeeding years: the most successful importations being made to Taymouth (Perthshire) in 1837 and 1838 . . . Since that date the species has firmly established itself in Scotland and has extended and is extending its range.
>
> 'At Dunkeld 69 Capercaillies were killed on the Craig and Barns and Ladywell beats (Perthshire) on 4th November 1910, by seven guns . . . This is believed to constitute the record bag for Great Britain since the 107 said to have been killed at Fothringham (Angus) in one day in November 1894, were in reality the result of three consecutive days' shooting. The statements that 150 Capercaillies have been killed at Blackhall (Kincardineshire), and 84 and 73 at Monymusk (Aberdeenshire) in one day are erroneous: the most killed at Blackhall was on 14th December 1910 when 60 were killed and 63 and 54 were killed at Monymusk in 1910 and 1911 respectively . . .
>
> 'It was long thought that the largest bag of Blackgame (black grouse) obtained in one day was that of 247, besides 69 other head of game, killed at Glenwharrie (Dumfriesshire) on 4th October 1869 by eleven guns . . . I have been told that this bag of 247 Blackgame included over 200 cocks.
>
> 'This record, however, was beaten about 1860, when 252 Blackgame were killed in a day's driving on Cannock Chase (Staffordshire) . . .
>
> 'The largest bag of Blackgame, obtained in recent years, is 114 (of which 74 were cocks) . . . at Auchenbrac (Dumfriesshire) on 25th October 1910 . . .

J G Millais 1907

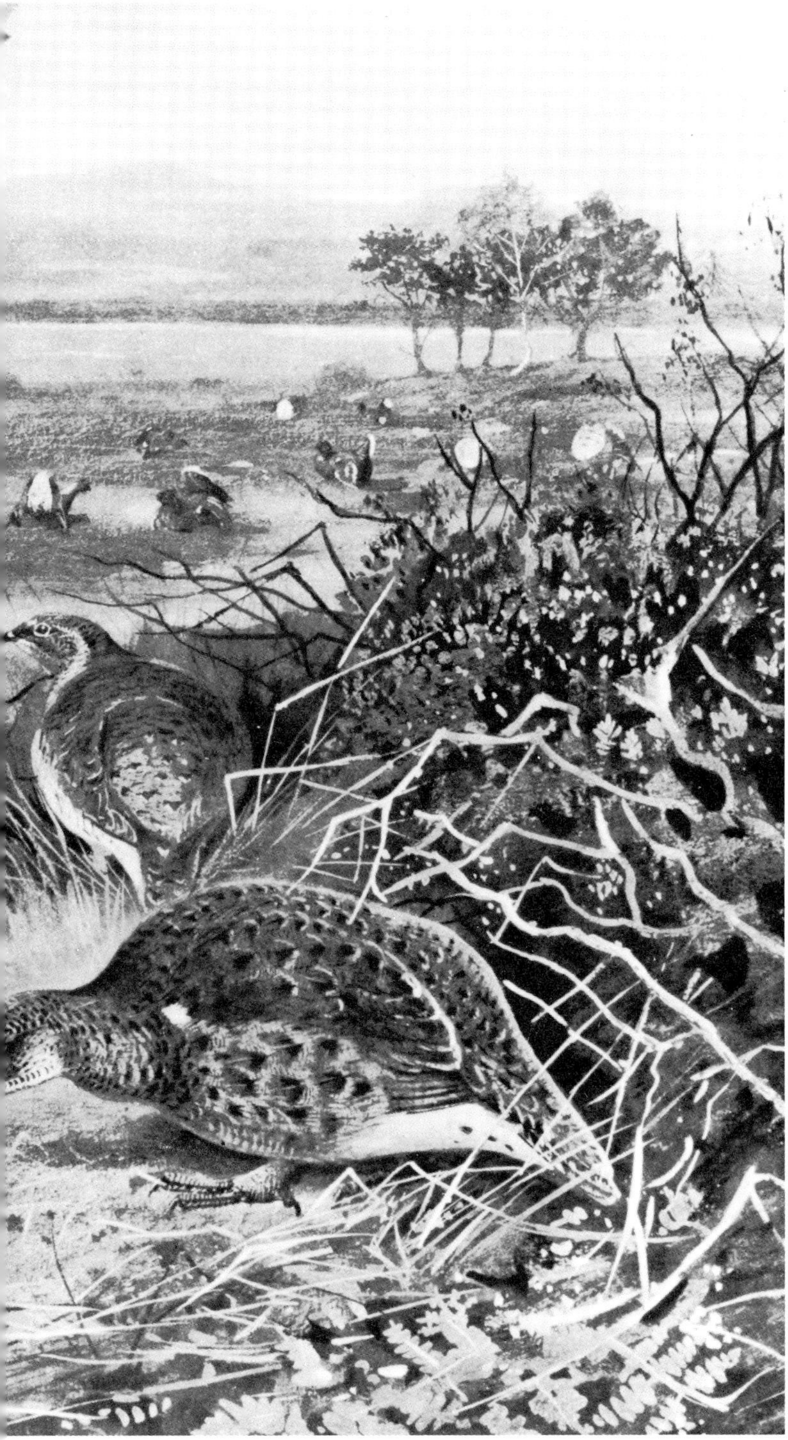

31. Black Grouse at the Playing Ground *by J. G. Millais (1907)*

> 'No less than 18 Blackgame are alleged to have been killed at one shot; this extraordinary feat is said to have been performed by a Mr. Wilson, in Dumfries-shire, who fired just as a large batch of Blackgame settled on a rail running along the top of a stone dyke: the birds' heads were looking in different directions – "heids and thraws" as the Scots express the position.'

Knox's *Game Birds and Wild Fowl* (1850) contains some interesting notes on both capercaillie and ptarmigan.

> 'The noble capercaillie, or cock of the wood (*tetrao urogallus*), after having disappeared from the Scottish forests about sixty years ago, has now been restored through the spirited exertions of a few large landed proprietors, among whom Lord Breadalbane stands preeminent.
>
> 'The successful establishment of the pheasant in England, though a native of the distant shores of the Caspian sea and even of the yet more remote regions of Cathay, might appear to encourage the hope that a similar attempt would, under certain restrictions, prove equally so with the great game bird of the North. But the wild and roving habits of the capercaillie are less favourable to naturalization in the highly cultivated districts of England than those of the comparatively docile Colchican. The capercaillie is essentially a forester. He shuns the open plain, and scorns such a limited range as could be provided by any artificial plantations for which the heaths and commons of the southern parts of England might be adapted, while in the pinewoods, and extensive tracts of the Highland forests he can yet find space to roam comparatively at large. Even the craggy mountains of North Wales would not appear to offer him a favourable resting place, for though their wild grandeur and lofty peaks would seem to have tempted the ptarmigan – so peculiarly a mountaineer in his habits – yet from some cause, as yet imperfectly understood, this member of the grouse family seems to have abandoned the Welsh hills; and even their loftiest eminences, being so bleak and destitute of trees, would fail to attract the capercaillie. Nevertheless, as numerous wide-spreading plantations of larch and fir have of late years been formed on the hill sides, in some of the larger estates of Caernarvon-shire, Merionethshire, &c., it is not perhaps too much to hope that they may be tenanted in some future day by the gigantic Norwegian.
>
> 'Some English proprietors have indeed attempted the introduction of the cock of the wood – but ineffectually. So many circumstances must combine to conduct the experiment to a happy issue, that the absence or failure of any of these conditions has in several cases led to disappointment of the most sanguine expectations. One of the most essential requisites however, and that which is absolutely the "*sine qua non*", is a vast range of pine forest, a moderate or even a wide, extent of moor and heath, though interspersed with large plantations, is insufficient for the bold range of the capercaillie. He is not to be restrained within ordinary boundaries, but soon wanders beyond the circuit of any limited protection; when his large size, comparatively defenceless habits, and tempting

singularity of appearance, expose him to many casualties, and thus it has but too often happened that the endeavours to establish this species, by the introduction of a few birds of both sexes into a circumscribed territory, have been, by some unlucky disaster, crushed in the outset.

'Through the kindness of a relative of Lord Breadalbane, I am enabled to add a few particulars connected with the present state and condition of the capercaillie at Taymouth (July 1850), furnished by the intelligent head keeper, Mr. Guthrie . . . Mr. Guthrie found that the treatment of the chicks, after the eggs had been hatched under domestic hens, was attended with much more difficulty than in the case of the pheasant. Experience showed him that it was necessary to move the coops to different parts of the forest according to the state of the weather; placing them, on a sunny day, under the shadow of trees or among tall grass or fern; but during damp or wet weather removing them to dry, bare, or sandy spots. While transporting them from one place to another he "put the chicks into a small woollen bag, and the hen into a basket covered with a cloth to keep her in the dark." When a fortnight or three weeks had elapsed he did not think it necessary to move the coops. He remarks, "After a time I gave the young birds very little food out of hand, except wild berries, and as soon as I got them to feed on the larch branches, I considered them safe. The Scotch fir is rather hard for their bills when young."

'In 1838 and 1839, Lord Breadalbane received from Norway fifty-four adult capercaillies; about two-thirds of which were females. Some of them were liberated in the forest, and others kept in a large aviary for the purpose of procuring the eggs. The plan of placing these in the nests of grey hens, subsequently pursued by Mr. Guthrie, proved eminently successful. The birds have steadily increased of late years, and now "all the old woods about Taymouth Castle are full of capercaillie, such as Drummond Hill, Kenmore Hill, Croftmorraig Hill, &c. Several migrate every season down to Strath Tay, Blair Athol, Dunkeld and the woods about Crieff"; so that the truly noble enterprise originally undertaken by Lord Breadalbane has been crowned with perfect success, and the king of the game birds may now be said to be restored to his hereditary dominions . . .

'There are not many sportsmen who devote much time to the exclusive pursuit of the ptarmigan; for, though naturally unsuspicious and easy of approach, yet the toil to be endured and difficulties to be overcome before these Alpine heights can be reached, are much increased by the impossibility of following the birds from one rocky corry to another, separated perhaps by a giddy precipice, over the edge of which they have suddenly disappeared from the view of the wearied shooter. A circuit of considerable extent must frequently be taken, and many a steep acclivity or dangerous descent encountered, before they can be found, again; while there is small chance of relieving this tedious interval by a stray shot at any other bird or quadruped, except the grey hare, who seems to share with the ptarmigan the occupation of these inhospitable regions, while they both undergo a nearly analogous change in their seasonal variations of fur and feather.

'It is certainly a remarkable circumstance in the natural history of our game birds, and a striking instance of the merciful dispensations of Providence, that those which inhabit the most northern and inclement quarters are the earliest in season; or, in other words, arrive first at full growth, and are therefore soonest enabled to brave the rigours of the coming winter. Thus, the young ptarmigan is able to fly before the red grouse poult can flutter above the heather. The latter, again, when strong on the wing, has fallen in thousands before the gun of the sportsman, ere its report can be legally heard among the birchen glens and the lower valleys where the black-cock loves to dwell; while he, in his turn, now come to maturity, may be bagged nearly a fortnight before the partridge; who has been peppered throughout the length and breadth of the land for a whole month, before the gorgeous pheasant – who as an exotic might have been suspected of precocity – is considered ripe for slaughter.

'Most persons have noticed the vast numbers of ptarmigan which appear in the shops of the London dealers, and in the stalls of the principal metropolitan markets, during the latter part of winter and the early months of spring, even as late occasionally as the beginning of May; but comparatively few are aware that scarcely one of these birds has been killed on the Scottish mountains. They are imported from Lapland and Norway: the greater number from the western ports of the latter country . . .

'The profit to the importer must be great, as a single ptarmigan, which is seldom disposed of in London for less than two shillings or two and sixpence, is sold in the market at Drammen for the trifling sum of fourpence. Strange as it may appear, all these birds are taken in separate horse-hair nooses during the winter; and so brisk a traffic is carried on by the peasantry at that season, that one of them, we are told, will set from five hundred to a thousand of these snares.'

(*Game Birds and Wild Fowl*)

But of all the minor game birds most sportsmen would probably put the woodcock in pride of place. A 'right and left' at woodcock is to the shooter what a hat-trick is to a cricketer or a hole-in-one to a golfer. The double right and left scored by Lord Balfour of Burleigh at Kennet in 1890 when four woodcock were flushed towards him simultaneously seems likely to stand as a record. Hawker describes the pursuit of woodcock with good spaniels as 'the fox-hunting of shooting!' but then curiously confines himself to a miserly two hundred or so words on the subject. John Watson, in his book *Poachers and Poachings,* gives more detailed information.

'At the time of the heaviest bird migrations in autumn, vast flocks of woodcocks pitch on the English coasts. They stay through the winter, and in spring the majority again cross the wild North Sea *en route* to their northern breeding haunts . . .

'In coming to this country, woodcocks generally travel in the night and

32. The Ptarmigan (Lagopus mutus, *adult male and female, summer plumage*) *by Archibald Thorburn (1908)*

against a head-wind. Those which are exhausted pitch upon the east coast, and here lie resting until nightfall, when they pass on. The probability is that if these birds had not experienced a rough passage they would not have touched the eastern seaboard, but would have kept well in the upper currents, of the air, and first dropped down in our western woods or even those of Ireland . . .

'Every sportsman knows that woodcocks are here to-day, gone to-morrow. He often finds that where there were plenty yesterday not a single 'cock remains. Ireland, perhaps, affords the best shooting. It was here that the Earl of Clermont shot fifty brace in one day. This feat was the result of a wager; and the bag was made by two o'clock in the afternoon, with a single-barrelled flint-lock. The birds were shot in a moist wood; and it is in such spots on the mild west coast that the woodcock finds its favourite haunt. In England the birds affect coppice-woods, frequenting most those which are wet, and such as have rich deposits of dead and decaying leaves. Most of these copses are of oak and birch and hazel, and being only of a few years' growth are thick in the top. Killing 'cock, as they dash through the twigs of these and seldom rising above the bushes, is one great test of a shooters' skill. Then the birds have a habit of dropping down at a short distance, which almost invariably deludes the inexperienced gunner. When they are put up from their resting places during the day the flight is rapid; at evening it is slow. It is now that they are easiest to shoot; though in some parts of the country they are still taken in nets as they fly at dusk through the paths of the woods . . .

'None of the denizens of the woods conforms better or more closely to its environment. The browns and duns and yellows of its plumage all have their counter-part in the leaves among which it lies; and it has been pointed out that the one conspicuous ornament of the bird is covered by a special provision from the gaze of those for whose admiration it is not intended. This is the bright colouring of the tail feathers, which cannot be seen except at the will of the bird or in flight. Its protection lacks in one thing, however, and that is its large dark eye; this is full, bright, and (so to speak) obtrusive. It is not often that a special provision of this kind is injurious to its owner; but the lustre which beams from the woodcock's eye is apt to betray its presence, and even to negative the advantage of its protective colouring. This has long been known. Hudibras has it that:

'Fools are known by looking wise,
As men find woodcocks by their eyes . . .

'One of the most interesting traits about the woodcock is the fact of its occasionally conveying its young through the air; which is done by only one or two other birds. This is no recent discovery. The fact was known as early as the middle of last century; though Gilbert White rightly surmised that those observers were mistaken who fancied the young were conveyed either by or in the bill. It is just as erroneous, however, to substitute the claws, as some have

33. Woodcock Shooting (*19th-century engraving by Howitt*)

done, for the bill. The truth is, that when the parent bird wishes to convey her young one from a place of danger to one of safety, the tiny thing is gently pressed between the feet and against the breast, the aid of the bill being resorted to only when the burden has been hastily taken up. In this way the whole of the brood is sometimes removed from one part of a wood to another, if the birds have been much disturbed. This trait may be confirmed by any one who will look out the bird in its haunts, and is all the more interesting as it seems to be quite an acquired one. The bird is in no way adapted to transport its young through the air.'

(*Poachers and Poaching*)

Charles Dixon's account of the *Scolopax rusticula* includes much information on the bird's amazing migratory habits, discriminating however between the birds which breed in Britain and those which do not.

'Speaking from a naturalist's point of view, and with a full knowledge of the habits of birds during the moulting season, I should say emphatically that the Woodcocks breeding in the British Islands are stationary, that is, in the sense of not crossing the seas. I am glad to say that this opinion is confirmed by several intelligent gamekeepers, on whose ground the bird breeds in fair numbers every season. After the breeding season is over the Woodcock is a most skulking bird until its moult is completed; in this respect it resembles the Snipe. Not only so, but many of these resident Woodcocks are actually breeding even before the return migration of this species in spring, when the birds that breed further north pass our Islands on their way thither. The migrations of the Woodcock are both marked and regular. The bird may be traced leaving its winter quarters in the Mediterranean basin at Gibraltar in the west during the latter half of February, and in Asia Minor in the east during the first half of March. We find it in the British Islands on its way north in March, and it reaches Scandinavia by the end of that month or early April. The return migration in autumn, which is much more pronounced and noticeable than the vernal one, begins early in October, and continues with varying intensity through the month into the first half of November.

'. . . The Woodcock almost invariably migrates by night, up wind, and at a considerable elevation. This species is seldom or never caught in the flight nets, because it continues its lofty course until over dry land, and then drops down almost perpendicularly into the cover below. I have met with great numbers of tired-out Woodcocks in the early morning before actual sunrise on the shores of the Wash, skulking in the hedge-bottom amongst the drifts of autumn leaves, or on the sea banks amongst the long dry grass. Here they generally remain, if not much disturbed, until the evening, and then, under the cover of darkness, continue their flight inland to their favourite and more suitable winter haunts. Many migrating Woodcocks come to grief at the lighthouses, attracted by the glare of the lanterns. The Woodcock very often arrives on our coasts, especially in autumn, in considerable numbers, or "rushes", but the bird, notwithstanding, is eminently a solitary one, even on passage, and these unusual arrivals are caused by a prolonged spell of unfavourable weather detaining them on Continental Europe and causing them to accumulate whilst waiting for a favourable passage. As soon as this is presented, all start off, eager to get to their journey's end, and consequently arrive simultaneously on our coasts, but as soon as they reach land they separate and each bird, or at most a pair, retire to their own particular haunts. Even in districts where the Woodcock is common during winter no gregarious tendencies are ever observed, and the birds are flushed with rare exceptions one after the other from certain favoured spots.'

(*Game Birds and Wild Fowl*)

CHAPTER THIRTEEN

Man's Sporting Character

'Be a good animal, true to your animal instincts.'

(D. H. Lawrence)

ALTHOUGH Herbert Byng Hall, writing at the time of Dickens, in the full flood of Victorian England's self-esteem, might have found fault with this Laurentian simplification, he was able to trace a direct link between the healthy outdoor life of the field and the continuing glories of British arms. In the following light-hearted chronicle of the nation's hunting history, he makes due acknowledgement to God's benevolence in this matter – though not specifically to Diana's.

'As the love of liberty induced our forefathers to become warriors, in like manner necessity compelled them to pursue, for the means of subsistence, the antlered monarch of the mountain, and the feathered tribe of the woodland. Indeed, the fact scarcely needs comment, that the activity and physical energy acquired from the pursuit of game, comprising every species of outdoor amusement termed sport, has, even to the present day, greatly contributed to that success which, under God's blessing, the armies of England have, and it is to be hoped ever will maintain, over those of foreign powers.

'During the period termed The Golden Age, our ancestors looked on the chase not only as a means of diversion, as by peers and commoners of the present age implied, or as a means of unlawful gain by poachers and pot-hunters, but simply as that which nature had liberally provided them for the well stocking of their larders, and the consequent sustenance of themselves or their followers. Nevertheless, they sported, in every sense of the word; and, by this active and manly pursuit – which caused them to be constantly under the canopy of heaven, in all weathers and during all seasons – they gained health, strength and nerve, for the more serious bloodshed of the battle-field.

'Dwelling during the summer months on the moorland or the mountain-top, when the rigours of winter approached they sought the sheltered valley and the glen, no millionnaire, with boundless acres – no unnecessary preserver of pheasants, and consequently, in many cases, destroyer of foxes – no velveteen-clad forester presented himself in person, or by the ruinous arm of the law, to disturb their wandering footsteps o'er the land of liberty. Ramblers in pursuit of game, no circumscribed limit for their sport was marked; their footsteps were free and unmolested – killing all they could, and eating all they killed. Those were not days of entails, or rent-rolls – no agents – no pilfering lawyers: unthinking, unshackled – free, wandering – merry lads were they. Industrious labour was, however, soon taught by nature to appreciate the gifts which she so bountifully supplied, and they, good men! with equal bounty appropriated; for, in those days, men hunted as they fought, and fought as they hunted – the best sportsman killed the most game and ate it; the best fighter, having won the battle, selected the best land and kept it. Many centuries have, however, elapsed – having a bad memory, we forget how many – since that pleasant sporting and fighting era. It is, nevertheless, vastly agreeable to reflect, as we now write in an easy chair, that it was long, long ago. We refer more particularly to the fighting; for, as regards the hunting and shooting, the love of rural sports then engendered in the hearts of Britons, has, from age to age, been handed down from generation to generation, and the passion burns in the breasts of Englishmen with an ardour undiminished; and a very pleasant passion it is, without fear of contradiction; but, like all other passions, it is sometimes sadly abused. In fact, the transports which excite the mind of all true lovers of field sports, at the relation of a glorious day's fox-hunting – a good run with harriers – a shooting excursion – a coursing meeting – indeed, any sporting details, to all a source of amusement, to most is a source of unmitigated delight.

' "The Golden Age" defunct, we come to the Middle Age. Then there were kings with their horses, and hounds, and henchmen; and they sallied forth from their castles and palaces with a noble retinue of fair ladies and bold barons, and they brought a stag to bay; and the king looked on, and the ladies looked pleased, and the barons blew their horns, and they all went home to dinner. And the next day, the weather being fair and the sky clear, the palfreys stood caparisoned before the baronial hall, and a sprinkling of sporting neighbours and pages were in attendance, and they all went forth to a hawking expedition, *selon le règle* of sporting barons in baronial times.

'Then came the Age of Squires, real *bona fide* squires – not squires in their present undefined title, but real solid squires, with their packs of hounds, and well filled stables of hunters, and their equally well filled cellars and larders; and we are told they rose before day break and started to hunt the fox; and that they rode some twenty miles to covert on a strong, half-bred, docked-tailed horse, which identical animal also carried them through a long and hard day's chase, and home again. After which, they hospitably and bountifully entertained their friends as well as themselves, with barons and sirloins of beef, and sundry bottles of good old port. These gentlemen had robust limbs, fat faces, and red noses; and their sporting costume was generally a very thick pair of yellowish ancestral buckskins, with brown tops to their boots. They invariably attended the parish church on the Sabbath, whatever might be the weather; and afterwards, in the society of the parson, who was always a Sunday guest at the squire's table, they drank two bottles of port – to the prosperity of the chase, in the first instance, and then to the king's health; and were termed, perhaps justly so, by their neighbours, good and honest men, who injured none but themselves; and, as this injury was, of course, the fault of the port, they were sinless.

'Swearing and tippling, in those days, were considered simply as sporting accomplishments; to be d-----d by a master of foxhounds was merely to be addressed in sporting language – as our legislators, in those days of refinement, sometimes courteously address each other in parliamentary language, which is easily learnt, with a little attention to the duties of your constituency, during one session. And as for coming drunk into the presence of ladies after dinner, it was supposed to be simply the natural consequences which followed the excitement of the hunting field; and a sound nap in an easy chair, from which issued a chorus of snores, was, doubtless, highly pleasing to the fair sex.

'[The present age, i.e. mid-nineteenth century] . . . came with the rapid strides of a race-horse, as did those of battues, grouse-shooting, and latterly deer-stalking. The hour for meeting hounds was later, the horses better bred, with more natural tails; till at length we find thorough-bred horses and first-rate riders, and tails in the fulness of nature's beauty, unadorned by docking – thus decidedly, as regards the horse, adorned the most – assembled at the covert-side at a reasonable hour in the morning.

'French and English male artistes have taken the place of female roasters of sirloins, who nevertheless serve eatables more agreeable to the palate, and more conducive to keep the frame lighter for the saddle – though no offence to roast-beef and Yorkshire pudding, excellent both in their way. Good claret in moderation, is now drunk instead of bad port in abundance, and very white and well-made leathers have banished the yellow buckskin; whereas well cleaned tops adorn the legs of peers and commoners, instead of dirty ones. The provincial counties have followed in the wake of Melton – foxes are killed in one hour instead of four; and more pheasants are found on one estate, and more partridges in one turnip-field, than heretofore lived and flew in a county.

'Young England has made rapid strides in the character of sportsman, and, as regards ourselves, we feel perfectly satisfied with the system of the present age, without entering into any discussion with reference to the merits or demerits of the Game Laws. As in all matters of life's career, there are unquestionably many objections to be found in the selfish bigotry and illiberal monopoly of game, and the no less objectionable manner of its undue preservation by some extensive landholders; happily, however, they are in the minority; and where you will find one man of this nature, you will find twenty open-hearted and real sportsmen, who preserve simply as a means of sport and recreation to themselves, but far more so for their friends; liberally compensating their tenants for injury done, allowing them also in many cases to participate in their pleasures, and in fact doing far more good than harm to their neighbours and their farmers.

'. . . Good horses, good hounds, and better riders than heretofore were ever known, notwithstanding their apparent dandyism, in dress and appointments, are to be met with in every hunting field; and hunting has become a source of unequalled delight and excitement, instead of a comparative toil mixed somewhat too copiously with the source of your enjoyment. You may now have a splendid day's hunting, ride home afterwards, make yourself agreeable to the fair sex, play a game of billiards, and then dress for dinner – drink a glass or two of sherry and a pint of claret, and be fit society for women, as well as for those men who do not exactly participate in your sporting propensities. Cigars, disagreeable as their aromatic effluvia may be to some, even in a hunting field, nevertheless close the lips of many heretofore given to d---n a little. Then, as regards shooting, in these days of sixty miles an hour by express – oh! 'tis a pleasant pastime to see your dogs range with a certainty of finding game, instead of walking o'er hill and dale for twenty miles in search of a brace of birds for your next day's dinner.'

(*Highland Sports and Highland Quarters*, 1847)

Hall's dilettante approach would not have met with William Scrope's approval. In his definitive work on deer-stalking, Scrope abjures all indulgence – even in refreshment – and would surely have scorned such pastimes as *après-chasse* billiards!

'Should a deer-stalker eat and snuff? – should he pamper the inward man? Shade of Abernethy forbid! He should go forth light and shapy as a gazelle; to restrict him entirely from venison pasty would be a cruelty from which our indulgent nature would be averse; we wish to be liberal in these matters, especially as the concern somewhat touches ourselves; we would therefore say in the words of Gay:

Go, but be moderate in your food,
A chicken too might do me good.

He may dilute with tea and possess himself with a few grapes to cool him. Peaches and nectarines may be put in his pocket, because as he will be sure to sit upon them, they will do him no earthly harm, but rather confer a benefit by moistening the outward man.'

Scrope, his tongue happily in his cheek, also describes the constitution of the ideal deer-stalker, in which the characteristics of the Spartans should be combined, apparently, with those of the ibex.

'Your consummate deer-stalker should not only be able to run like an antelope, and breathe like the trade-winds, but should also be enriched with various other undeniable qualifications. As, for instance, he should be able to run in a stooping position, at a greyhound pace, with his back parallel to the ground, and his face within an inch of it for miles together. He should take a singular pleasure in threading the seams of a bog, or of gliding down a burn, *ventre à terre*, like that insinuating animal, the eel; accomplished he should be in skilfully squeezing his clothes after this operation, to make all comfortable. Strong and pliant in the ankle, he should most undubitably be; since in running swiftly down precipices, feet will unadvisedly get into awkward cavities, and curious positions; thus if his legs are devoid of the faculty of breaking, so much the better – he has an evident advantage over the fragile man. He should rejoice in wading through torrents, and be able to stand firmly on water worn stones, unconscious of the action of the current; or if by fickle fortune he loses his balance, and goes floating away upon his back (for if he has any tact, or sense of the picturesque, it is presumed that he will fall backwards), he should raise his rifle aloft in the air, Marmion fashion, lest his powder should get wet, and his day's sport come suddenly to an end. A few weeks' practice in the tilt will make him quite *au fait* at this. We would recommend him to try the thing in a speat, during a refreshing north wind, which is adverse to deerstalking; thus no day will be lost pending his education.'

(*The Art of Deer-Stalking*)

It is no surprise to find that however extreme the specifications there are always men to meet them, even to go beyond them. According to his own accounts, Charles St John must have been such a paragon.

'The hounds were in pursuit of a roe; and I was partly occupied in listening to their joyous cry, and partly in admiring the beautiful light thrown by the low rays of the winter sun on the bright trunks of the fir trees, contrasted as it was with the gloomy darkness of their foliage, when I heard the foot of a roe as it came towards me, *ventre à terre*. Taking a cool aim, I sent a cartridge through the poor animal's head, who, of course, fell rolling over like a rabbit. I went up in order to bleed her, according to rule, when just as I was knife in hand, I heard the hound come up in chace of another roe. I dropped the knife on the heather, and at that instant the dying roe gave an expiring plunge, as animals almost always do when shot in the head. Her hind foot struck the hilt of the *couteau de chasse*, driving it straight into my foot. Having, not without some little difficulty, drawn it out, I had next to cut off my shoe, when the blood came out like a *jet d'eau*. Making a tourniquet of my handkerchief and a bit of stick, I managed to stop the bleeding, not however before I began to feel a little faint. Then not waiting for my companions, I hobbled off to a forester's house, where I rebound the cut, and having directed the man where to find the roe, I made my way homewards as well as I could, and luckily meeting on the road one of my servants exercising a pony, I got home without more inconvenience, but I had to pass many a long day upon a sofa. Had a similar accident happened on some of the wild and distant mountains of the country where I often shoot, I should probably not have been seen again, till the ravens and the storms of winter had left nothing but my bones.'

(*A Tour in Sutherlandshire*, 1849)

Peter Hawker was another, though even this amazingly resilient and hardy man apparently drew the line (along with 'the perfumed young men') at the rigours of the Highland pub; for whatever hardships a sportsman may endure in the cause of his sport, he does at least expect a few creature comforts when rain stops play.

> 'Scotland is the best place for grouse shooting, as the heather being much higher; they will lie closer than in Yorkshire, and the other moors of England: add to which, the sport there, has, in many parts, the pleasant addition of blackcock and ptarmigan shooting. Such, however, is the misery of the Highland public houses, and particularly to our perfumed young men of fashion, that I have generally observed nine out of ten of them, however good may have been their sport, come home cursing and swearing most bitterly about their wooden berths, peat fires, and oatmeal cakes . . . We will suppose one of my young readers to have arrived at the miserable hole alluded to, and that the first salutation, after the knock at his bedchamber door, in the morning, is "A wet day, sir!" and instead of being able to pursue his sport, either after breakfast, or at noon (the most usual time for the weather to clear up, if it clears up at all), he is consigned a close prisoner to the pot-house; looking alternatively to the windward clouds, and the plastered walls of the room; hearing, through a thin partition, the discordant merriment of drunken fellows; and inhaling the breezes of a smoky wood fire, with the fumes of their shag tobacco!'
>
> (*Instructions to Young Sportsmen*)

It may have been that Scrope had the primitive conditions of Scottish inns at the back of his mind when he drew up his list of deer-stalking qualifications; but the pleasures of the chase were never really those of the sybarite.

At the time of Richard Blome, less stress was laid upon the physical attributes of its adherents, but severe restraint was recommended in the pursuit of worldly pleasures. However, it is difficult not to believe that Blome's 'Necessary Rules for a *Faulconer* to observe' were more honoured in the breach than in the observance.

> 'Whosoever intends to apply himself to his Art, and to become Master, must for some time bestow all his Care and Endeavours therein; He must be diligent to learn and observe the Natures, Inclinations, Strength, Mettle and Conditions of his *Hawks*; He must treat them with a gentle and loving Hand, and pass by their Faults with Patience: He must not be addicted to Tables, Cards, or playing of Good-Fellow; for many an excellent *Hawk* hath been lost, through the Intemperance of her Keeper; nor can he be term'd a good *Faulconer* that is apt to be led away by these, or the like Disorders. I grant he may be expert in Reclaiming, Enseaming and Flying his *Hawk*; nay, he may attain to great Skill in the Ordering and Managing her in her Flights, and whilst she is in the Field: But if then he betakes himself to Pot and Pipe when he is return'd Home, and peradventure let his poor tired *Hawk* to hang by the Heels, such a one cannot deserve the name of a good *Faulconer*. He that is a Smoaker must not chew the *Hawk*'s *Meat* in his Mouth for some good time after; for it will make her cast her Gorge, or stand upon her Meat, which will occasion a Disorder in her, if not kill her.'
>
> (*The Gentleman's Recreation*)

When it comes to shooting, however, the rules of etiquette are most stringently enforced. As Sir Ralph Payne-Gallwey remarks in his comprehensive treatment of the subject, the most unpleasant thing that can happen to a young sportsman is having to admit to shooting a beater!

> 'Fair play towards fellow-shooters is a good quality in a young shooter. If, for instance, a bird rises before him in covert, and offers a low and easy, I may say stupid, shot, he should certainly not fire if another shooter happens to stand forward, as by the time the game reaches the latter it will probably afford him a high and sporting mark for his gun, Such little compliments as these tend to good-fellowship out shooting, and are usually repaid with interest when the time comes.
>
> 'Be very careful not to fire at a bird that rises nearer to another shooter than yourself; or which is a fair shot for your friend and a long one for you; or at a bird that rises too far from or too near you and which, if left alone, will afford your neighbour a fair mark. Above all things, avoid anything approaching jealous shooting, even though your companions may be foolish enough to indulge in it; *jealousy* makes shooting *a very dangerous sport*.
>
> 'On no account should you fire at game till the man to whom the first chance at it properly belonged has discharged both barrels. Then if it offers you a fair shot, you can have a try; though, if you kill, you had better half-apologise for doing so, and account for your success through the bird having given you an easy chance; for to "wipe a man's eye" may be all very pleasant for you, but the man who has had his "eye wiped" is not, perhaps, so satisfied – especially if he be a much older sportsman or confessedly a superior shot to yourself. So, if you are fortunate in doing the latter feat, do it delicately, I advise.
>
> 'It is well for a young shooter to recollect, if he is one of a party, that he cannot always be in place for obtaining shots, and that he will have to take his turn with the other sportsmen and trust to his luck, and certainly not endeavour, if he is in an unfavourable place for obtaining shots, to try and better it without directions from the person in authority. In a well-organised shooting party it is the object of the host to deal out the best places to his friends in turn, whatever their rank or powers of markmanship may be; and should a bad shot chance to enjoy the best place, a good marksman can always be placed behind him to back him up and prevent the game escaping. I recollect hearing on one occasion of a head keeper placing the noble lords continually in the best places in a day's shooting, till at length one of the party, without a handle to his name, losing patience at being always sent to walk up with the beaters, exclaimed, in a well-assumed injured tone, "Where am I to go this time, keeper? Perhaps you are not aware I'm a banker, and the fifth son of a bishop!"
>
> 'It is very unsportsmanlike to edge up to another gun who is enjoying plenty of shooting, with the object of sharing his luck and taking some of his shots, unless your assistance is requested, as it may be, if the game rises too fast for your neighbour to kill a good percentage. Nor is it ever correct proceeding for a shooter to

change his place, especially when standing for driven birds, even should he be able to kill more by doing so. It is best for him to previously inquire if he may move in case of the game breaking away out of his reach; else, should a young shooter take it upon himself to alter his position, he may hear hard words spoken to him for having intercepted the birds from being driven in a proper direction for future sport.

'When walking in line, a shooter cannot well alter his course, unless he does so wilfully. He should be cautious to keep in line. Few lag behind, but some men will *gallop* forward of the rest. *Nothing* seems to cure them of this annoying habit; whether they do so under the mistaken idea that they procure more shots, or for some other reason, has always been a mystery to me. By walking ahead of a line of guns, though but a few yards forward, a shooter gently drives the birds, as they rise, to either side of him, for the other guns to kill. This is of no consequence, as it serves him right; but he also often prevents his companions from killing the game through his being in the line of fire – shots that neither he nor they can safely take by reason of the irregular line caused through one gun marching ahead of the others.

'This sort of behaviour is always looked on with disapprobation by other sportsmen, as, whether correct in their surmises or not, it gives them the idea that the man who persistently walks forward of the line is endeavouring to jockey his fellow-shooters, and obtain more than his fair share of the sport.

'It is not an uncommon habit with a young sportsman, should a bird rise or fly past when two or more shooters are standing together, to be the first to blaze off. Unless the game is palpably his shot, either from its or his position, he should not fire. If it is as much another gun's shot as it is his, he had better leave it alone, and, to prevent the shot being lost through mutual hesitation cry, "Yours" to his neighbour – just as when fielding at cricket a "catch" may come to two fielders, either of whom could hold the ball if left to do so without interference.

'When out shooting with one friend, be sure you do not fire at the same birds as he does, else your four barrels may bring down but a brace out of a covey rising between you, and these, moreover, so riddled with shot as to be only fit for soup. Take the birds in the covey that are *nearest* to you, whether you be walking or standing. If you are on the right of your friend you will take the right-hand birds, and he the left-hand ones, or the reverse, according to your respective positions. When walking in line, this equally applies to the gun on your right and the one on your left.

'It is from a little want of knowledge on the part of shooters as to how the game, when it rises, should be divided among their guns that it so often occurs, when a couple of easy birds and one or two very easy are flushed at the same time, that the contents of the sportsmen's barrels are showered into the latter, and the former fly away unharmed, when, by a little exercise of judgment, all the birds might have been killed. For the above reason a man may be a good shot, and yet not be so *successful* as another man, of perhaps less accurate aim, who, from his better discrimination of the position of the game, takes full advantage of every chance that offers.

'A young sportsman's reputation in connection with shooting can be easily spoilt: one or two dangerous or unsportsmanlike shots, and the argument of the proverbial dog with a bad name holds good. There is no excuse for the former style of shot; though for the latter an apology, and future care not to repeat the mistake may set matters straight.

'There are more people in a party of shooters who watch with critical eyes the behaviour of an inexperienced shot than he suspects; and let me tell him he should take just as much care not to fire too near a beater as if the latter were a "prince of the blood". One of the neatest hints I ever heard of to be more careful in their aim was given to his friends by a host who printed on his game cards, after the usual list of pheasants, hares, rabbits, &c., *keepers, beaters, dogs, windows*!

'I have seen shooters, who though they never aimed near a friend's person, yet would kill rabbits all round the legs of the beaters, as if the lives of the latter were of secondary consideration.

'The most unfortunate and unpleasant thing that can occur to a young shooter, after he has fired a careless shot, is to hear the cry of "Who fired that shot?" then to see a beater limping out of covert, and be forced to admit *who* fired the shot, and have to hand out a guinea as a solatium for the present, with a chance of a doctor's bill looming in the future – to say nothing of the sportsman's reputation as a safe marksman being irretrievably damaged.

'In a day's shooting, the shooters are the actors whose every act is criticised, and the assistants are the audience in the theatre of sport; and very critical and capable observers the latter usually are, too.

'There are, however, many points of etiquette in the shooting field that require to be learnt intuitively, and from experience rather than from print. For example, never call attention to your own skill; this can easily be seen by your friends without your impressing it upon them; doing so only leads to the conclusion that to shoot well is an unusual and not a frequent attainment on your part. Nor should you make excuses for missing; explanations of the latter kind are absurd if you are a poor marksman, and if you are a good shot they are not required, as everybody fails to kill at times. Some shooters – good shots – apparently look upon missing as a crime, and fancy all present notice their failures; though probably the other guns do not care a straw one way or the other, and are much too intent upon their own performances to criticise those of their neighbours.

'The shooters who are the worst marksmen generally make the most excuses, as if it were quite an exceptional occurrence for them to miss at all. I call to mind the story of the gentleman – a notably bad shot – who missed in fine style all day, and who, grumbling furiously at every failure, finally lost his temper completely, and exclaimed to his own keeper, who was attending him, "I can't shoot a bit to-day,'' and was met with the crushing reply, ''You *shoots* well enough, Squire, but you *hits* nowt.''

'There are certain rules you should always adhere to when shooting. For instance, if you are walking a covert out towards other guns posted forward outside, never fire at low birds that rise in front of you, however tempting the shots appear; nor should you even fire at rabbits, unless they are near and the forward guns are at a safe distance. In the same way, if a forward gun yourself, on no account fire at low birds coming towards you out of a covert, and only at ground game between you and the guns walking up when the latter are at a perfectly safe distance; in any case, it is better to stand quite still, and take your shots as the game passes overhead or behind you.

'Counting game you have killed at a stand, or in a day's sport, and letting others know of your success, is always unsportsmanlike, unless it is a matter of general conversation or enquiry. Killing more game than anybody else is oftener the result of good luck than of good shooting. A young shooter seldom counts correctly, and the more he adds up as his total (he does not often subtract), the less he leaves for the other guns. I give an amusing example of this that I can vouch for. One of the best shots in England invited several young shooters to his grouse moor; the bag was a heavy one, and all save the host were full of their own shooting, and what each gun had killed as his share. After a deal of dispute as to how this shooter had brought to bag fifty birds, and that one sixty, they finally arranged everything to their satisfaction – a satisfaction somewhat marred when the host, who had to every eye shot splendidly, quietly remarked that ''he was afraid he should have to give up shooting, because during the day, he had failed at least a hundred shots, and after subtracting the bag accounted for by his friends from the real total brought in by the keepers, it appeared that he had *only killed three birds*.''

'A young shooter needs cure himself of any tendency to excitement in the field, such as may occur to him when the game is in abundance. It is always the man who is cool and collected who is not only the safest shot, but the one who kills his game in the most sportsmanlike style. However plentiful the game may be, an absence of excitement will certainly enable a shooter to use his judgment in discriminating between safe and dangerous shots, and what he ought to fire at and what he had best leave alone. Such a man will also make up his mind instantly, whilst the nervous sportsman will point his gun and take it down, and point it again, and then perhaps hesitate between one bird and another, and finally pounce upon somebody else's shot, or else fire at a bird too near or too far, though a fair shot offered in front of his nose.

'It is thoroughly sportsmanlike behaviour of a shooter who, being the host, takes a ''back seat'', and places himself where he may rather have the worst of the sport than the best. When he shoots with his friends, he will probably have every chance of a ''front seat''. I like to see a host manage his shooting, rather than participating in it, and throughout the day arrange that his friends have the best of the sport. To my mind, there is on these occasions just as much, if not, indeed, more, pleasure in acting the part of head keeper and seeing that all goes well, than there is in slaying your own game.'

(*Letters to Young Shooters*, First Series)

Is the pleasure then, after all, as much in the form as the substance? Eric Parker nostalgically conjures three memories of a day's shooting which underline the importance of the frame into which every sportsman puts his own picture.

'One is the quiet of the morning before the keeper moves off his line; you can hear nothing then but the distant tap-tap of stops, jokes go in undertones, and it is with a sort of attack that the line moves forward at the whistle, with sticks belabouring bushes and trees. Another is the break-off after lunch, when the merry are merriest, and the gauntest have got new looks, and you see the jolliest of English holiday life, beef and beer and jovial countrymen.

'And the third is the end of the winter afternoon, when the shooting is over and the guns have gone into the house, and the beaters stand in groups in the yard, with a stray boy toiling up the hill out of the gathering dusk, to add his burden of game to the rows counted by the keeper. There are lights coming in the house windows, and a jug going round at the kitchen door; and that is a genial end to a village day, with coins clinking, heavy footsteps trudging off into the dark, good night called down the drive.'

(*Shooting Days*, 1918)

The Roman writer Oppian may be left to sum up:

'No man once taken captive by love of the charms of hunting can ever forsake it again of free will – so overpowering are the bonds that hold him.'

(*Cygnegitica*, II, *c*.A.D.180)

CHAPTER FOURTEEN

'First Catch Your Hare . . .'

'It resteth now that I proceed unto Cookery itself, which is the dressing and ordering of meat, in good and wholesome manner; to which when our Housewife shall address herself, she shall well understand that these qualities must ever accompany it; First, she must be cleanly both in body and garments, she must have a quick eye, a curious nose, a perfect taste, and ready ear; (she must not be butter fingred; sweet-toothed, nor faint hearted) for the first will let every thing fall, the second will consume what it should increase; and the last will lose time with too much niceness. Now for the substance of the Art itself, I will divide it into . . . Sallers and Fricases . . . boyld Meats and Broths . . . Rost meats and Carbonadoes . . . Bak't meats and Pies . . . banquetting and made dishes, with other conceits and secrets.'

(Gervase Markham, *A Way to Get Wealth*, 11th edition, 1660)

WHATEVER ARGUMENT there may be about any other aspect of game there is scarcely a dissenting voice when it comes to table and for that and other self-evident reasons it seems fitting to conclude this book with some aids to the pleasures of the end game.

Colonel Kenney Herbert, writing in 1896, on the cookery of venison, plays the part of banqueting manager:

> 'Turtle and Venison! – they are the symbols of civic luxury. We dare to say that the typical haunch, with all that precedes and follows it, from the iced punch and Madeira to the curious old cognac, has done more than the example of Whittington or Gresham to animate aspirants to the gown and golden chain . . . Surfeit will lead on to satiety, and venison and burgundy with sedentary habits end in gout, dyspepsia and doctors' fees.
>
> 'Vert and Venison with us were strictly guarded by the atrocious severity of the Norman forest laws. The deer were preserved, under pain of death or mutilation, for the sport and table of the sovereign. Even under the Tudors there were still 70 royal forests, 13 chases, and no fewer than 700 parks . . . The barons and monastic orders were granted privileges in their own domains by special licence. We may be sure that the Church took excellent care of itself. Landseer's picture of "Bolton Abbey in the olden time" carries us back to the

jovial days which preceded and hastened the dissolution of the monasteries. The portly prior, with the flower of the holy brotherhood, is standing over the slaughtered deer. The good monk is grateful for the gifts of God, and though the smile of expectant complacency is benignant, woe be to the brother who presides in the kitchen if he "sins the mercies" by careless cookery.

'That Shakespeare loved venison we know . . . There is a memorable scene when Sir John is befooled by the Merry Wives in Windsor Forest. When he comes in disguised in hide and antlers, he says "For me, I am here a Windsor stag; and the fattest, I think, i' the forest." Falstaff was a bon vivant if ever there was one, and his thoughts flew at once to the fat – to the inches of grease on the brisket. He may have been groaning over his own obesity, though well used to it; but he naturally thought of the savoury venison as it would be served by mine host of the Garter or by Mistress Quickly's cook in Eastcheap.

'Venison was of course the staple dish at the great mediaeval banquets arranged on a scale of lavish profusion. Fortunately no meat keeps so well or so long with ordinary care, for the deer must have been sent in from many a distant forest and chase to furnish out those sumptuous boards . . . At the installation of George, the youngest brother of the Kingmaker, as Archbishop of York, all the world of the Court society was bidden to the feasting. Upwards of 500 "stagges, bucks and roes" were served entire, and 4,000 cold pasties of venison figured on the bill of fare . . . The guests brought Gargantuan appetites to those feasts, and the caterers went in for show and quantity rather than quality. We can imagine the amount of pains which could be spared on the dressing and the serving when half a thousand deer were turning simultaneously on the spits.

'Those ancestors of ours must have been men of heroic mould and iron stomachs. They breakfasted, with their ladies, on salt beef and beer, they spiced their wines into infernal concoctions, and when the cuisine went beyond plain roasting and boiling, the good meat was bedevilled by incompetent cooks.

'Some of the recipes in *The Noble Boke of Cookery*, (reprinted from a rare manuscript in the Holkham collection) are curious, but we can recommend few conscientiously for modern imitation. That for the "rosting" of venison – when the deer was not served entire – directs you to cut the meat into slices, spit them and powder with salt and ginger. The "side of high grease" is to be mangled in similar fashion; but as if the scorched slices had not suffered sufficiently, they are to be subsequently boiled in red wine.

'The liver and kidneys, we admit, are excellent, and black puddings of the venison are not to be despised. But the Umbles or Numbles, which were much in favour, simply meant the entrails in general. "To make numbles, tak hert middrif and kidney and hew them smalle and prise out the blood and sethe them in water and ale and colour it with brown bred or with blood and fors it with canell and galingalle and when it boilithe kole it a litille with ale and serve it." In the dish made of those modest materials we have the obvious origin of humble pie.

'Serving the venison is a matter of no little consequence, for the fat has the unfortunate defect of congealing with extraordinary celerity . . . Always sensitive to the fleeting nature of earthly pleasures, the bitter lesson is never more forcibly brought home to the epicure than when the venison fat and gravy are congealing visibly on china before his eyes. The evanescent joy eludes him unless he bolt the delicacies American fashion, which is fatal to his hopes, obnoxious to his principles, and attended by indigestion, dyspepsia and remorse.

'. . . Venison may be kept with due care for a fortnight or even three weeks. When it has been hung in the larder the precautions are simple, though close attention is needful. Cut out the pipe running along the backbone, which is likely to taint, and wipe away the mould which gathers on the surface and in the folds of meat. You may dust from time to time with flour or pepper or pounded ginger.

'When the haunch is to be dressed, sponge the surface with lukewarm water, and rub it with butter and lard. Cover with sheets of paper well buttered or steeped in salad oil, and over that lay a paste of flour and water half an inch thick. Swathe with strong paper again, secure with greased string, and drench the whole in melted butter to prevent the paper from catching fire. Baste incessantly before a strong, clear fire, using a cradle spit; the time depending on the size of the haunch. A large joint may need at least five hours. Half an hour before it ought to be done remove the swathings and test with a skewer. Then reduce the fire, and baste every few minutes with claret and butter. Celerity in sending from the fire to the table is everything, and the brown gravy poured over the meat should be as hot as the dish on which it is served.

'The recipes for the gravy are various, although all suggest similar ingredients. A very good one is a pound of currant jelly, a gill of port, and the rind of a lemon with a flavouring of cinnamon. Other experts substitute claret for port, and suggest the addition of cloves and nutmegs, cinnamon and cayenne . . . the sauces most relished by the Cleikum Club were, first, a glass of claret with three times the quantity of venison or mutton gravy, and a small glassful of raspberry vinegar, or, second, a plain piquant sauce of white wine vinegar and white sugar, heated in a stone jar.

'We have had our say elsewhere against the practice of mixing wines at dinner, and serving various vintages, however rich or rare, with the several courses. We said it was a sound rule to stick to champagne, nor have we anything to retract. But no rule is without its exceptions, and . . . with venison Burgundy goes as naturally as iced punch with the turtle, and with far more obvious reason. The bouquet of one and the savour of the other were evidently predestined to make a happy love match.'

If the foregoing account whets your appetite, perhaps the following recipes, by Ena Baxter, will encourage you to prepare your own 1973-style banquet.

Hare Soup (Scotch Style)

1 hare, freshly killed
Mixed herbs and peppercorns
Onion, carrot, turnip
Port wine

Skin hare and clean thoroughly, holding it over a large basin to catch all the blood, which contains much of the flavour. Joint the hare and put into a pot with water, carrot, onion, turnip, peppercorns, herbs, salt and pepper and simmer for 3 hours. Strain soup. Cut the meat into small pieces and return to the pot with the stock, add a handful of oatmeal. Strain the blood and gradually add to the soup, stirring all the time and bring to the boil. Then add a glass of port wine and serve. A boiled potato should be served for each person and eaten with the soup.

Pheasant Normande

1 Pheasant
2 ounces butter – melted
1 pound cooking apples
4–5 tablespoons single cream
Salt and Pepper

Set oven at 350° (Mark 4). Melt butter, brown pheasant evenly all over. Peel, core and slice the apple thinly. Layer half the apples in a 2½-pint casserole. Pour a little butter over the apples, put in the pheasant. Surround with the rest of the apples, seasoning each layer. Pour over the rest of the butter and the cream. Cover tightly and cook in the oven at 350°F (Mark 4) for about 1 hour. Serves 4.

Roast Grouse

Said to be at its best from mid-August to mid-October and one of the finest of game birds, perfect roasted. Allow 1 for 2 persons. Grouse should be slightly underdone, pink, not 'blue', and may be roasted at 450°F (Mark 8) for just 15 to 20 minutes or at 400°F (Mark 6) for 30 minutes. If liked, insert a sprig of lovage inside the bird, but do not use strongly scented herbs. Mash cooked liver into a little stock and spread on a piece of toast. Serve the grouse on this.

Accompaniments:
Clear gravy, bread sauce, fried crumbs, game chips, roast or mashed potatoes, green salad. If a hot vegetable is preferred, serve cauliflower, onions or green beans. Garnish with watercress.

Roast Pheasant

Hen pheasant is smaller and more tender than the cock bird. To get the true flavour, the bird needs to be hung for a week or even up to 10 days, depending on taste, weather and storage conditions.

Allow a plump bird for 4 to 5 persons. Choose young birds and do not over-cook or they will be dry. Set the oven at 450°F (Mark 8).

Season ready-to-roast bird inside and out with salt and pepper. Cover the breast with rashers of green fat bacon. Put a knob of butter inside the bird. Stand pheasant on a trivet in a roasting tin, spoon over 1 tablespoon melted butter.

Cover with a lid or leave uncovered and baste (frequently). Roast at 450°F (Mark 8) for 10 minutes, then reduce to 400°F (Mark 6) for 30 to 40 minutes, altogether. Five minutes before the end of cooking time, froth the breast to give a delicious crisp skin. To do this, remove bacon rashers, baste with the hot butter, dredge with flour and baste again. Return to oven at 450°F (Mark 8) uncovered, until brown and frothy.
N.B. A glass of red wine can be added halfway through the cooking time.

Serve on a croûte of toast hollowed out and spread with liver pâté.

34. A medieval feast, from Jean de Wavrin's Chronique d'Angleterre

Accompaniments:
Clear gravy, bread sauce, fried crumbs, game chips, or wafers, watercress, green salad. Hot vegetables, braised celery with butter and lemon juice.

Venison

'I have heard the excellence of venison disputed by sportsmen, and others who have tasted it in the north; but I attribute this entirely to the age and condition of the sort of creature it was their lot to taste, or to the time of year in which it was killed. A hart, like most other animals, has little fat when he is growing; and if sportsmen do not distinguish, or have not the means of selection, the haunches will cut but a sorry figure at the table. But in the estimation of all the numerous guests it has been my good fortune to meet in the hospitable halls of Blair, the red-deer has been infinitely preferred to the fallow; and I could name many such guests, whose judgement would be pronounced paramount in such matters. On the contrary, the haunch of the fallow-deer, when brought to table at Blair, although perfect in its kind, was always neglected. There must, however, be a wide difference between the quality of the red-deer which are fed in English parks, and such as wander freely over the mountains, and browse on the sweet grass and heather.'

(William Scrope, *The Art of Deer-Stalking*, 1838)

Cooking of Venison

Due to the rather dry texture of venison meat, it is essential to marinate. Here are two excellent recipes for marinades.

Marinade 1

$\frac{1}{2}$ cup oil
$1\frac{1}{2}$ cups red wine
12 peppercorns crushed
1 bay leaf
$\frac{1}{2}$ medium onion sliced

Marinade 2

$\frac{1}{2}$ cup oil
1 cup red wine
1 cup water
4 tablespoons mild vinegar
12 crushed peppercorns
2–3 cloves
1 bay leaf
$\frac{1}{2}$ medium onion sliced

All cooking is done in preheated oven (Moderate: 350°F (Mark 4)).

Venison Goulash

2 pounds venison
2 ounces dripping or lard
¾ pound onions thinly sliced
1 level tablespoon flour
1 level tablespoon paprika
1 level tablespoon concentrated tomato purée
Garlic salt
Black pepper
¾ pint stock
½ level teaspoon caraway seeds
1½ pounds potatoes
5-ounce carton soured cream
Chopped parsley

Oven temperature: warm (325°F (Mark 3)).

Cut the venison into serving pieces and fry quickly in the fat until sealed and brown. Drain the meat from the fat and place in a casserole. Fry the onions until soft and golden brown. Add the flour, paprika, tomato purée, garlic salt, pepper and stock, bring to the boil and pass through a sieve or liquidise in an electric blender. Pour the sieved ingredients over the meat, stir in the caraway seeds and cover tightly. Cook in the oven for about 1½ hours, add the potatoes, roughly cut into ½-inch cubes, and return the goulash to the oven for a further hour to finish cooking. Pour the soured cream in a small pan and bring gently to the boil. Pour over the casserole, top with chopped parsley. Serves 4–5.

Medallion of Venison

1. Place medallions with a smear of French mustard in Marinade No. 1 for 8 hours.
2. Lightly drain and place straight in oiled sauté pan, quickly turning the meat to seal, and cook for 3–4 minutes.
   Medallion size – 2½ inch round by ½–¾ inch thick.

Venison Medallions in Sour Cream Sauce

1 pound venison medallions (marinate in No. 1 for 8 hours)
Salt
3 tablespoons margarine
4 slices fat bacon, diced
1 large onion, finely chopped
2 tablespoons flour
1 cup sour cream
Nutmeg
2 tablespoons redcurrant jelly
Butter
4 slices thick white bread
1 cup black cherries to garnish, canned or fresh

Lightly drain and sprinkle the venison medallions with salt. Heat the margarine and fry the meat on both sides for about 3 minutes. Place on a warm dish and keep hot. Pour off the margarine, heat the bacon until the fat runs, add the onion and fry until soft. Add any gravy from the meat. Stir in the flour, blend thoroughly then add the sour cream, whisking all the time. Simmer for 2 minutes, season with salt and nutmeg to taste and stir in the jelly. Heat enough butter to fry the bread on both sides until brown and crisp. Place these on a warm flat dish, put the venison on top and cover with the sauce. Heat the cherries and add as a garnish.

Boned Shoulder of Venison

Roast:
1. Marinate in No. 2 for up to 24 hours or overnight.
2. Remove from marinade, smear with bacon fat and wrap in tin foil and roast for 25–30 minutes per pound.

Roast Haunch of Roe Deer

1. Marinate in No. 1 for up to 24 hours or overnight.
2. Remove from marinade, smear with bacon fat, wrap in tin foil and roast for 12 minutes per pound.

Roast Haunch of Red Deer

1. Marinate in No. 2 as for boned shoulder.
2. As per instructions for shoulder and haunch of roe deer, roasting for 25 minutes per pound.

Venison Pasty

2 pounds venison (with bone)
2 onions
$\frac{1}{2}$ cup port or claret
$\frac{1}{4}$ cup good vinegar
$\frac{3}{4}$ pound puff pastry
A little allspice or mace
Mutton fat or butter

Make sure meat has been well hung. Remove meat from bone and beat well. Rub the allspice, mace, salt and pepper into the meat and rub it lightly with mutton fat. Make stock from the bones. Roll up and tie the meat; sprinkle it with a little more allspice. Strain the stock, return it to the pan, add the venison roll and onions and cook slowly for 3 hours. When the meat is tender, untie it and leave overnight in its stock in a cool place.

Next day, skim off the layer of fat which has formed, cut the meat into thick pieces and place in a pie-dish with a little of the stock, adding the port and vinegar. Cover with puff pastry and cook for 30 minutes. Serve with pickled walnuts. Serves 4–6.

Fillet of Venison Strathspey

2 tablespoons oil
6 ounces finely chopped onion
1 teaspoon oatmeal
½ pint fresh cream
4 tablespoons Scotch (malt) whisky
3–4 pounds fillet venison
2–3 ounces butter

Cook venison in sauté pan in small amount of oil. When cooked, remove from pan, sweat off the onions, add a little butter and allow to foam.

Add the oatmeal, then cook until butter has been absorbed. Add whisky quickly, then the cream. Pour over the venison and garnish with watercress. Serves 8.

Steak Balmoral

4 8-ounce haunch steaks of venison
8 ounces tomato concassé (skinned, roughly chopped tomatoes, sautéd in butter with bay leaf and ¼ clove garlic)
8 ounces duxelle (chopped mushrooms, shallots and onion, sautéd in butter)
8 asparagus tips
1 pint demi-glace (rich brown sauce)
4 ounces watercress

Cook steak in sauté pan, removing from pan when cooked. Add a little demi-glace to the residue and de-glaze (remove pan juices by adding liquid and scraping out). Pour the sauce into serving-dish, place steak in dish, then arrange concassé and duxelle longwise on the steak. Finally, add the asparagus down the centre. Garnish with watercress. Serves 4.

Cairngorm Pie

1 pound mixed game (at least 3 types,
e.g. pheasant, hare, venison, grouse)
4 ounces mushrooms (flat, preferably)
Demi-glace (a rich brown sauce)
Game bones or carcasses
Malt whisky (to taste)
$\frac{3}{4}$ pound puff pastry
6 ounces onions

Cut meat into irregular-sized shapes, not too big for one mouthful. Place bones in a large russe (heavy pan) with a little lard and brown well. When brown remove the bones, replace with demi-glace then de-glaze (remove pan juices by adding liquid and scraping out: liquid may be wine, stock, water or cream).

Sweat off the diced onions and the mushrooms.

Place meat and onions in individual pie dishes. Pour the malt whisky into the sauce, stir well and pour over meat. Finely sprinkle the whole unsliced mushrooms on top. Cover with puff pastry, brush with beaten egg, and cook until pastry is done. Serves 3–4.

Hare Brawn

1 pound hare
6 ounces diced cooked ham
1 shallot (minced)
Parsley
2 ounces redcurrant jelly
Salt and pepper

Mince hare, cook with a little water and then remince finely. Add other ingredients and mix thoroughly. Place in small moulds and brush the top with melted butter.

Place in a bain-marie and cook in a moderate oven (350°F/Mark 4) for 15 minutes.

Barron of Hare

Rub barron over with moist sugar and leave for 2–3 hours.

Turn onto back and brush well with bacon fat; add minced onion and finely chopped parsley. Brush the top with bacon fat. Wrap in tin-foil. Bake for 1 hour at 375°F (Mark 5).

Unwrap and baste with 2 glasses of port. Return to the oven for a further 10–15 minutes.

Take hare out, keep hot in oven while making sauce. For sauce, add $\frac{1}{2}$ pint good stock and 2 ounces redcurrant jelly to roasting pan. Reduce liquid to half quantity, season and serve. Serves 4.

Stuffed Partridge

$\frac{1}{2}$ pound Concord grapes
1 pound fresh vegetables: e.g. leeks, carrots, onions, celery
$\frac{1}{4}$ clove garlic
$1\frac{1}{2}$–2 pints veal stock
$\frac{1}{2}$–$\frac{3}{4}$ pint cider
4 ounces white panda (equal quantities kneaded flour and butter)

Stuff cavity with Concord grapes (USA species), stoned and skinned. Braise on a bed of fresh vegetables, covered $\frac{1}{3}$ way up with veal stock. Cook in a moderate oven (350°F/Mark 4) for 50 minutes.

When cooked, remove bird and reduce liquor to half quantity. Add equal quantity of cider, thicken slightly with a white panda, and season. Replace bird in sauce and take temperature up to near boiling. Serves 2.

To vary: stuff cavity with green grapes, and cook as above, exchanging champagne for cider. Serve on a bed of sautéd cabbage along with sauce boat of champagne sauce, made as above, but substituting champagne.

Salmi of Duck

1 duck (N.B. any game suitable)
1 ounce flour

Break up the duck carcass and place in a russe (heavy pan) with any giblets, feet and duck gravy available. Cover with cold water and simmer gently for at least 1 hour.

Melt $1\frac{1}{2}$ ounces duck fat in a russe, adding 1 ounce flour. Stir and cook until russet brown, then slowly add 1 pint of the duck stock, stirring constantly and well until thickened.

Place the meat in the russe and bring temperature up to about 190°F, but do NOT allow to boil or the duck will be tough. Keep at this temperature for $\frac{1}{2}$ hour. Serves 2–3.

Pancakes

Grouse: bind together pieces of meat with demi-glace (rich brown sauce), red wine and cream.
Pheasant: bind together pieces of meat with cream and white wine sauce gratinated with Orkney cheese.

Potted Grouse, Partridge or Pheasant

Cold cooked breasts of bird
Lamb and tongue
Butter
Salt, pepper and mace
Lemon juice and parsley
Worcester sauce and clarified butter

Using *only* breast meat and skin, remove fat from meat and mince, then pound until smooth with lamb and tongue. Add $\frac{1}{2}$ pound butter to 1 pound meat. Season with salt, pepper and a pinch of mace, then add a few drops of lemon juice and Worcester sauce. While still soft, force into a mould and brush with clarified butter and chopped parsley. Store in refrigerator.

Grilled Blackcock

1 young blackcock
Seasoned flour
Melted bacon fat

Sauce:
Blackcock giblets and liver
6 ounces shallots
$\frac{1}{4}$ clove garlic
3 ounces butter
$\frac{1}{2}$–$\frac{3}{4}$ pint mild stock or brown sauce
1 glass port
Seasoning

Split and skin the bird, dip it in seasoned flour, brush over with melted bacon fat, place on grill and cook for 20–30 minutes, turning frequently.
For the sauce, sauté the giblets with the shallots, garlic and butter. Cover with a mild stock or brown sauce and cook for 10 minutes. Strain. Sauté the liver in butter and smooth with the back of a heavy knife. Add the strained stock, then a glass of good port. Season. Serve with blackcock. Serves 2.

Cooking Times for Game

	Electric	*Gas*	*Time*
Blackcock	425/375°F	7/5	45/50 mins.
Capercaillie	400/375°F	6/5	50/60 mins.
Wild duck	425/375°F	7/5	35/40 mins.
Grouse	450/425°F	8/7	20/25 mins.
Pheasant	450/400°F	8/6	45/50 mins.
Pigeons	(casserole) 375°F	5	60 mins.
Venison	400/350°F	6/4	2¾/3 hours
Guinea fowl	400/375°F	6/5	55/65 mins.
Hazel hen	400/375°F	6/5	35/40 mins.

All meats should be either cooked on a bed of root vegetables and basted with white or brown stock, or barded (covered with bacon fat) and wrapped in cooking foil.
N.B. The chart temperatures indicate the sealing temperature (5/10 minutes) and the cooking times.